THE BILINGUAL COCKATOO

John Gatt-Rutter was born and raised in Malta, graduated in Modern Languages at Cambridge and has held academic posts in Italian studies at British and Australian universities, including the Vaccari Chair at La Trobe University in Melbourne from 1991 to 2008.

Also by John Gatt-Rutter

Italo Svevo: A double life (1988)

Alias Italo Svevo: vita dello scrittore triestino Ettore Schmitz (1992)

Oriana Fallaci: The rhetoric of freedom (1996)

The Bilingual Cockatoo:

Writing Italian Australian Lives

John Gatt-Rutter

HYBRID
PUBLISHERS

Published by Hybrid Publishers

Melbourne Victoria Australia

©John Gatt-Rutter 2014

First published 2014

National Library of Australia Cataloguing-in-Publication data:

Gatt-Rutter, John, author.

The bilingual cockatoo: writing Italian Australian lives /
John Gatt-Rutter.

9781925000269 (paperback)

Includes bibliographical references and index.
Subjects: Biography as a literary form.
Italians–Australia–Biography–History and criticism.
Immigrants–Australia–Biography–History and criticism.
Australia–Biography–History and criticism.

Dewey Number: 808.06692

Cover design: Grant Gittus ©

Contents

This book is dedicated
to all those
who have come from Italy
to make a new home in Australia.

Acknowledgements

Of all those with whom I have shared the making of this book, I owe most to Richard Freadman for his comradeship which extends well beyond his generosity in discussing my work at many different stages and over several years. Other good friends have also read the work in whole or in part and have given me valuable feedback for which I am grateful – Paolo Baracchi, Stephen Kolsky, Gay Miller, Robert Nitti and Luisa Percopo. Piero Genovesi has given me unstinting friendly and professional support and made available to me the institutional resources of the Italian Australian Institute, for which I am also grateful to the Grollo Ruzzene Foundation. Other good friends and colleagues who have led me to texts which I might otherwise have missed and with whom I have profited from discussion are Antonio Pagliaro, Gerardo Papalia and Luigi Gussago. I have also enjoyed the support of my friends and colleagues conducting the Italian studies program at La Trobe University: Nicole Prunster, Brigid Maher and Abigail Liggieri, as well as the ever-willing professional help of the La Trobe University Library staff. My family have sustained me joyously through all the ups and downs.

I acknowledge with thanks the kind permission of the respective editors to publish revised versions of articles which appeared in the following volumes:

2006 "Bello the bilingual cockatoo: writing Italian lives in Australia", *Annali d'Italianistica* (Univ of N Carolina), 24, pp. 107-31.

2007 "Translating lives: Italian-Australian biography and translation", *Life Writing*, 4.1, pp. 41-58.

2007 "Scrivere la biografia di un siciliano d'Australia. *Sebastiano Pitruzzello: l'uomo, la famiglia, l'industria* di Piero Genovesi", *Studi Emigrazione*, XLIV.168, pp. 877-86.

2007 "Writing the life of an Italian Australian: Piero Genovesi's *Sebastiano Pitruzzello: l'uomo – la famiglia – l'industria*" in *Literary and social diasporas: an Italian Australian perspective,* edited by Gaetano Rando and Gerry Turcotte, Brussels: Peter Lang, pp. 97-107.

2008 "'You're on the list!' Writing the Australian Italian experience of wartime internment", *FULGOR: Flinders University Languages Group Online Review*. Vol. 3, Issue 3, November 2008, pp. 46-56.

2012 "Fosco Antonio's *My Reality*: A rogue Italian Australian autobiography", *Spunti e Ricerche*, vol. 27, pp. 100-14.

Finally, my warm thanks go to Co.As.It. Italian Assistance Association in Victoria and Anne Parnis for their financial support which has made this publication possible.

John Gatt-Rutter

Chapter 1

Bello the Bilingual Cockatoo

Which lives? What stories? What language?

In his 1993 study on *The Politics of Language in Australia*, Uldis Ozolins draws on an earlier report by Erwin Koch-Emmery on Italian immigrants in Canberra in 1953 – that is, during the early part of the period of mass migration from Italy and other parts of Southern Europe into Australia which mainly covers the 1950s and 1960s. Koch-Emmery found himself drawn into the problems faced by the Italians through witnessing incidents such as the following, which took place in a canteen when Italian and Australian workers were queuing for lunch:

> One Australian came late and pushed in front of some Italians. The Italians protested. The Australian, obviously trying to amuse his fellow-workers, hit the nearest Italian in the face, called him a b… dago and told him to go to the end of the queue. The Italian left the queue without saying a word, and put his arm under a circular saw that was running nearby. When I saw him in hospital a few days later he admitted that he had been absolutely crazy with indignation, not so much at the man who had insulted him, but at the fact that none of the other Australians had taken sides with him and that he had felt that, as he did not know enough English, he just had to find another means of making his protest. [Koch-Emmery 1953; quoted in Ozolins 1993: 61-2]

The factors and motivations making for silence or publication of a life experience are extraordinarily variable, and the anonymous protagonist of this incident does not appear to have committed his life story to print or to have it done for him. Most people do not write their autobiography or have a biography written about them. What is more, certain life experiences tend not to surface in formal genres of life writing, and come up, if at all, only in response to purposive socio-anthropological or ethnographic, or even clinical, probing.[1]

A telling instance of this emerges in a paper by Diana Glenn [2004] about some informants who, like her own parents, came to South Australia from Campania as part of the mass migration of the 1950s and 1960s. "There is a wealth of information still to be collected and analysed about," writes Glenn: among other things, "the survival stories of young girls being hidden in abandoned wells, in barns, in holes dug deep underground and in the hillsides, in secret places where they wouldn't be found by the occupying German forces." [Glenn 2004: 128-9] Glenn explains: "The process of enculturation in the second and third generations living in Adelaide was mostly based on experiential narratives, evoked through memory (not transcribed onto paper)" [119].

Glenn herself transcribes one of these onto paper, "The story of Uncle Fred and the Chooks", a hilarious anecdote which goes back to the 1930s or 1920s in South Australia, extends over three good pages of print [120-3], and represents "enculturation" in the sense that it dramatises the language gap between Italian and English as it affects the larger than life Uncle Fred who rejoices in the Italian name of Ferino. Ferino, in fact, through an interlingual misunderstanding, finds that he has acquired six cratefuls of chickens at an auction, without the crates, and has to carry the thirty-six birds home in his brand new saloon car, and then live on chicken broth for days to come.

This brings us closer to the heart of my present enterprise in this book, which is not "information", but the link between discourse

---

1   Individual lives are projected within a social survey perspective in Morag Loh (ed.), *With Courage in their Cases: The experiences of thirty-five Italian immigrant workers and their families in Australia.* Carlton, Victoria: FILEF, 1980. In this book I focus on full-length life narratives. However, this issue is further discussed in chapter 5 below on "Autoethnography".

and experience, and experience *as* discourse, and the publication of both in print.

Through the print medium, discourse and experience circulate among a new and less easily definable social group. Koch-Emmery's story and Glenn's may differ in that Koch-Emmery as eye-witness is author of the former and addresses it to non-Italian Australians like himself, while Glenn picks up a more comically catastrophic tale that has been circulating orally as part of the folk culture of South Australia's Italians for over half a century. But the two instances have some things in common. One is the language barrier (the immigrant's lack of English), and another is the fact that "enculturation" – the adaptation and development of personal identity in relation to a group identity or awareness, but also the collective group identity or awareness as such – is shown in process (sometimes abruptly, and sometimes negatively), first through life experiences and then through the narratives of those life experiences circulating among more or less defined social groups. Neither personal nor group identity is fixed, but each is more or less fluid and perpetually mobile, forever being reconstituted, and this dynamic evolution of identity is most marked at moments of marked interaction between different social groups, as in a situation of mass migration.

All the texts discussed in this opening exploratory chapter are written in English, except the autobiographies by Olga D'Albero Giuliani and by Carlo Zaccariotto (this latter co-authored by Pino Bosi) and the biographies of Sebastiano Pitruzzello and Joe Maffina (*Cammina per me, Elsie*), written by Piero Genovesi and Flavio Lucchesi respectively. Genovesi's book has also been translated into English by Walter Musolino, and the translation will be briefly discussed here and studied in some depth in a later chapter. Flavio Lucchesi is the only non-Australian author discussed (and his book has also been translated), while Judith Armstrong, Michal Bosworth (New Zealand-born co-author of Emma Ciccotosto's book), Helen Garner and Mark Thomas are non-Italian Australians. The market for some of these works may be presumed to be small, but nevertheless, some texts have been re-published. Apart from the conspicuously special case of Bob Santamaria, there are those of other *notabili* or self-made men – Bonutto, Alcorso, the biography of Pitruzzello, as well as the other rather different case of Garner's book about Joe Cinque. And Emma Ciccotosto's autobiography not only inspired a successful play, *Emma*, by Graham Pitts and the Deckchair Theatre, but also an augmented second edition with a culinary-anthropological section, under the title *Emma: A recipe for life*.

A clear-cut distinction in these texts between biography and autobiography cannot always be made. Of the texts in Italian, only that by Olga D'Albero Giuliani is straightforwardly autobiographical in that the author writes her own life story (covering one ten-year period with sporadic diary entries and another ten-year period with sporadic letters), and the same is true of the texts written in English by Claudio Alcorso, Rino Baggio and Adele Bentley. Maria Pallotta-Chiarolli's *Tapestry* interweaves the story of the author's own life in the third person with those of five generations of her family, from great-grandmother to daughter.

Conversely, the first-person "autobiography" of Amelia Musso Tilbury, *Amelia, a Long Journey*, is actually written, with great conviction and vivid immediacy, by her granddaughter, Maria Triaca, from tape-recordings and conversations with her grandmother, and from other sources [Triaca 1985: "Acknowledgements"]. Carlo Zaccariotto figures as the author of *"Me ricorde …"*, which is in fact the story of his life narrated by the well-established bilingual writer and journalist, Pino Bosi, predominantly via lively conversations and monologues by Zaccariotto.

Emma: A translated life, as the title hints, like its extended version, *Emma: A recipe for life*, is the autobiography of the Abruzzo dialect speaker, Emma Ciccotosto, rendered into a coherent narrative in brisk English by her co-author, Michal Bosworth, who explains: "It was truly a joint effort. Every word I wrote she had to understand, so I had to use as much of Emma's vocabulary as I could, and as little of the historian's jargon as I could manage. We have aimed at a clear and understandable script which everyone from a non-English speaking background can read … The whole question of language is a troubling one for me."[2]

---

2   See Ciccotosto and Bosworth [1990: 12-13] and also Emma's own comments

Diana Ruzzene-Grollo, inserting her own childhood story of growing up as an Italian immigrant in a 1950s Melbourne suburb within the widening circles of the histories of related families in the Veneto and then in Melbourne over several generations, and of the well sourced and referenced histories of both their former and their adopted home areas, acknowledges having her English grammar corrected in *Growing Through the Brick Floor*, and the Italian version of the same book, *Noi gente d'emigrazione*, done by Piero Genovesi, is a fresh redaction of the author's original material prior to its editing for the English version.[3]

From this spectrum of more or less straightforwardly autobiographical texts, it is not a long hop to Piero Genovesi's biography of the Pitruzzello family, largely based on interviews with Sebastiano Pitruzzello himself and with family members and friends, and a further mediation in the English translation of Genovesi's book by Walter Musolino.

The hop is only a little bit longer to Judith Armstrong's resourceful exploitation of the interview method, and of her own role as friendly enquirer, in *The Cook and the Maestro*, with the brothers Sergio and Stefano de Pieri and their circle, both in and around their native Dosson near Treviso and in Melbourne and Mildura and other locations in Victoria.

Flavio Lucchesi approaches the life of Joe Maffina, after his death, by drawing copiously on the memoirs about her father written in English by his daughter, Ersilia (Elsie) Enright, which he translates into Italian to form nearly half the text of his *Cammina per me, Elsie* (*Walk for Me, Elsie*), alternating sections of social history of immigration from the Alpine region of the Valtellina into Western Australia with the corresponding narrative of the Maffina family's personal experiences.

Furthest out (but only in the sense I have been pursuing) is Helen Garner's *Joe Cinque's Consolation*, where the interviewing and investigative technique cannot get her directly to her eponymous

in Ciccotosto and Bosworth [1995: 151].

3   See Ruzzene Grollo [1997: v; 1999: "Nota del traduttore"].

subject, who had been murdered two years earlier.

In all these cases, except possibly the straight autobiographies, there is at least one intermediary between the subject of the life history and the published text, and in all these cases this mediation is marked by what Kyrkilis, Nicolacopoulos and Vassilocopoulos [2005] have called "solidarity", or sympathy and understanding with a sociocultural and political inflexion, towards the subject (in their case, Greeks who had migrated to Australia). Jennifer Burns, [2003] for the parallel and converse case of non-European immigrants into Italy writing in Italian, invokes Derrida's *Politics of Friendship* and Homi Bhabha's notion of the mediating "third space" (between and across the two cultures in contact) to similar effect.

This sympathetic mediation minimises the risk of the imposition of one personality or culture on the other, such as that, identified by Alison Ravenscroft, of the "whitening" of Australian Aboriginal life writing texts by "white" Australian editors to make them conform to the norms of mainstream society and culture [Ravenscroft 2005].

How hard it is to eliminate this risk altogether, however, can be seen in Musolino's translation of Genovesi's biography of the Sicilian Sebastiano Pitruzzello. Despite the fact that Musolino is a fully bilingual and bicultural Italian Australian, his mediation between the two cultures tends subtly but pervasively to Australianise Genovesi's text. Italian (or Sicilian) experience comes across in translation as less "lived" (*vissuto*); the migrant experience is presented much less as an "adventure" (a term commonly used in Italian life writing to describe the move to Australia). Italian or Sicilian identity is reduced to a "heritage" or "memory", despite the fact that modern communications can keep it fresh and immediate. Thus, even a sympathetically inclined translator like Musolino can, perhaps unconsciously, apply what students of translation call a "cultural filter", which tends to over-interpret the culture of the source text in terms of the dominant culture of the target language. This instance is more fully explored in one of the following chapters of this book.

Emma Ciccotosto and Michal Bosworth's *Emma: A translated life* appeared only a year after Eva Hoffmann's classic 1989 autobiography, *Lost in Translation: A life in a new language*, the story of a Polish Jewish girl moving to Vancouver in the 1950s at the age of thirteen, and later to the United States. But, like the other texts examined here, *Emma* is not, as is Hoffman's text, an introspective intellectual enquiry into the subject's negotiation between two different linguistically and culturally formed modes of consciousness. Rather, it is conceived as a chronicle of survival and adaptation to a new and harsh physical environment within a very different society. Nevertheless, as we shall see, virtually all the texts examined in this chapter, beginning with those by Koch-Emmery and Glenn, in one way or another, in greater or lesser degree, highlight, at the level of raw social interaction, often involving survival, the struggle of the (auto)biographical subject or self to accommodate two or three different language worlds – Italian and/or dialect, and English.

One variable index of this struggle, or of its transcendence, is the presence of English words or phrases or of anglicisms in Italian texts or of Italian or dialect words or phrases in English texts. These are visible markers of the crossing and dilution of linguistic and cultural boundaries. D'Albero Giuliani's autobiography displays some English uses of Italian words, and uses the English words relating to Australian officialdom. Bosi, evidently aiming at maintaining his subject's Italian identity, avoids anglicisms in his colloquial Italian life of Zaccariotto, but occasionally uses *ritornare* in the sense of *restituire*. In the more formal Italian of his biography of Sebastiano Pitruzzello, Genovesi uses English words only when absolutely unavoidable. These works keep faith with the continuity of an Italian identity component in Australia and keep open an easy line of communication with potential readers in Italy. (Genovesi's text is in fact used as a school reader in Pitruzzello's native Sortino).[4]

Musolino's translation of Genovesi's biography, conversely, keeps to a minimum the use of Italian words (*ricotta, mozzarella*) in apparent pursuit of Australian acceptability. Likewise, autobiographies and biographies of Italian Australians written in English (Bonutto, Triaca, Bentley, Ciccotosto / Bosworth, Alcorso) strive to establish their subjects' Australian credentials by cultivating an easy, engaging

---

4   P. Genovesi, personal communication, 1 November 2005.

English idiom, native to Australia but not flaunting Australian linguistic idiosyncrasies, and (except in Triaca's case) with little or no use of Italian or dialect in the service of cross-cultural reference or "authenticity".

Like Triaca, Armstrong enjoys importing bits of Italian into her English text but, with greater insider's assurance than Triaca, moving eagerly into an Italian space, does not always provide the English equivalent. In these works, with a tendency that becomes more marked as we enter the third millennium, a mutual interest in, and appreciation for, Italianness and Australianness develops that fluid "third space" hypothesised by Bhabha, amid that multi-dimensional space within a Western world open to promiscuous migration, transverse identity, and varying degrees of ethnic mixing or interaction. Acceptability of the non-Australian origins by the Australian society, or reassurance of a continued Italian identity component for Italians in Australia, is the dominant goal of the discursive strategy.

By contrast, Rino Baggio's defiant autobiography contests this linguistic and cultural boundary in more ways than one, but also in his educated irreverence towards established English usage, his unceremonious use of Italian and dialect words, and his introduction of a chapter devoted to a glossary of words and phrases of the hybrid "Italo-Australian" *lingua franca* used by most Italian Australians, employing English lexis with Italian phonology, grammar and syntax [cf. Paul Carter 1992].

Compensatory auto/biography

If one judges by Gillian Whitlock's 1996 anthology *Autographs: Contemporary Australian autobiography*, Italian Australian autobiography had not had much impact on "mainstream" Australian consciousness.[5] Her anthology has 42 extracts by 36 authors. Of

---

5   This is borne out by the fact that neither the earlier *Penguin Book of Australian Autobiography*, ed. by John and Dorothy Colmer (1987) and *Stories of Herself When Young: Autobiographies of childhood by Australian women*, ed. by Joy Hooton, Melbourne: Oxford University Press, 1990, nor the slightly later *Australian Lives: An Oxford Anthology*, ed. by Joy Hooton, 1998, include any Italian Australian.

these, several are by indigenous Australians and a few by Australians from non-Anglo-Celtic backgrounds. There are none by Italian Australians, though Rosa Cappiello's transgeneric *Oh Lucky Country*[6] is listed as an autobiography, and also listed is a piece by Lilian De Angelini.[7] This exclusion is no doubt largely unconscious and accidental. It was not Whitlock's plan to include samples from every major ethnic group in Australia. Also, relatively few straightforwardly autobiographical Italian Australian texts had appeared in English by the mid-1990s, when her anthology was going to press, and most had limited circulation. But does another consideration apply? In her introduction, Whitlock, following Joy Hooton, remarks:

> Sadly, reading autobiography has often been part of the process whereby thinking about Australian identity is confined and confirmed. There has been an ongoing assumption that autobiography will prove a quarry for confirming familiar national myths, that the "quest for personal identity" must involve asking fundamental questions about national identity. This approach has resulted in some self-fulfilling tendencies ... depressing the variety of the genre in Australia, "re-establishing received perceptions of a homogeneous national identity even while claiming to explore the relevance of the concept".[8]

This might seem to apply equally to Italian Australian life writing. Though academics may focus on issues of "ethnic" identity, identity boundaries may be precisely what those living and/or writing the lives of Italian Australians wish to overcome. As I hope to show, their stories mostly have a two-fold and interlinked vocation: the

6   Rosa Cappiello, *Paese fortunato*, Milan: Feltrinelli, 1981; as *Oh Lucky Country*, trans. Gaetano Rando, St. Lucia: Queensland University Press, 1984.

7   G. Whitlock, *op. cit.*, p. 311

8   G. Whitlock, "Introduction: disobedient subjects", in G. Whitlock (ed.), op. cit., pp. ix-xxx (see p. xix). Whitlock's embedded quotation is drawn from Joy Hooton, "Australian Autobiography and the Question of National Identity: Patrick White, Barry Humphries and Manning Clark", *a/b: Auto/Biography Studies* 9 (Spring 1994), pp. 43-63, p. 44.

affirmation of their survival and success in a new and difficult material and social environment and adverse circumstances; and their claim to be accepted as Australian. Neither of these vocations seeks to challenge the established Australian polity and socio-economic order except in broadening the Australian identity construct to make it include the laboriously modified construct of their own identity.

Whereas Whitlock searches Australian autobiography for "disobedient subjects", the writing of Italian Australian lives is inclined towards obedience as long as it does not involve deleting their identity of origin. As Sneja Gunew argues, ethnic minority narrative writing expresses nostalgia for a unified subject and for legitimation [Gunew 1994: 112-13]. This is especially true of Italian Australian life writing (as of most life writing generally). For Italian Australians, such "nostalgia" exhibits a characteristically complex duality: a yearning for the place of origin, whether personal or ancestral, as the origin of identity; and the memory of ordeals endured and overcome as the anvil on which identity is re-formed: the two compounded by being encoded in different language worlds and cultures. What may not apply so generally is Gunew's claim that "the machinery of nostalgia … releases the uncanny" as the return of the repressed [Gunew 1994: 15]. This is one of the things we shall be watching out for.

What sorts of challenge, if any, do Italian Australian life writing texts present to the restrictive identity constructs of ethnicity, whether the "Australian" majority ethnicity or the "Italian" minority ethnicity? Rando presents one possible answer. Discussing Italian Australian writing generally, and not exclusively life writing, he sees it as an expression of sociocultural and personal identity conflict, of marginalisation and crisis, and he sees it as presenting a highly critical, even negative, view of Australian society, through the experience, which is unique to the immigrant, of an irreconcilable clash between two worlds and ways of being, forcing a reappraisal of Australian principles of "equality" and "non-discrimination".

This view from the periphery, Rando suggests, challenges the hegemonic discourse from the centre as represented by Australia's then current (and second longest serving) Prime Minister, John Howard [Rando 2004: 262-4]. "Ci si potrebbe chiedere", writes Rando, "se questi scritti … in alcuni casi potrebbero rappresentare il tentativo da parte dello scrittore di risolvere certi dilemmi personali." [One might ask whether these writings … might in some cases embody an attempt on the writer's part to resolve certain personal dilemmas Rando. 2004: 261]

The motives for writing one's own life, or having it written, have an added poignancy when that life crosses two cultures and, especially, two languages. To convey that experience to those that have never known it, having lived safely monocultural and monolingual lives, or to share it with others who have lived cross-cultural lives, can itself be an existential imperative, of which I shall consider some instances in this first chapter, before looking at the entire corpus in the rest of this work.

Crossing the linguistic and cultural divide can itself be traumatic, or at least an awesome challenge, depending on the subject's prior knowledge of the new language and his or her language learning opportunities. The overwhelming majority of Italians coming to Australia have had to face that challenge or trauma. But, beyond that linguistic ordeal, and at least until the inauguration of multi-culturalism in the 1970s, Italians in Australia, seen as competitors in the workforce, have often, from as early as primary school, faced hostility, discrimination, and persecution, sometimes amounting to outright violence, especially in northern Queensland during the 1920s and the Western Australian goldfields in the 1930s.

Many Italians, especially the most prominent, even if naturalised Australians, or even born in Australia, were interned as "enemy aliens" during the war years 1940-43 [Rando 2005b: 22; Elkner, Martinuzzi O'Brien, Rando and Cappello 2005]. A much higher percentage of Italians living in Australia were subjected to this treatment than in either the USA or Britain. The trauma inflicted on those concerned by this experience of imprisonment was so great that it has remained largely a "storia segreta".

Here we have a hint of the "uncanny", which is borne out by the intense memories of the internment experience directly or indirectly inscribed in the autobiographies by Bonutto, Dalseno (which we will look at in a later chapter, as part of a more detailed study of accounts of internment) and Alcorso, in Lucchesi's biography of Joe Maffina, and perhaps most suggestively in the silence of Bob Santamaria, who escaped that experience. Rando, researching the matter, found that "Only one third of the pre-war [Italian] migrants interviewed were willing to talk about wartime experiences and of these only one … was willing to speak extensively about his internment" [Rando 2005b: 25].

Emma Ciccotosto almost makes light of the fact that at the age of fourteen she was left to run the family market garden when her father was interned [Ciccotosto and Bosworth 1990: 44-8], but the bitterness provoked by one or more of these traumas, and compensatory self-vindication, are conspicuously foregrounded in the autobiographies by Osvaldo Bonutto and Claudio Alcorso and the biography of Joe Maffina by Flavio Lucchesi. Bonutto felt unable to mention his experience of internment to his children for twenty years,[9] and Alcorso elsewhere also admits that for many years he felt unable to talk about it.[10] It was not until the early 1990s that Australia's Federal and various State Parliaments passed unanimous motions of apology for the wartime policy.

Italy's exit from the war in 1943 saw the end of internment of Italians in Australia, but not the end of fairly widespread discrimination and hostility. Furthermore, during the 1950s and 1960s, Italian and other immigrants were often held waiting many months in reception camps (converted from military camps) for promised employment, so that their frustration sometimes led to unrest, most signally the riots in the Bonegilla reception camp in 1952. (The most coherent circumstantial account of the troubles at Bonegilla and elsewhere at this time is that by Idini [2012]). On the other hand, Olga

---

9   Don Dignan, "Foreword", in Osvaldo Bonutto, *A Migrant's Story: The struggle and success of an Italian-Australian, 1920s–1960s,* 2nd ed., St Lucia: University of Queensland Press, 1994, p. x.

10 Claudio Alcorso and Caroline Alcorso, "Italians in Australia during World War II," in Stephen Castles, Caroline Alcorso, Gaetano Rando and Ellie Vasta (eds.), *Australia's Italians: Culture and community in a changing society*, North Sydney: Allen & Unwin, 1992, p. 34 (quoted in Rando, "Italo-Australians During the Second World War", p. 43).

D'Albero Giuliani's autobiography gives a rather heart-warming picture of the people and facilities at Bonegilla in 1957 [D'Albero Giuliani 1994: 307-25].

Double lives

In his greatly abbreviated 1994 version of the text originally published in 1963, Bonutto's linear narrative, in matter-of-fact, unaffected English, of his experience in, and identification with, Australia since his migration from the Veneto to Queensland in 1924 at the age of 21, clearly climaxes with the sixth of his seven chapters, titled "'J'accuse': internment", forcefully associating his wrongful victimisation with that of Alfred Dreyfus which had been the subject of Emile Zola's famous open letter of that title in 1898 [Bonutto 1994: 51]. Bonutto's vividly detailed memorial recall or reconstruction (a quality of all the life writing narratives examined here) and factual or documentary evidence are coupled with a sustained argument against intolerance, prejudice and discrimination inspired by xenophobic rivalry or envy which recur in episodes both preceding and following that sixth chapter. Bonutto's autobiography is courteously but firmly couched as an argument for the host society to accept those newcomers like Bonutto himself who are eager to be accepted as Australian without renouncing their origins.

The dominant theme is expressed in the seventh chapter, where Bonutto reports the outcome of an attempted boycott of his hotel at Gympie: "The majority of the people of Gympie showed their true Australian nature by rallying to my support" [Bonutto 1994: 86]. This is in keeping with the book's subtitle, "The struggle and success of an Italian Australian". First appearing in 1963, Bonutto's work served to spearhead the campaign for a more inclusive and open Australian society and polity than that based on the "White Australia" policy of Anglo-Celtic dominance which had re-emerged from the Second World War.

Alcorso foregrounds his bitter internment experience differently, making it the first chapter of his autobiography, *The Wind You Say*, after a brief "Prologue", and then following it with two chapters recounting his earlier life based in Rome from his birth in 1913 to

1937 and his first three years in Australia. This dramatically (but not radically) disturbs the book's longitudinal paradigm of chronologically sequential and implicitly incremental narrative which is typical of the life writing that endeavours to build up a unified self through time on the model of the *Bildungsroman* – the model adopted in Bonutto's autobiography and in most of the other life narratives concerning Italian Australians.

The written self-construct predicated on the union of Italianness and Australianness (with Alcorso's vestigial Jewishness almost wholly elided) thus starts from crisis, but in one major respect it still repeats the model expressed in Bonutto's subtitle "struggle and success": Alcorso follows the chapter on his internment with a sequence of chronologically ordered episodes presenting the author's endeavours and achievements, "fragments from the life of a perplexed, fortunate man" [Alcorso 1993: 170].

These (like Bonutto's) are conceived always in terms of an identification of the personal project with the national, but also more widely humanistic, project of advancing Australia, whether through anti-Fascist journalism, artistic innovation in textile design, pioneering the silk commerce with China in the 1950s, chairmanship of the newborn Sydney Opera House autonomous company and the Australian Elizabethan Theatre Trust, activism within the environmental movement in Tasmania, the introduction of wine-making to Tasmania and the building of his residence on the model of a classical Roman villa at Moorilla outside Hobart.

This parallels Bonutto's achievements in progressing from cutting sugar-cane in northern Queensland to establishing the tobacco industry in southern Queensland and running hotels at places in between, Alcorso starting with higher educational qualifications (including a year's postgraduate study in England) and good connections. But it is notable that what stimulated Alcorso to pen his autobiography was his being asked to contribute a chapter describing his experience of internment to a collective volume on *Australia's Italians*, his archival research into the official records relating to his own internment and the interminable proceedings involved in securing his eventual release.

Internment is simply ignored in what must be one of the most widely read life narratives to have been written by an Italian Australian, B. A. Santamaria's *Santamaria – A Memoir* (1997, published in an earlier version as *Against the Tide* in 1981). Bartholomew Augustine, generally known as "Bob", Santamaria, born in Melbourne of Sicilian parents in 1915, has probably had more impact on Australia than any other Italian Australian. His anti-Marxist campaign split the Australian Labor Party and kept it out of government during the third quarter of the last century. Italian identity played no overt part in this. Santamaria's memoir mentions the Second World War as perfunctorily as could be and does not at all refer to the internment of Italians as "enemy aliens". This is despite, or because of, the fact, that the Catholic Archbishop Mannix, with whom Santamaria worked closely, ensured that Italians in the State of Victoria were far more leniently treated than those in other States.

Santamaria's memoir devotes only a few early pages to his own Italianness. He remarks:

> From the food we ate to the music we enjoyed, our way of life was unmistakably Italian. Perhaps this explains why a deep love for all things Italian, from its history to its literature to its music, prevails in me today. Whether it is the Italy of reality or the Italy of the mind that plays on my imagination and excites my affection, I do not know. [B. A. Santamaria 1997: 5]

Of himself and his fellow-Italians at school, Bob says:

> We knew by instinct that what we call cultural affinity was one thing and political allegiance another. We all knew that we were Italian by blood but Australian by national allegiance. Should a conflict between both arise – as it did during the course of World War II – national allegiance must prevail [ibid].

Yet Mark Thomas' *Australia in Mind: Thirteen influential Australian thinkers* opens as follows:

> B. A. Santamaria has often been depicted as a European intellectual who happens to work in Australia, rather than as an Australian thinker with distinctive national roots,

loyalties and interests. That view of Santamaria's alienness has been compounded by his opponents' emphasis on other ostensibly foreign traits: Santamaria's Italian ancestry, his reliance on secrecy, his links to the Vatican, his affinities with European Christian Democrats, and – in Dr Evatt's notorious phrase – his use of "methods which strikingly resemble both Communist and Fascist infiltration of larger groups".

And Thomas gives it as his own view that "the assumptions and premises in Santamaria's thought just seem alien in Australia" by virtue of Santamaria's historical perspective and his view of "Anglo-Saxon" foundational myths from the outside [Thomas 1989: 24]. Thomas may simply be implying that the Catholic Church-centred world-view, with its ultimate loyalty to the Vatican, had always been subordinate in Australia. The ethnic majority ("Anglo-Celtic") is constituted as "Australian" in subordinating other value systems (the family,[11] religion) to the polity and marginalising them as "alien".

If the life writing impetus for Alcorso and Bonutto came from the outrage inflicted by internment on their desire to be accepted as Australian, that same smarting desire is at work in Rino Baggio's *The Shoe in My Cheese: An immigrant family experience* (1989). Baggio, born of parents from the Veneto in 1937 and brought up in Little River in rural Victoria just outside Melbourne, conjures up a vivid and indulgent reconstruction of how the local policeman enjoyed a superior lifestyle in terms of fresh farm produce during the war years by playing on the fear of internment on the part of Baggio's father and other Italian farmers. To an even greater extent than Bonutto and Alcorso, Baggio goes beyond vivid reconstructions of a vanished past and lost scenarios (which he does as well as anyone) to engage polemically with the wartime policy of internment and, more generally, the recurrent xenophobia of some Australians. But he also irreverently and learnedly lambasts the Church's long history

---

11 Ross Fitzgerald identifies the experience of Italian (or Sicilian) family life and family values as central to Santamaria's life project: "The break-up of the family as a consequence of industrialisation echoed throughout Santamaria's adult writing" [Fitzgerald 2003: 7].

of unforgiving power-struggles and its doctrine of transubstantiation in the Eucharist, as well as the secular follies of empire and government, giving the reader a running debate with history, from a remote Mediterranean past to the personally experienced Australian present.

As his title hints, his irreverence extends to language, which, in Baggio's ink, overflows Australian niceties, felicities, complicities and proprieties, coining new and hybrid words and resurrecting old and exotic ones, injecting instability and idiosyncrasy, a moderately immodest excess whose occasional admixture of erudition and Italian will sometimes leave some readers out of the game. A half self-confessed Joyce *manqué*, not for nothing has Baggio encountered academic criticism for his discursive misdemeanours [Musolino 1988-89: 141-5].

Baggio's is only a mildly roguish text as compared with that outrageous projection of the "lucky country" in sub-proletarian multiethnic Sydney as hell which is Cappiello's 1981 quasi- or pseudo-autobiographical *Paese fortunato* [*Oh, Lucky Country*, 1984],[12] or as compared with Fosco Antonio's *My Reality*, which is the subject of a later chapter of this book, but Baggio makes a stand for the acceptance of difference rather than the imposition of sameness and the demand for a fake facsimile of Australianness which, however perfect a copy, can never pass as the equivalent of a presumed original [Baggio 1989: 92-102]. As is more discreetly mooted by Bonutto and Alcorso, Baggio's is a plea for a more expansive and inclusive Australianness which does not reject Italianness (or other cultural affiliations) as "alien".

The post-war success stories of Carlo Zaccariotto (another native of the Veneto) as a construction entrepreneur and Sebastiano Pitruzzello (from Sicily) as a processed cheese manufacturer do not have to face the experience of internment and do not dwell on instances of hostility or exclusion. They tell a tale of initial toil and struggle and then of more or less rapid success, pitched in terms of

---

12 This is one of the best-known texts of Australian ethnic minority writing (or, more precisely, of Italian writing in Australia), and has been extensively discussed, e.g., in Gaetano Rando's introduction to his translation of Cappiello's book, in Gunew [1994] and in Kirkby [1996].

life as an "adventure". The tone is light-hearted, personal and chatty in the conversations and anecdotage between Zaccariotto and his scribe Pino Bosi, while it acquires epic resonances in Piero Genovesi's biography of Pitruzzello, which goes back to the ancient Greek ruins of Pantalica in Sicily and situates the Pitruzzellos' transmigration within the context of that mass exodus of over a quarter of a million Italians who moved to Australia during the 1950s and 1960s.[13]

As in all the other life stories under consideration, great emphasis is placed on "helpers" – insiders, established Australians of whatever standing – who offer friendship and help and support the immigrant at key moments, whether psychologically or economically. The fact that these life stories were written and published in Australia in Italian fits in with a long (but now rapidly fading) tradition of Italian-language writing and publishing in Australia, and denotes that their subjects are relaxed about sporting their Italianness in print within their adopted country.

This last point applies also to a very different subject of auto-biography, Olga D'Albero Giuliani, a Neapolitan who moved to Melbourne in 1957 at the age of thirty-two while expecting her fourth child. Her long text, *Piccola quercia: la vita di Olga* [Little Oak-Tree: Life of Olga], is divided equally between Naples and Melbourne, but being Italian in Australia never figures as a problem for Olga.

Battling all her life, whether in Naples or in Melbourne, in domes-tic work, cleaning or catering, mostly as an employee, occasionally self-employed, it is her mother's indifference towards her, and then her husband's, culminating when he deserts her after she has had her tenth child, that torments her; it is love that drives her: love for her uncaring mother, for her wayward husband, for her family of origin, particularly her physically disadvantaged brother Alberto, for her own children; above all for God, to whom she addresses the poem that closes her life story, and whom she regularly refers to as an interlocutor. Love, for Olga, entails romance, and in her

13 Flavio Lucchesi uses the word *epopea* in the subtitle of his biography of Joe Maffina, which he places both in broad historical perspective and in detailed historical context, but he does not deploy the epic literary trope. Genovesi's work is discussed more fully in chapter 4 below.

eight-year-long clandestine courtship with Franco she sees herself as the heroine of a novel, "l'eroina d'un romanzo" [D'Albero Giuliani 1994: 117], with Liala (the Italian counterpart to Barbara Cartland) as her intertextual model: a romantic delusion which is doomed to disillusion. The absence of love, or its loss, produces a void, like the end of that happy period of childhood before both her parents died, a void which she tries to fill with memories: "Anni di sogni dolcissimi, che mi destarono troppo presto, lasciando nel mio cuore un vuoto enorme, che durante tutto il corso della mia vita ho cercato di riempire con la dolcezza dei ricordi." [Years of sweetest daydreams, which awoke me all too soon, leaving in my heart an enormous void, which I've endeavoured throughout my life to fill with the sweetness of memory. – D'Albero Giuliani 1994: 61]

Autobiography for Olga is emotional reliving: "Narrando la storia della mia vita, io l'ho rivissuta: ho rivisto volti adorati, luoghi carissimi, ho riso, scherzato, pianto e amato nuovamente, e tutto ciò mi ha fatto tanto bene." [Relating the story of my life, I've relived it: I've seen once more adored faces, beloved places, I've laughed and joked, wept and loved all over again, and all of this has done me so much good. "Prefazione"]

Olga's is the traditionally gendered life-story of family, of the policing of social and sexual roles, of domesticity and domestic or related labour (rising to the status of chef to a club), of the female body (menstruation, non-consensual artificial insemination, pregnancy, attempted seduction and actual rape, fulfilment and disappointment in the marriage bed, issues of infertility or excessive fertility), of the struggle with the Victoria Housing Commission to retain her family's right to subsidised accommodation, of dreams of having her own *pizzeria* and economic self-sufficiency – all recounted with an impressive show of frankness, and a retrospective astonishment at her own compliance with male domination: "Perché tacqui, perché obbedii, perché non mi ribellai? Sono domande che mi faccio solo oggi.; … una marionetta nelle mani di Franco …, io confusi terribilmente l'ubbidienza con la stupidaggine." [Why did I keep silent? why did I obey? why didn't I rebel? Only today do I ask myself these questions. … A puppet in Franco's hands …, I had hopelessly mixed up obedience with stupidity. – D'Albero Giuliani 1994: 266] Her autobiography is therefore, for her, a retrospective emancipation, as well as her vindication of herself as a *piccola quercia*, having survived, even prospered, as a single mother of ten children, and in a new country and a new language.

Other women's life stories play variations on these themes – endurance in the struggle with poverty, setting up home (possibly several times over), negotiating gender and familial roles, self-realisation. Vitality is claimed in the title of the second edition of Emma Ciccotosto's autobiography, *Emma: A recipe for life*, and the apotheosis of her life as a worker in a Fremantle biscuit factory is a world cruise with her husband, followed by a lively and sociable Third Age.

As Emma, then aged thirteen, and her family left Casalbordino near Vasto in the Abruzzo to join her father at Waroona, south of Perth, in 1939, they were just in time to escape the blows of the war years in Italy and to brave the blows of the war years in Australia. One blow was internment for Emma's father, with Emma left to run the vegetable farm. Another blow was the call-up for her fellow-Abruzzese fiancé, Peter, who was caught dodging the draft and imprisoned when Emma (up to then ignorant of the facts of life) was already pregnant, but released from Fremantle prison for the day of their wedding.

Emma's is, among other things, a story of integration despite encountering some hostility and, as in other Italian life stories, largely thanks to the decency of Australian "helpers". It is also a story of survival amid apparently desperate circumstances (at one time, Emma was living in a shed with her four infants) [Ciccotosto and Bosworth 1990: 80)]. Her longitudinal narrative achieves its strongest effect in the evolving relationship, over some thirty years, with her formidable mother-in-law. The latter was convinced that Emma had trapped Peter into marriage, and never accepted her, until the end of her life when, a helpless and difficult invalid, she found herself neglected by all her own family, and cared for only by Emma.

Amelia: a Long Journey, the autobiography of Amelia Musso Tilbury written by her granddaughter, Maria Triaca, begins and ends with a return: in 1936, after thirty-two years in Australia, Amelia takes her seventeen-year-old daughter, Gina, back across the oceans to visit her birthplace of Moneglia, near Genoa, and to establish the Italian component of Gina's identity by means of a course at Perugia's University for Foreigners.

The following nineteen chapters circle back to that point in a chronological account of Amelia's astonishing life from her poverty-stricken 1890s childhood with a widowed mother drained of affection by thrift, to the "grand adventure" of her journey to Australia in 1904 to join her great-uncle, a shaggy gold-miner in a squalid shack in Daylesford, Victoria, where, she says, laconically, "I discovered the horror of being different" [Triaca 1985: 45].

Vivid scenes recapture the drama of past moments with richly descriptive detail – a feature of most good (auto)biographies – in choice but unostentatious English, and in a rather understated manner. This applies also to Amelia's meeting during the First World War with the English sergeant Teddy Tilbury, wounded in action, who nevertheless went back to the front, returning safely to Melbourne at the end of the war, only to die of Spanish 'flu shortly after marrying Amelia and leaving her pregnant. She never remarried, but devoted the rest of her life to bringing up her daughter, Gina, as an Italian Australian. Identity is not so much discussed as embodied in the narrative, including its silences, such as that over her vocation for widowhood from the age of twenty-nine.

Fitting in as an Italian in Australia is part of the long journey, for Amelia and for her daughter Gina. The author, Maria Triaca, in her "Epilogue", ends the "autobiography" she has just penned by offering an interpretative key: "She always craved security and the warmth of family life, something she never knew as a child. Today … she has found what she was looking for in Melbourne, Australia" [Triaca 1985: 137]. The narrative itself had ended with Amelia and Gina's return journey back from Genoa to Australia in 1938, not long before the start of the Second World War, when Australia had already applied sanctions against Italy on account of the latter's invasion of Ethiopia.

The almost half-century interval between that date and 1985

elides the trauma of the war years and of the post-war mass migration but Amelia alludes to it obliquely in recollections about her participation in Italian social and cultural circles in 1930s Melbourne, which Mussolini's regime tried to dominate. On behalf of herself and her daughter, she attempts to square the circle of conflicting loyalties: "… our loyalty in the 1930s was to Australia. Yet part of being Australian meant embracing this Italian side of our lives" [Triaca 1985: 134]. With differing inflections, all the Italian Australian life narratives discussed here express this commitment to Australia as a home that does not involve denial of a home of origin. "World War 2", she continues, "when you knew never to speak Italian on the tram and when people who had lived here as Italian Australians for the best part of thirty years were interned and separated from their families, was still ahead of us."

The return visit to Italy is differently and more emphatically foregrounded in Adele Bentley's *Between Two Cultures: Italian-Australian, an autobiography* (1996).[14] Here, the linear chronological narrative proceeds in eight chapters, each designated by the new location, from an account of hard-pressed peasant origins in the province of Belluno in the Veneto and Adele's passage to Australia at the age of two in 1928, through the Depression in 1930s Balcatta near Perth and a sequence of other market-gardening and poultry-farming locations in the same vicinity, climaxing in chapter 9, "Italy – the search for my roots", which accounts for a quarter of the book's total length.

A first point of arrival is chapter 5, "Carmel, a place of our own", though it does not spell the end of hardship for Adele and her Anglo-Australian husband, Bob Bentley. But it is not until two moves later, in chapter 7, "Armadale", that Adele, by this time (in the 1950s) working in a hotel, discovers her autonomy as a person, playing a leading role in organising social life and amenities for the incoming working-class immigrants from Britain (nicknamed in Australia "Ten-Pound Poms" on account of the assisted passage granted them by the Australian government) and for local youth.

---

14 For the socio-economic aspects of return visits to Italy by emigrants to Australia, see Baldassar 2001.

The ninth chapter, describing her tour of Italy in 1988 after fifty-nine years' absence, is a long travelogue of estrangement as Adele recognises and does not recognise Italy as her country in her encounters with her presumed fellow countrymen: "It was then I truly felt the culture shock of Italy's history" [Bentley 1996: 121]. The differences between Italians, and the transformation of Italians over those fifty-nine years, gradually dawn on her as she tours the cities: "If only they knew how strongly I identified with the peasants in Italy – the feel of the earth under my bare feet ..." [Bentley 1996: 130; suspension points in the original]. She describes herself as having been near to screaming, and appeals directly to her readers: "Dear readers, if my description of the tour reads like a travelogue, it is because I felt like a stranger looking on. I ask you to bear with me while I continue the journey ..." [ibid].

Adele dutifully subjects herself and her readers to Rome, Florence, Pisa, Elba until she is met at Mestre, near Venice, by cousins whom she had never met before, but who treat her as if they had always known her, and who drive her through landscapes which she recognises from her parents' descriptions and their stories of the First World War related in the opening chapter [Bentley 1996: 139]. So begins the reunion of a family that had never been together before, and the rediscovery or reintegration of Adele's Italian identity. The process of reintegration climaxes on her return flight to Australia, Adele's account showing her emotions brought drily under control by her discourse as an Australian public figure of some local standing:

> ... I began sobbing under my breath. The realisation suddenly hit me just how deep were my psychic roots. For many years I had been acutely aware of the necessity for mental negotiations; being a citizen of foreign descent meant a constant meshing and blurring of loyalties. However, although there have been many painful moments, the experience has broadened my perspective and in the final analysis has enriched my life. [Bentley 1996: 148]

So an Italian sense of self is subsumed in an Australian discourse: Adele recognises life, personhood, as "being change". "And what am

I?" she asks, and replies: "One thing is now clear. I am an Australian of Italian descent. Australia is my home." And she adds: "Writing my story has been a catharsis." She had already stated, "I especially want my grandchildren to know" [Bentley 1996: 161-2], sounding a note often explicit, always implicit, in these life narratives, in which the print medium supplements, perhaps supplants, the oral narratives that, within a single language world, and before the age of electronic entertainment media, used to maintain continuity between generations.

This conversion of family life narrative from the transgenerational oral tradition into the print medium is spectacularly visible in Maria Pallotta-Chiarolli's *Tapestry: Interweaving lives.* [1999]. "I come from a Southern Italian peasant family oral storytelling tradition as a way of teaching and discussing political and sensitive issues", the author has declared. "In this tradition the anecdote *is* the explanation" [Pallotta-Chiarolli 2004: 154]. Like *Amelia*, this work also opens and ends with the "visit home" to Italy and, as for Adele Bentley, Maria's initial experience of Italy is of estrangement, which changes to a sense of belonging only when she arrives at the *paese* of her parents' origins and reconnects to her extended family, releasing a discharge of emotional self-recognition [Pallotta-Chiarolli 1999: 32].

But that opening and closing spiral intermeshes with numerous other narratives spiralling backwards and forwards in a timeless present or simultaneity, splicing and cross-cutting at countless points between her great-grandparents' generation at rural Montesarcchio [*sic*], near Squillani in the province of Benevento, and her own homes at industrial Adelaide and Melbourne in Australia. Chronology is flagged at virtually every narrative hop so that a sequential order could be rather unnecessarily reconstructed out of the scrambled narratives that are linked together by a different logic of memories, stories heard and repeated, linked issues of courtship and childbirth, school and toil, repression and rebellion, tradition and innovation, identity-forming experiences within one country or the other, all highlighted typographically and by art photographs.

Ancestral continuity, in Pallotta-Chiarolli's family life narrative, is not identified with conformity to the rigid rules and authoritarian male hierarchy of peasant society and its migrant afterlife; nor is it rejected in favour of conformity to a new Australian suburban lifestyle. The author has given us her own highly lucid and conscious self-exegesis in terms of ethnography by herself as participant observer overflowing all visible boundaries, revelling in hybridity, *mestizaje*, inhabiting "multiple life-worlds … inside / outside / no-side both Italian and Australian identities" [Pallotta-Chiarolli 2004: 152].

Though the author remarks that "the anecdote *is* the explanation", her already very pointed anecdotes in *Tapestry* are usually also accompanied by explicit commentary and judgement. To take only one example, old *nonna* Maria Giovanna tells her granddaughter Maria Giovanna, after an incident of male despotism: "They're afraid of us, you know. That's why there are rules" [Pallotta-Chiarolli 1999: 99].

The Italian Australian *mestizaje* that Pallotta-Chiarolli's characters inhabit is not a bipolar world, centred around two fixed poles. The Italian country town and suburban Australia are both presented as sites of struggle and flux, each of them shifting across the decades and the century which the "tapestry" spans. Even the Church is seen as no longer monolithic, as Maria's quest ends with her encountering at a remove a gay priest, a friend of friends in Australia, involved in youth reclamation in the outskirts of Rome in 1996, when, at thirty-five years of age, Maria finally goes to Italy. In all this, the family is emphatically enacted as collective subject and discursive centre, as a network or tapestry, and the hard-won dynamic, open-ended combination of Italianness and Australianness is confidently proclaimed.

Two narratives about Italian Australians by non-Italian Australians, both of them professional writers – Judith Armstrong's book on the brothers Sergio and Stefano de Pieri and Helen Garner's *Joe Cinque's Consolation* – have in common the tale of the chance by which each biographer was drawn into her subject (thus drawing the reader in also) and a warm feeling for the warmth of Italian family feeling and for its expression through hospitality, but have virtually nothing else in common except for the unaffected Australianness of their discourse.

Armstrong gets quite close (though not intrusively) to the

convivial brothers, respectively the eldest and the youngest of six siblings from near Treviso, in her second chapter, "Convivio!", before launching into the classic biographical chronicle of family origins and scene-setting and thematic chapters tracking each of the two brothers through their schooling and early ventures, their widely spaced, and adventurously undertaken, transfers to Australia (in 1961 and 1974 respectively), both their engagingly picaresque careers and social and amorous lives, to their contributions, in Sergio's case, as an organist in two countries, in Stefano's case, to politics and social action, and in both cases to good food, at home with friends in Sergio's case, and for the public at large in Stefano's, combining these things in arts festivals in Victoria's country towns. Recipes by both brothers and poems by Stefano variegate the text.

Armstrong not only conveys two appealing personalities, but situates them in an appealing Australian cultural and social environment, challenging but welcoming, which she knows intimately, giving the sense of two societies made of friendship networks of real people.

Helen Garner's book, *Joe Cinque's Consolation* [2004], opens as follows:

> The first time I saw Joe Cinque among his friends and family, the first time I ever heard his voice, was in the living room of his parents' house in Newcastle, in the winter of 1999.
>
> By then, of course, he had already been dead for nearly two years.

Unlike all the other books so far discussed, which are all more or less abundantly illustrated with photographs, Garner's reportage on the trial for the murder of Joe Cinque and its segue is bare of images until the very end, when Garner and Joe Cinque's mother, Maria, view a video which shows him at a wedding: "We gazed in silence on her undefended son" [Garner 2004: 328]. So the book concludes, and on the facing blank page is a small black-and-white photograph of Joe, as enigmatic and unknowable as Mona Lisa.

The three-hundred-odd pages in between that beginning and that ending carry Garner's account of her own personal quest to come to terms with the pre-announced poisoning and killing of Joe, still in his twenties, by his girlfriend, a fellow-student of Indian descent, and with the light sentence which the latter had received on grounds of diminished responsibility. This wholly modern, late twentieth-century high-life chronicle of a death foretold, gradually draws Garner in to Joe's grim-faced parents at the trial, and subsequently to his circle of friends, first in an effort to understand the extraordinary circumstances and personalities involved, and subsequently, as the law appeared to let his death pass so lightly, in response to Maria Cinque's plea: "All I want is my son to be acknowledged" [Garner 2004: 269].

So we come to know something – a little, and at a remove – of a likeable young second-generation Italian Australian, born to hard-working Southern Italian immigrants, and lured by a yuppie lifestyle combining fast cars, tertiary education, girls – especially one girl – and "recreational" drugs. And we come to know something – a little, and at a remove – of the lifestyle and attitudes and social networks of successfully integrated Australian Italians in a multi-ethnic Australia in which one of the young Italian Australian man's closest female friends is of Spanish parentage and the other of Indian parentage, while the judge who presides over the trial for his murder, as well as the investigating biographer, are both Anglo-Celtic Australians.

The bilingual cockatoo

This brief exploration of fourteen Italian Australian life writing narratives does not allow any but the most tentative of general observations. The spectrum examined is broad in some senses, as it comprises both autobiographies and biographies and texts in between the two; texts written in English as well as Italian; and texts written by non-Italians and by a non-Australian; texts by or about Italians bred in Italy and Italians bred in Australia in diverse periods; but only one text by or about a political or social activist (B. A. Santamaria), apart from the partial exceptions of Adele Bentley and Stefano de Pieri, and some other incidental mentions.

It would be unproductive to apply to this particular assortment of Italian Australian life writing texts the evolutionary interpretative grids elaborated first for American ethnic minority literatures by Aaron Daniel and then for Italian Americana in its entirety, over a much longer time-span, by Fred L. Gardaphé and by Anthony Julian Tamburri respectively [Aaron 1964, 1985; Gardaphé 1996: 11-28; Tamburri 1998: 8-14]. Xenophobia and hostility directed at Italians, culminating in the Second World War with the experience of internment, looms much larger in Italian Australiana than in Italian Americana, so that it strongly marks even a text like *Amelia* where it does not enter the narrative. The long silence inflicted by that trauma accentuates the generational profile of life writing which, since it usually requires an achieved life, implies advanced years, and in most of these texts it is a grandparent that is writing or being written about, and largely for the benefit of ensuing generations.

This generational dimension, in turn, coinciding with the twentieth-century transition from oral transmission between generations to electronic saturation, makes of printed life writing an alternative medium with an undefined alternative circulation, largely within local friendship networks, and also an archive of stored and storied experience. But autobiography is also a process of self-discovery, first in the retracing of the individual's life trajectory and the negotiation and assertion of an Italian Australian self, then, for the Italian Australian, in the "return home", which reveals differences within Italianness itself, as well as a local belonging. Life writing by Italian Australians represents a claim to recognition as members of the Australian community, with full citizenship. This claim for recognition is honoured in the life narratives about Italian Australians written by non-Italian Australians.

The texts by Judith Armstrong and Helen Garner involve discovery by the non-Italian Australian of the Italian, not as an Other, but as an alternative Self. Homi Bhabha's fluid "third space" of "hybridity" is occupied not only by the massive effort on the part of Italians to cross the linguistic and cultural border into "Australia", but also, and no less importantly, by less strenuous effort on the part of Australians to visit Italianness.

Back in the 1920s, as related in Maria Triaca's limpidly

ventriloquial English "autobiography" of her grandmother Amelia Musso Tilbury, Amelia's household in Melbourne boasted a pet sulphur-crested white cockatoo (of a large and handsome species common in the area). This one was called Bello, which he rhymed with "hello", and had a considerable repertoire both in Italian and English, as well as at least two dogs' voices, all of which he addressed to the appropriate interlocutors. Bello also knew how to answer the question: "Bello, vuoi pane o biscotto?" (Do you want bread or biscuit?), though with a pronounced lisp, and could also mimic the gardener's Italian-English [Triaca 1985: 125-6]. He may serve as an auspicious emblem of cross-cultural and interlingual, as well as interspecies, sharing and conviviality.

I first published this last preceding paragraph in 2006 and was delighted to find, six years later, that William McInnes, in his interweaving of Australian life-stories that makes up his book *The Making of Modern Australia*, opens with a foreword titled "History as a Caged Cockatoo". This describes how his little daughter, during a family visit to a folk-history Apex Park in outback Australia, is held spellbound by a great white cockatoo, clinging to the wires of his cage, addressing a hello to her. McInnes adopts this as his symbol for the voice of history addressing us. McInnes' book is hospitable to Australia's multi-ethnic society, though Italian Australians, with the exception of B. A. Santamaria, do not come under his spotlight. Amelia Musso Tilbury's Bello speaks history with the gift of tongues.

Chapter 2

"You're on the List!" Writing the Italian Australian Experience of Wartime Internment

Writing the internment experience

"You're on the list!" This, as recounted in Peter Dalseno's lightly fictionalised third-person autobiography, *Sugar, Tears and Eyeties* [Dalseno 1994: 192], was the new greeting that circulated among the Italians of the Herbert River sugar-cane district of North Queensland when Italy's entry into the Second World War in June 1940 triggered the Australian military authorities' reaction of interning resident Italians. It dovetails sardonically, as we shall see, with more straight-forwardly factual reports emanating from the life histories of another Queenslander, Osvaldo Bonutto, of Claudio Alcorso from Sydney, and of Joe Maffina from far-away Fremantle in Western Australia. It dramatises the historical situation in terms of personal interactions and rumour-mongering even among the Italians themselves, not always without malice.

Factual objectivity is hard to establish in life writing. Dalseno casts his narrative in the third person and calls his protagonist Peter Delano. Other personal names and factual details have also been changed. This is a transparent disguise and distancing device, a bridle on subjectivity, and of itself does not make Dalseno's account any less reliable or "truthful" than a frankly autobiographical or biographical account.[15] In fact, *Sugar, Tears and Eyeties* (like all the life histories

---

15 Dalseno's "Preface" dwells on his having opted for "preciseness" over "praise" or "flattery" [Dalseno 1994: v], while declaring "... I have taken licence ... to substitute names, locality and in some cases omit a specific appendage to an event, for the sake of camouflage" [Dalseno 1994: vii].

referring to the internment of Australian Italians) is securely moored to its historical context, both global and local, at every turn, but this is in itself no guarantee of authenticity. It is also not really the point as far as this present study is concerned (though a historian could critically evaluate the evidential value of the life histories discussed here by correlating them with other sources).

Rather, the issue addressed here is discourse itself – what topics are canvassed, and how they are canvassed. Life narratives tend to approximate to the novelistic model (in their narrative articulation of time, scene-setting, characterisation, the use of dialogue, and in other respects), and, as far as communicating the experience of internment is concerned, Dalseno's well-developed novelistic treatment is, as we shall see, in some ways more revealing than other more direct life narratives (as well as occasionally being intriguingly in conflict with them). What all these life narratives, of course, have in common is precisely their capacity to engage the first-hand subjective experience – history as experienced by the individual, rather than as captured by archival records and documentary data, vital though these are in their different way. "Singular voices" feed into that collective construct which may be questionably thought of as objective history, and Davis, Aurell and Delgado, introducing a volume of essays on *Ethnic Life Writing and Histories*, offer a rich discussion of the "mediation" between those two terms flagged in its title, and, following Rosenstone, suggest that "The reality of the past does not lie in a collection of data but in an accumulation of stories" [Davis, Aurell and Delgado 2007: 10-11)]. The two terms point to different sorts of facticity.

This has been taken very seriously by historians of the internment of Italians in Australia during the Second World War, and the contributors to *Enemy Aliens* [Elkner, Martinuzzi O'Brien, Rando and Cappello 2005] draw very effectively on individual life histories to flesh out a broader experiential history of the episode. Martinuzzi O'Brien recalls the differing effects of internment on two individuals of Italian origin in North Queensland – Alf Martinuzzi and Giuseppe Cantamessa – and makes good use of the internment diary left by the cane-cutter Mario Sardi; and Rando does something similar with the 1984 interview given by the fisherman Andrea La Macchia – an almost unique instance of a former internee being willing to recount his experience [cf. Rando 2005a and 2005b]. Rebecca Huntley [2012] likewise attempts a reconstruction, through family memories and archival researches, of the impact of internment on members of her family, since deceased, in the area around Innisfail in North Queensland.

The purpose of this chapter is somewhat different. It will not focus particularly on further building up a detailed factual reconstruction of the historical episode of the internment of Australian residents of Italian origin, so much as on gauging the discursive valence of crafted, written and published life histories (autobiographies or biographies variously mediated), of such individuals, trying to identify silences as well as outcries, examining attitudes. Issues of belonging, citizenship and nationality foreground the tension between traditional ascription (ethnically determined) and individual choice (legally sanctioned) and acculturation into the host society [cf. Martinuzzi O'Brien 2005: 29-30].

But, whilst piecing together a factual account of the internment of Australia's Italians is not the objective of this present exercise, nevertheless the perusal of memoirs by Italians may nuance our reading of the statistics, and it is with the seemingly solid objectivity of the statistics that we should begin. Altogether, out of 7711 men and women interned in Australia as "enemy aliens" (including Germans and Japanese and citizens of other Axis nations) during the Second World War, 4727 were of Italian origin, comprising just over 10%, [Alcorso and Alcorso 1992: 19] or, according to another count, about 20% [Martinuzzi O'Brien 2005: 15, 18], of Italians resident in Australia. (This percentage is much higher than the 2% of enemy aliens interned in Britain or the 0.2% in the United States.) The percentage of Italian residents interned, however, varied enormously between the component States of the Australian Federation, on account of their differing internal histories and politics. Victoria, Australia's second most populous State, interned only 3% of its "enemy aliens", including 170 Italians, as compared with 1346 Italians interned by Western Australia and 2107 (representing 43%

of Italian males) interned by Queensland [Lamidey 1974: 51-3, quoted in Douglass 1992: 33 and in Elkner 2005: 3-4; Bevege 1993: 62, quoted in Elkner]. But we find, reading the life histories, that Western Australia's harsh treatment of its Italians is slightly mitigated by instances, some of them funny, some of them heart-warming, narrated by Elsie Enright in Flavio Lucchesi's *Walk for Me, Elsie*, as will be seen below, and also by the experience of Emma Ciccotosto, who recounts that when she was aged fourteen "my father and brother and all the other Italian men like them were rounded up and sent to holding camps". With her mother pregnant, Emma was thus left to run the family dairy farm. However, she complained to the local policeman in Waroona, with the result that her father was back home in two months, and her brother two months after that [Ciccotosto 1990: 45-7; 1995: 41-2].[16]

Conversely, Rino Baggio, who grew up in rural Victoria, relates in *The Shoe in My Cheese* how his father, a market gardener, suffered from the permanent threat of internment through having to humour the local policeman on his regular visits of inspection and to keep him supplied with fresh farm produce. After one such visit, when the situation was saved by his mother's tactful intervention, Baggio remarks, "Once again, my father's holiday at Murchison internment camp would be postponed, until the next time the policeman called around on his inspection of enemy aliens" [Baggio 1989: 49]. Though the author does not explicitly broach the connection, his father's wartime experience, his literal "alienation", fits in with the book's overarching argument about Italianness and Australianness via the puzzle of the father's alcoholism. This is introduced with an unmistakable Italian inflexion which raises the timbre of the author's completely natural Australian English: "Why did he drink so much, my father? Was he frustrated? … Was he unhappy?" Both these hypotheses are dismissed, leaving the puzzle unresolved: "This unrelentingly normal man was able to use alcohol in a way that was no different from a

---

16 Incidentally, Emma shared the mistaken assumption that British citizenship exempted Australian residents of Italian origin from internment: "The Ciccotosto men were all naturalised Australians [*recte* British subjects], so they had not been interned" [Ciccotosto 1990: 46; 1995: 41].

man who might be incurably sick of life, and disgusted with himself. I never understood why my father drank so much" [Baggio 1989: 89-91]. But textually the puzzle set by the father haunts the quandary faced by his semi-estranged son as his autobiographical text comes to its end: "So why cling to the yarmulke of differentness?" Should he act Australian? "I could do it but I would have to fake it." Faced by "the paradox where you have to fake Australianness to be genuinely Australian", he answers, "I won't do it. ... I am who I am, and Australian with it" [Baggio 1989: 98-9].

Two individual cases, then, two life experiences, that of Emma Ciccotosto's family in Western Australia and that of the Baggio family in Victoria, which divergently illuminate the application and the impact of the internment instrument in different States.

Thus, explicitly in Rino Baggio's case, implicitly in that of Emma Ciccotosto, the discourse of internment finds its place in each text as part of an overarching argument about the survival of Italianness within Australianness, as part of Australianness, signalled by its expression in Australian English: Ciccotosto's scribe, Michal Bosworth, uses a plain idiom intelligible to non-native speakers of English; Baggio challenges Australian idiom from within, stretching it in various directions. (See Ch. 1 above.) In both texts, however, the topic of internment is tangential to the overall argument of the narrated life history. Four other life histories, on the other hand, make it pivotal.

Four accounts of internment

1. Osvaldo Bonutto's autobiographical essay (1963, 1994)

Osvaldo Bonutto's *A Migrant's Story* first appeared in 1963, when postwar Italian immigration to Australia was at a peak, and courageously opened up the issue of the injustice of the wartime internment of Australian residents of Italian origin who were loyal to their adopted country. Bonutto had felt unable to talk about his internment experience for twenty years even to his children [Dignan 1994: x].[17] The

---

17 Claudio Alcorso admits something similar [Alcorso and Alcorso 1992: 34], and Gaetano Rando reports this to be general among ex-internees [Rando

inhibitions against voicing his protest were almost overpowering. As Bonutto himself put it: "It nearly shattered my faith in and love for Australia. I have not yet told my son and daughter the story of my internment ... so as not to poison their minds against their native country" [Bonutto 1994: 77; 1963: 112-13].

In its 1963 edition, *A Migrant's Story* opens with a twelve-line dedication to the author's wife Egle Piccini "who unflinchingly and uncomplainingly shared all my troubles" and who prevented him from burning the notes for his book: "'Don't be silly,' she said, 'for every ten enemies that you may make you will be sure to make at least one hundred friends'" [1963: v].

This first version of Bonutto's life history is much longer than the 1994 version, which omitted its chapter II (a historical account of emigration from Italy), III (on Italian immigration into Australia), IV (on Mussolini's Italy, and the disarray of its armed forces and its economy), and VII (on the Italians in Australia and the ethnic divide between Northerners and Southerners). The remaining chapters, partly rearranged but textually unchanged, make up the 90 pages of the 1994 edition, as against the 139 pages of the 1963 first edition. This means that the two versions are considerably different books, the 1963 edition being a much more general essay on emigration from Italy to Australia, promoting understanding of Italy and Italians by Australians, with Bonutto's own life history inserted as an extended case study as well as a personal polemic over his own individual griev-ance, whereas the 1994 edition is much more sharply focused on Bonutto himself.

Bonutto's autobiographical life history takes him from his depar-ture from his native Veneto and his arrival in north Queensland in 1924 at the age of twenty-one to start labouring as a cane-cutter in the most primitive conditions, and then on to his rise as an agricul-tural entrepreneur who introduced the tobacco-growing industry in southern Queensland, acquiring an excellent command of cultivated English along the way, of which his autobiographical text is itself an admirable example. He then recounts how, on the eve of Italy's

---

1995b].

declaration of war against the British Empire, he called a meeting of Italian tobacco-growers in southern Queensland and the adjoining area of northern New South Wales, who declared their loyalty to Australia. "As a reward for my efforts," he comments drily, "I was interned the very first day war broke out, and some suggested that our meeting had been an attempt to cover up our disloyal schemes" [1994: 50; 1963: 91].

In both the 1963 and the 1994 versions of *A Migrant's Story*, the chapter on Bonutto's wartime internment is the longest of the book. It represents its climax, as marked by its title, "J'accuse", and its explicit parallel with the infamous persecution of the innocent Dreyfus in France at the beginning of that century purely as a result of racial prejudice [1994: 51; 1963: 92].

Bonutto's invective is restrained, however, and his life history is resumed, as hitherto, in narrative scenes: the arrest, imprisonment, transportation, appeals, temporary release and re-internment. The arrest ("a police officer from Texas [a country town in southern Queensland] accompanied by half a dozen burly looking men, whom I took to be detectives, armed with fearful looking revolvers appeared on the farm" [1994: 51; 1963: 92]) is followed by a series of car journeys via Texas and Stanthorpe, to Warwick. Here Bonutto is made to spend the freezing mid-winter night in the watch-house (or police cell) on straw and unwashed blankets which "had a foul smell of stale liquor and something worse" [52/93].

This is the initial shock (similar to that experienced and related by Claudio Alcorso who, like Bonutto, was interned soon after Italy's declaration of war) which leaves a permanent scar in memory and, at the time of its occurrence, threatens the victim's very sense of reality: "The whole thing made me sick in mind and body. I kept asking myself, 'Is this true? Is it actually happening to me or is it just a dream?'" This sense of unreality and depersonalisation pursues Bonutto as he is transferred to the Gaythorne army staging post near Brisbane, "where, for the first time in my life and through no fault of my own, I became a number … For the first few days I walked around the compound as if in a trance trying to get my bearings"

[1994: 53-4; 1963: 94].

It is notable, however, that Bonutto does not mention (presumably finding the memory too demeaning) the strip inspection and body search to which he must have been subjected like other internees. What he records is the financial blows which rain down on him, leaving him unable to support his family: the Taxation Department arbitrarily confiscates all his liquid assets, and the licensee of the hotel which Bonutto owns in Texas refuses to keep up his lease payments on the ground that he has lost his customers. Bonutto recounts: "I had lost faith in everybody and everything, and all I wanted at that particular moment was oblivion. The world, which only a few months before was smiling on me, had all of a sudden become an ugly, fearsome monster" [1994: 54-5; 1963: 94-5].

So the resilient, resourceful, self-made man, Bonutto, who had struggled with tough conditions to become a prosperous and respected businessman, is brought to his knees, at least temporarily. His account of his internment, however, focuses almost entirely, and in considerable detail, on the injustice and lack of evidence surrounding his internment, and on his subsequent energetic efforts to have the decision reversed, succeeding temporarily on his first appeal, only to realise that his release depended on his having to sell all his property at giveaway prices [1994: 55-9; 1963: 95-8]. A second appeal failed owing to the obduracy of Army Intelligence (the decisive authority regarding internment) [1994: 62-6; 1963: 101-3], and finally his third appeal was successful, after Italy had signed the armistice [1994: 69-70; 1963: 105-8]. By this time, most Italian internees, other than diehard Fascists, were being released.

The dignified juridical vindication by Bonutto of his injured innocence takes up most of the long chapter, with just one page devoted to a description of life at the purpose-built Loveday internment camp beside the river Murray in South Australia, where all internees were eventually confined. Characteristically, Bonutto's description is almost entirely interested in the productive activities carried out by the internees, but pays no attention to the internees themselves or to personal relations with them [1994: 68; 1963:

105]. No negative notes are struck, but internment comes across as a locus of non-existence. However, in common with the other three life histories discussed below, Bonutto's account singles out appreciatively several instances of human warmth and sympathy shown to the internees by Australian service personnel or civilians. This is in keeping with those internees' common sense of belonging, or of a desire for belonging, to an Australian community.

2. Claudio Alcorso's autobiographical narrative (1993)

While Bonutto's autobiography, lively as it often is, has the orderly character of a business report, or of forensic testimony, Claudio Alcorso's *The Wind You Say* has a more reflexive and introspective character which is immediately signalled in his Prologue: "When I closed my eyes to let recollections emerge, the images that emerged were always related to emotions", and the first of these emotional images which he recalls is "the dreadful first sight of Long Bay Gaol", where Alcorso was taken immediately upon his being detained in Sydney, soon after Italy's entry into the war in June 1940 [Alcorso 1994: 2].

And while Bonutto's chapter on internment stands out clearly as the climax of his narrative, in Alcorso's life history the corresponding chapter is foregrounded by coming first, before and outside the loosely chronological sequence followed in the rest of the book. As with Bonutto, however, the traumatic memory of that sordid first night of incarceration is indelible, and Alcorso describes the venereal diseases section of the prison to which he is consigned, with "grimy nets" slung outside the windows at every level to forestall attempts at suicide leaps. "… I sat on the cot bewildered and overcome by revulsion. I had seen this type of gaol in American movies … but now that I was inside a real one, the impact was very different from watching a movie. The vision of people condemned to spend years inside those cells was too desperate to contemplate …" The new reality of his situation is forcibly impressed on his memory as he gets his hand immediately slapped when he reaches out for a slice of bread out of turn. Yet a little Italian among the internees, "Joe Spaghett", relieves the tension somewhat by his clowning [Alcorso 1994: 5], the first of several novelistically constructed scenes that are one component of the chapter.

Alcorso supplements this component with analytical comments, observing that most of the Italians arrested held no political views and "migrated to Australia to try to evade the class bondage into which they were born", so much so, that the judges hearing their appeals said that they were politically so little informed that bank passbooks were the only books they knew [Alcorso 1994: 6-7]. As emerges in the course of this chapter, and as is laid out more plainly in the second, Claudio Alcorso (and his younger brother, Orlando) was anti-Fascist and had in fact attempted to join the Royal Australian Air Force in his enthusiasm to fight Nazi-Fascism [Alcorso 1994: 7], having done military service in Italy as a fighter pilot. Alcorso was a Roman, a free-thinking Catholic but of Jewish descent [Alcorso 1994: 52] who had come to Australia in 1937 at the age of twenty-four with a Master's degree from the London School of Economics and industrial knowhow, good connections, and financial backing in textile design and production, as he recounts in his second chapter. Not a self-made man of mature years then, like Osvaldo Bonutto (or Joe Maffina), when arrested, he was on the brink of a promising business career. The two brothers had changed their surname from Piperno.

From the outset, and at intervals throughout his first chapter, Alcorso dwells on the laughably flimsy evidence which led to his internment – an abundance of French and Swiss hotel labels on his suitcases and a few pro-Fascist publications in his well-filled multilingual bookcase [Alcorso 1994: 8], this "evidence" being subsequently put on display as part of the Sydney exhibition purporting to demonstrate the existence of a "Fifth Column" of German and Italian secret agents seeking to undermine security in Australia [Alcorso 1994: 9].

Alcorso makes the case (also made in the life histories of Bonutto and Maffina and, at least implicitly, of Dalseno) that there was no juridical evidence justifying his internment, but that Army Intelligence consistently overrode the appeal judges, apparently on the basis that an educated Italian was a potential danger, and all the more so if moneyed or influential. Alcorso's text is silent about the fact that he, and more so his brother, were on friendly terms with Mussolini's two sons, and about the likely fact that the *Duce* had facilitated their leaving Italy and taking capital out of the country ahead of the passing of anti-Jewish legislation in 1938.[18]

Internment for Alcorso proved to be a key formative experience, a key chapter in that *Bildungsroman* which is his autobiography, a falling in love. Through internment, he discovers the Australian outback and the world of nature, he discovers the Italian working class and Marxism-Leninism, he discovers oriental religion, he even learns to read Pushkin's poetry in Russian.

His acquaintance with the Australian landscape begins with the train journey out of Sydney and via Orange to the newly built Hay internment camp in outback New South Wales: "As first light appeared I looked outside the train's window to see a perfectly flat, almost treeless plain. I had never seen such a landscape. Nothing indicated human activity or presence. It looked eerie, limitless, hostile" [Alcorso 1994: 10-11].

Later, when he ended up in Loveday, beside the great river Murray in South Australia, he developed an intimate relationship with that landscape through being engaged in tree-felling outside the camp, a skill he acquired by working with Italian internees from north Queensland. He records having learned to swing an axe from Giovanni Villanova [Alcorso 1994: 25]. He feelingly describes the Murray landscape, and writes: "I loved the beautiful straight gums. I ran my hand on the smooth bark, as if to caress the tree to be felled" [Alcorso 1994: 26]. He reflects retrospectively: "I did not know that the bush had started to talk to me, and that I looked at the big river as a companion. I did not know that I had commenced to love this

---

18 See Venturini 2007: 703, and footnotes 40, 41 and 42. Venturini states: "There is no question that, even to be as generous as possible, the Piperno Alcorso brothers and their father largely profited from their acquaintances with Mussolini and his family. Documentation is overwhelming … A change of mind – if that is what it was – occurred to Claudio in London: having just finished a residual six-month service with the Fascist Air Force, he offered to fly for the British Air Force … There is an air of disbelief arising from all of this, and a suspicion of opportunism."

land." The outdoor work lent itself to a bucolic idyll: "At lunchtime we swam in the river and caught fish in primitive cages" [Alcorso 1994: 25]. And he recapitulates at the start of the following chapter: "Despite the squalor and hatreds of the camp, the routine of going out to cut timber on the uninhabited, beautiful sunny banks of the Murray together with people I had come to love, had become an oasis of warmth, a protective cocoon" [Alcorso 1994: 34]. Leaving that cocoon was to precipitate a crisis.

While in captivity, Alcorso gets to know many people, several of whom he was to "come to love", beginning with the first Italian camp leader at Hay, Prince Alfonso Del Drago, who proved not to be a sufficiently enthusiastic Fascist for some of the internees in the camp and was physically attacked one dark night [Alcorso 1994: 12].

Another was Phil Bossone, an industrial worker originally from Genoa, whose vegetable patch at Hay spectacularly out-performed those of the interned professional market gardeners. It turned out that Phil had been recycling the contents of the latrines to fertilise his crops [Alcorso 1994: 13]. Bossone was an outspoken Communist and had enjoyed the solidarity of his Australian fellow workers before he was interned. Alcorso struck up a lifelong friendship with him. "My discussions with Phil Bossone left me disoriented. It was my first encounter with a militant worker." This was to lead Alcorso, when he was later moved to Loveday, to become friendly with a more intellectually inclined German Communist, Herman Behrens, at whose suggestion he read works by Lenin [Alcorso 1994: 14-15].

At Hay (as later at Loveday), Alcorso's sociability, in his account, proved both broad and deep, though implicitly excluding Fascists and Nazis: "Confinement leads to familiarity … Now I knew virtually every man in my new community." He names Italo Rossi as a lifelong friend whom he met at Hay, and his future father-in-law, Ned Zavattaro, who had been a gold-miner in Papua New Guinea, as another among many [Alcorso 1994: 15]. He also singles out Enrico Piombo, a former anarchist, who had become a follower of the Indian guru Krishnamurti and introduced Alcorso to his ideas of "wholeness" and "global interrelationship" [Alcorso 1994: 17].

Alcorso conceived a collective admiration for his Italian

fellow-internees. He admired the skill they revealed at wood-carving and clay-modelling: "Unsuspected creativity emerged ... a portent perhaps of the resources latent in most human beings, given time and opportunity." This leads him to endorse an insight which he gathered from reading Colin Ward several decades later: "The artist is not a special type of person. Every person is, or could be, a special kind of artist" [Alcorso 1994: 17-18]. After the move to Loveday in 1942, Alcorso's admiration and affection was to extend to the cane-cutters and farmers from Ingham, Mareeba and Stanthorpe in Queensland and from Griffith in New South Wales whom he met there: "I came to feel that I knew Ingham well, even though I had never been there. ... I listened to how tobacco grew at Mareeba, and fruit at Stanthorpe. I heard tales from the irrigation farms and the vineyards around Griffith. The people who had worked on the land had more to say than the city greengrocer or the terrazzo worker. Behind their talk there was love for the land; through their talk I started to perceive unsuspected aspects of life in Australia." And he observes: "... they leaned towards anti-Fascism almost naturally" [Alcorso 1994: 31-2].

Given this ample testimony to Alcorso's sociability and enthusiastic discovery of his fellow Italian Australians, it must appear extraordinary that Peter Dalseno, who was at that time a young man from the sugar-cane area of northern Queensland, should, in his *Sugar, Tears and Eyeties,* single him out for his aloofness and *lack* of sociability:

> The only exception was found in the Italian Jew. There were two such Jews in the camp, and they were brothers. They were fluent in English – obviously domiciled in Australia for some length of time. Tall of body, fair of complexion, their body movements suggested much athletic preoccupation. They were masters in the art of segregation. They mixed with no one, restricted their conversation to matters of import and guarded the privacy of their lives. They could afford to do so. Massive wealth simplified their attitude. [Dalseno 1994: 245]

Dalseno is clearly wrong in his inference that the Alcorsos had been long-term residents in Australia, as he is also at least half wrong about their "art of segregation". The apparent discrepancy may be attributed to the fact that Dalseno's alter ego in his narrative, there called Peter Delano, was camp secretary, and therefore inevitably seen as being associated with the camp's internal Italian Fascist hierarchy (though "Delano" may have had no sympathy with Fascism). It is therefore entirely understandable that the Alcorsos should have kept their distance from him, and that therefore he did not really know them. Alcorso himself does record the generally accepted fact that Army Intelligence put Fascists in charge of the Italian internees, even though (according to Alcorso) the Official Visitor, K. F. Sanderson, advised against giving Fascists authority over anti-Fascists [Alcorso 1993: 23].

Alcorso mentions the presence within the Italian camp of various non-Italians, most intriguing among them, for him (as for Bonutto and Dalseno), being the Australia First anti-British internees, of Irish descent [Alcorso 1994: 26-7], and the aristocratic Arnold von Skerst, a descendant of the Teutonic Knights from Riga, who turned against Nazism when Germany attacked Russia, and who taught Alcorso to read Pushkin's poetry in the original Russian [Alcorso 1994: 27]. Meanwhile, Alcorso records, the Fascist leaders within the camp, when the war was going well for the Axis Powers, bragged of the compensation they would receive for their internment when the war was over, but turned vindictive when the tide of war swung against them [Alcorso 1994: 28].

It was in this atmosphere that, on 16 November 1942, Francesco Fantin, an anti-Fascist, was murdered in the Loveday camp. In researching for his book half a century after the event, Alcorso discovers a rough English translation of Fantin's diary *Pensieri e Ricordi*, more poetic than political in tone and content: "Reading Fantin's diary the vision of the camp reappeared before me. I shuddered recalling the atmosphere of hatred, of fear, mounting in the camp as the tide of war turned" [Alcorso 1994: 30]. Dr Piscitelli, the Fascist camp leader, alleged the death to have been accidental, but Dr Muggia, the camp medical officer, and a Jew (for whom Claudio Alcorso worked as an orderly), adduced evidence that Fantin had been deliberately murdered. The Fascist leaders whispered: "'Those who speak will die; there are six more communists to be killed.'" (The Fascists described all their opponents as Communists, even if, as in Fantin's case, they were not.) Fantin's killer, Casotti, was convicted of manslaughter [Alcorso 1994: 29]. Alcorso's tallies with other accounts of this well-attested episode.

The Alcorso brothers appealed against their internment, and their case was heard in Sydney in February 1941. The tribunal dismissed the evidence against them and recommended their release, but this was vetoed by Army Intelligence, despite affidavits in their favour from leading Italian anti-Fascists in the United States – Arturo Toscanini, Max Ascoli, and Randolfo Pacciardi. The Army's position was that the war was a conflict between nationalities and not between ideologies [Alcorso 1994: 21-2]. Release did not come until three years later, and with it the experience of radical estrangement, conveyed by the narrative equivalent of a cinematic dissolve.

This comes at the beginning of Alcorso's second chapter which states his total lack of recall of the period from his departure from Loveday, his rehabilitation at Adelaide, and the first few weeks after his return to Sydney. "I must have acted like a robot," he surmises:

> A cold feeling of anxiety crept up inside me, mixed with bitter hatred for the faceless men who controlled my life. … The self-confidence, the optimism of prewar Claudio Alcorso had vanished. Now I was 9221; my internment number had not been tattooed on my skin but it was deeply engraved in my psyche. I was conscious of my accent and that it would lead to questions the moment I opened my mouth. It meant that anyone I talked to would classify me as an enemy alien. The feeling of being outside of the real world, the apprehension that made me feel cold all the time, remained with me for weeks and weeks … [Alcorso 1994: 34-5]

The narrative dissolve is sparked off by seeing Sydney as the opposite of the beautiful "dreamtime" vision of arrival in the harbour seven years earlier: "My perceptions of time and place remained confused, as they do in dreams. The sight of George Street triggered visions of my native city, Rome" [Alcorso 1994: 35]. This leads in to the chronological reconstruction, in the second chapter, of Alcorso's previous life from early childhood through adolescence to early adulthood, and, in the third chapter, of his arrival and early experiences in Australia. The subsequent chapters pick up the narrative of Alcorso's life experience after internment. But the traumatic centrality of the internment experience is reiterated in Alcorso's brief Epilogue which suggests: "But there may be something to be learned from my wartime experience, namely the evil of racism and the need to ensure that the rulings of our courts of justice are supreme" [168]; and declares: "My love for freedom means that I am capable of feeling hatred for those who would destroy it" [Alcorso 1994: 170].

3. Peter Dalseno's autobiographical novel (1994)

Peter Dalseno, on the last page of *Sugar, Tears and Eyeties*, his narrative of the formative years of his autobiographical alter ego Peter Delano, sheds his lightly fictionalised persona and assumes that of judgemental author and ex-internee who has had the relatively uninhibited conversation with other Italian ex-internees that academic researchers such as Rando [2005b] had found it difficult to entertain. Here he is, half a century after the experience, in his own characteristic English, soberly but sharply criticising two opposed attitudes displayed by different categories of those ex-internees:

> There are no more internees … But, it is interesting to listen to the comments of those who were and who are still alive today. The boastful eulogises the 'paradise' enjoyed as a prisoner. The conservative calls for an apology and a recognition that internment was not necessarily the result of his political views. Unfortunately, neither attracts acknowledgement. In the first instance, the veneer of bravado is varnished with the smear of stupidity; in the second instance, the claim is ignorant of the penalties of war – wages, unmindful of discrimination and devoid of explanation. [Dalseno 1994: 280]

Elkner [2005: 11] quotes the warning by Iacovetta and Ventresca, in a Canadian context, against over-simplifying internment into a "story of political innocents hurt by a vindictive wartime state". This supports Dalseno's rebuff of "the conservative", and yet the perspective that emerges from all four of the extended accounts of the internment experience studied in this chapter – those already examined, by Bonutto and Alcorso, the one yet to be seen, regarding Maffina, and that now under examination, involving Dalseno/Delano – is indeed of a "story of political innocents hurt by a vindictive wartime state", and the issue at stake, which Elkner, Iacovetta, Ventresca, and Dalseno understate, is the quality of justice involved and the grossness of the criteria discriminating between belonging and not-belonging (particularly in the cases of those Australian Italians who had been naturalised as British subjects or who were British subjects by virtue of having been born in Australia). Certainly, Dalseno's book devotes the last ten chapters (from 17 to 26), amounting to ninety pages out of 280, to the internment experience, making it the culminating point of the *Bildungsroman* of his central character, Peter Delano, which is itself the central component of this multi-faceted book and supplies its connecting narrative thread.

Returning, however, to the opening quotation from Dalseno's finale, his vaunted independence from the cant of diametrically opposing persuasions is refreshing (which is not to deny that there may be some truth in those persuasions). This claim to independence is flagged in the very opening words of his Preface: "The foregoing [*recte* following] pages are factual!" [Dalseno 1994: v]. It is elaborated on the following page: "I must apologise to my co-nationals for exposing some of the uncongenial qualities of our character" [Dalseno 1994: vi].[19] And it is borne out by his recounting his story in the third person as part of a broad social community comprising first the Italians of the Herbert River sugar-growing area around Ingham in northern Queensland, and those connected with them, and then some of the same individuals, among many others, held in the Loveday internment camp between March 1942 and February

---

19 It is curious that Dalseno refers to Italian Australians as his "co-nationals", though his alter ego, Peter Delano, in *Sugar, Tears and Eyeties*, obtains Australian British citizenship shortly after the end of his internment (see below) and sets great store by being accepted as Australian.

1944. *Sugar, Tears and Eyeties* is therefore at once autobiography and social chronicle, firmly inserted in the history of the Queensland Italians and (in common with the other chronicles studied here) of the Second World War. It is documentary writing fashioned as a novel which might be ambiguously termed docufiction.

Fears and uncertainties about internment arise among the Italians as Italy enters the war in June 1940 (when Bonutto and Alcorso were interned), and mount as the war goes against Britain [Dalseno 1994: 187]. This is when the cry "You're on the list!" becomes a current, half jocular, half sinister greeting [Dalseno 1994: 192; the cry recurs, with opposite effect, towards the end of internment: cf. 269, 272, 273].

Dalseno's central character, the impecunious but high-school educated Peter Delano, is interned on 10 March 1942, at the age of twenty-one and just three days after his registry office marriage to his sixteen-year-old non-Italian bride. This is part of the mass internment of Queensland Italians that follows in the wake of the loss of Singapore, the attack on Pearl Harbour, and the very real threat of Japanese invasion, and Delano's experience is presented within the collective experience of the Italian internees, with scenes including that at the Ingham railway station [Dalseno 1994: 194] and the arrival of the trainload of internees at Castle Hill in Townsville [Dalseno 1994: 196], where Peter experiences a phantasmagoric hallucination which marks the life-changing experience which he is undergoing [Dalseno 1994: 197-8]. This is followed by the real-life nightmare of Stuart Creek Prison:

> It was no longer a matter of identification of an Italian as an Alien; he was now indelibly tattooed – an Enemy-Alien. It was traumatic. It carried a stigma. The Naturalization Certificate that attested to his allegiance to the Crown and that influenced his pride in citizenship, now remained suspect – valueless in a moral and civil sense. [Dalseno 1994: 199-200]

(The tattooing here is metaphorical, but none the less hurtful.)

Both the collective scenes and the individual experiences of the internment processes are unique to Dalseno's account, all the more so by the fullness of circumstantial detail and by the snatches of waggish backchat with which they are rendered. Such is the description of the interminable train ride through four States, starting at Ingham and ending at Barmera, the station for Loveday in South Australia: this features the cramped conditions aboard a bare cattle-truck, the incident of Frank Spertino being manhandled by a police guard, the jeers and abuse by the Australian crowd at Bundaberg as the internment train passed through on the way to the army staging post at Gaythorne near Brisbane, where a floodlit night-time transfer from train to truck was effected [Dalseno 1994: 201-5].

The narrator describes the astonishment of the internees when they are greeted at Gaythorne, before entraining for Loveday, with a Fascist salute by two Italians under whose instructions they are put [Dalseno 1994: 209]. The fact that the two are Sicilians provokes comment by the narrator about the differences and the divide between northerners and southerners from Italy, a note that recurs consistently from time to time in the book, Peter Delano and those close to him being mainly northerners, and mainly from the Veneto [Dalseno 1994: 211]. The narrator also records, without explicitly subscribing to it, the dictum of a character identified only as "a cynic": "Far better to have a death in the house than have a Britisher at the door" [Dalseno 1994: 217], which is later explained to young Peter by the corpulent Communist cook, Frederico [sic], in terms of the evils committed in the name of the British Empire [Dalseno 1994: 220]. This anti-British animus is given added substance when the train halts at Seymour in Victoria and the Italian internees are subjected to more jeers and insults by the Anglo-Australian crowd. Peter's sense of humiliation is slightly mitigated by the expression of sympathy from an Australian woman whose son is a prisoner-of-war of the Italians in Africa [Dalseno 1994: 219].

As the transport train and Dalseno's narrative bring us to Loveday, the reader is presented with what is probably the fullest existing description of the camp, its setting, and the living arrangements within it, beginning with a longish march from Barmera station to Loveday through vast vineyards [Dalseno 1994: 222-3], then the humiliating stripping and body search, followed by the change of

clothes into the burgundy-coloured internment uniform, registra-
tion and interrogation. Dalseno makes much of the questioning of
Peter Delano's national identity, his legal name being Pietro, and his
being unable to identify his precise place of birth in Italy [Dalseno
1994: 224-5].

The precise and detailed description of the layout, facilities and
arrangements in Loveday Camp 14D (the only one containing mixed
nationalities) [Dalseno 1994: 229, 234] is followed laconically and
pointedly by a glance at the night sky: "The beauty was there for every
living creature to enjoy" [Dalseno 1994: 231]. Peter is appointed
camp secretary (apparently for lack of competition, but presumably
also by virtue of his moderate level of education) [Dalseno 1994:
234], and the narrator delivers himself of this definition of Delano's
existential situation:

> Intimacies of yesterday were but straws in the wind. True,
> there was a persuasion that yesterday existed, but the
> awesome present, stark and unrealistic, conditioned him
> to believe that the mind was no longer his own. It now
> belonged to the compound. Yes, he ate with them; he
> drank with them; he showered with them. He lived, he
> laughed and he cried with them. Only experience would
> show that the concentration of humanity squeezed morale
> to a point where he saw nothing but a screen projecting a
> depressing kaleidoscope. [Dalseno 1994: 235]

This is a markedly more negative outlook than that offered by
Alcorso, though Delano/Dalseno, six years younger than Alcorso,
and raised bilingually in the north Queensland sugar-growing area
from which many hundreds of his fellow-internees had come, might
have been expected to enjoy the bonhomie. But he may have been
constrained by his position as camp secretary, as well as by his family
history, which had led him to claim belonging to Australia rather
than to Italy.

Thus, Dalseno, too, recalls a gallery of individuals and groups, but
none of them providing the individual or collective uplift acknowledged by Alcorso. There is the rather dubious Army interpreter,
the Maltese Sergeant Scibberas [recte Sciberras], there are the two

stand-offish and obviously wealthy unnamed Italian Jews [Dalseno 1994: 246] (discussed above), there is the brilliant Hungarian violinist, Julian Helji, who, in conversations including two German internees, bewilders Peter with high-sounding pseudo-metaphysical claptrap ("Peter sat agog. The discussion was beyond his understanding") [Dalseno 1994: 259, 264], the Nazi Paul von Hersfeldt, who regales Peter with contempt after the Italian armistice [Dalseno 1994: 260], a chance meeting with a broken Joe Cantamessa at the dentist's [Dalseno 1994: 265], and the murder of Francesco Fantin [Dalseno 1994: 267]. This is relieved by an account of the hugely successful camp entertainment organised and performed by the internees.

Following Mussolini's overthrow and Italy's withdrawal from the war in 1943, prospects improved for the release of internees. Dalseno presents the tribunal which presided over this process as "a farce" [Dalseno 1994: 270], which he illustrates with some of the questions put to Delano, including the final one: "Do you feel resentment for your internment?" [Dalseno 1994: 272]. The narrator's judgement is the relativistic one that: "War was war and the exigencies of human conflict were observed by different eyes from different perspectives" [Dalseno 1994: 271].

The ex-internees take the train to Adelaide for their transition back to civilian life, marked by the distribution of Borsalino hats [Dalseno 1994: 273], which is mentioned generally in the literature on the subject. Delano, like many others, is detailed to serve a spell helping the war effort in the Civil Alien Corps, which sees him making another train journey through the tropical night towards Maranboy in the Northern Territory to lay sleepers for the extension of the railway line [Dalseno 1994: 273-4]. But, while there, he has his application for citizenship approved, which meant that "He alienated himself from his former co-workers." Thanks to his good schooling, he soon graduates from labouring on the track to helping the Australian office staff, among whom "He came to understand the meaning of tolerance. He was addressed as 'mate'" [Dalseno 1994: 276]. A low-key melody of the quest for identity and acceptance as an Australian thus dominates the finale of Dalseno/Delano's internment narrative and of the docufiction as a whole.

4. Ersilia Enright's memoir of Joe Maffina (2002, 2008)

Of the internees considered in this chapter, Joe Maffina is the only one who does not tell his own story. The testimonial urge is that of his daughter Ersilia (Elsie Enright), who wanted justice and moral redress for her father. She compiled a history of her family origins and her father's experiences as an immigrant from the Alpine Valtellina region in Lombardy to Australia and made it available to an Italian researcher from Lombardy, Flavio Lucchesi. Lucchesi translated excerpts from Elsie's memoir to produce an intriguingly original work, alternating chronological slabs of "history from above" with corresponding slabs of "history from below" drawn from Elsie's account of her father's life experience [Lucchesi 2008: 10-11].[20]

The three chronological segments thus match up the collective and the individual histories, the scholarly overview and the experiential testimony. First, the migratory flow from the Valtellina to the Western Australian goldfields and the experiences of the immigrants in adapting to their new country across the turn of the nineteenth century; then the period of establishment of the immigrants in the face of considerable hostility from some of the resident population, culminating in the Australia Day riots of January 1934, in which there was much burning and looting of the property of immigrants from southern Europe, including that of the Maffinas, who had to flee into the bush; and finally, the Second World War and internment [Part 3 chapter 2 "The Story": Lucchesi 2008: 155-99].

The double mediation of Joe Maffina's internment experience, firstly through his daughter Elsie and subsequently through a non-Australian Italian, Lucchesi, brings with it a double emotional investment in rehabilitation – on Elsie's part, a vindication and acknowledgement of her father as an honourable Australian unjustly treated, and on Lucchesi's part, indignation at the injustice committed against a fellow Italian.

Born in 1886, Giuseppe (Joe) Maffina arrived in the Western Australian goldfields shortly before the First World War, and after various vicissitudes, progressed via farming to hotel-keeping, and by

---

20 For the sake of convenience, page references are to Margaret Downing's 2008 English translation of Lucchesi's work.

the 1930s had become a man of substance, but also an invalid, having suffered a heart attack. By the time the Second World War broke out, he had retired from active business and settled down with his family in a comfortable house on the Fremantle seafront. Elsie's account stresses Joe's principle of avoiding discussion of politics or religion. She mentions his being secretly a Freemason while outwardly professing Catholicism, and, sounding a consistent note of distaste, or at least distance, towards southern Italians, she links this with his having kept his distance from the social institution that was close to official Fascism: "He steadfastly and politely declined repeated urgings to become a member of the *Italian Club*, made up mainly of Sicilians" [Lucchesi 2008: 155]. As the only Italian member of the Fremantle Bowling Club, Joe took care not to discuss the war in that company [Lucchesi 2008: 158-9].

Elsie conveys the atmosphere among Fremantle's Italians as internment started, with dark hints spreading panic [Lucchesi 2008: 159], and recalls the viperish remark of one of her teachers, Sister Kevin, at St Joseph's College, when her friend's father, Cono Sgro, is picked up: "Your father will be next!" [Lucchesi 2008: 164]. This incident provides one of several lively scenes or anecdotes which inform Elsie's account. Another of these, like several other details in Elsie's narrative, does something to mitigate the undoubted harshness of the Western Australia internment policy, as well as pointing up its haphazard nature. It concerns the lone policeman at the outback station of Marvel Lock, Joe Farrell, who had only a bicycle, but was ordered to round up all the single Italians in the surrounding area. With only Henry Enright to help him, and a requisitioned beer truck for transport, he does so but, having nowhere to hold his detainees, he takes them to spend a night at the hotel, where they have a booze-up, and then lets them go [Lucchesi 2008: 160].

Elsie also records that there was much sympathy among the general public for the families of Italian internees who had been left destitute, and that many gave assistance [Lucchesi 2008: 161]. However, Joe was one of the most prominent Italians, and the Maffinas' home was searched three times for incriminating evidence that might link Joe to the Italian authorities. Joe was so careful to eliminate any such link that he took down the treasured picture of his brother Giovanni, who had received an Italian gold medal for having heroically given up his life so as to save a passenger train from an Alpine avalanche [Lucchesi 2008: 155-7].

Elsie says that it was after a Sicilian had made a complaint against Joe that her father was finally interned, on 2 September, 1941. She brings the scene vividly to life, as two police cars draw up on the wrong side of the road, and Joe, lying underneath his own vehicle which he is getting ready for a long journey, sees two booted feet and trouser-bottoms standing beside his head [Lucchesi 2008: 168]. Joe's internment, as it comes across in Elsie's account, is a curious mixture of sternness and indulgence. The officers who arrested him treated him with great consideration before taking him to prison. Elsie writes: "... in Fremantle Gaol ... he spent what was to be his first week of humiliation, isolated and locked in a cold, grey cell with a small barred window." Yet he was driven home secretly every night and left there over the weekend. No kindness, however, could soften the blow of being recorded as internee No. W15173, "which identified him like a common criminal" [Lucchesi 2008: 169]. Likewise, visits to the Harvey internment camp on the other side of Perth from Fremantle were difficult and costly because of the distance involved, but at least they were feasible, as they were not for the Queensland internees (and were not to be for Joe Maffina also, when he too was moved to Loveday in South Australia). "We children," writes Elsie, "only saw our father on three occasions ... the first time ... I could not keep back my tears." She describes the scene of the visit in a long wooden hut in Harvey Camp No. 11, and remarked that both Joe and his visitors "would feign a joyful countenance" [Lucchesi 2008: 171-2].

Information about life in the camp, no doubt relayed to Elsie by Joe, confirm the generally received impression that conditions in Australian internment camps were relatively benign and bland, almost indeed a sort of "holiday" for some internees, if not for family men like Joe: "Many [internees] were single men, who had been working for a long time in lonely areas. For them the enforced camaraderie of living together was almost enjoyable ... there was laughter and the sort of horsing around one would expect in a boys' school playground!" [Lucchesi 2008: 172]. Elsie comments on the internees' craftwork and reports that her father has a ring carved for her out of a shilling piece inscribed with her initials. Other artefacts included a grotto of Our Lady and a statue of Romulus and Remus.

She mentions that working parties would work outside the camp, and that, although he was not fit enough to work, her father was allowed to join them and received a shilling a day for it like the rest of them [Lucchesi 2008: 173]. Elsie also mentions the monkeying around at rollcall, causing numerous recounts (not very amusing for the older internees like Joe), and she tells the story about a lone Italian who had not been interned circling outside the camp on his motorbike on Saturdays and hugely entertaining the inmates with his exaggerated Fascist salutes, until he achieved his desired aim and was made to join them [Lucchesi 2008: 174].

Elsie complains about wartime propaganda with its grotesque misrepresentation of the enemy: "War taught us to hate or love people according to whose side they were on" [Lucchesi 2008: 177], but she also remarks on the "new sense of freedom experienced by Italian women when the men they loved were interned" [178]. Among the few women internees, she singles out the small and round but larger than life and indomitable Nina Gregorini, a founder member in 1935 of the Perth Casa d'Italia Italian Club [Lucchesi 2008: 181-2], and Director of the Perth Fascio, a Fascist out of sheer patriotism. Elsie relates how she and her mother overheard a comic conversation at a petrol station in which some army personnel recounted how they had found it impossible to get a grip on the rotund and resisting Nina, so that it had taken six of them to shove her into the truck. "We picked up a big fat dago bitch yesterday, and did she give us trouble." The conversation between the petrol pump attendant and the soldiers recreates the scene in some detail. As an internee, Nina proved no less intractable, and when, to everybody's surprise, she suddenly appeared to turn co-operative, it was only to bake a huge cake iced with the Italian national colours [Lucchesi 2008: 183-6].

In April 1942, the Harvey internees were secretly transported by night to Parkeston in the goldfields, without amenities, accommodation or provisions. Elsie constructs her narrative by piecing together what she could glean from her father with the eye-witness account of Renato Fomiatti, the barman at the Main Reef Hotel in Boulder, who saw the five hundred internees standing in the rain in an enclosure in Parkeston, among them, Joe Maffina [Lucchesi 2008: 186-8].

Joe's family were fortunately able to move to Kalgoorlie so as to be near him and continue their weekly visits, and, through his wife Maria's resourcefulness, coped with difficult conditions of wartime scarcity [Lucchesi 2008: 180] and courted favour with the camp officers with her stylish hospitality [Lucchesi 2008: 193]. While at Parkeston, Joe suffered the indignity of being very publicly escorted to Kalgoorlie (where he was well known) to have two molars extracted. "This particular incident," writes Elsie, "did more damage to my father's spirit than the riots of 1934 or even the initial shock of internment. The pain of this episode was still visible decades later when my father recounted the experience to me and to others" [Lucchesi 2008: 192].

The memory of the insults of the prison guards and soldiers also rankled within him: "Look at that dago bastard!" [Lucchesi 2008: 193]. There was another secret night departure in November 1942 which took the Parkeston internees, including the ailing Joe Maffina, on the long train journey to Barmera in South Australia, the station for Loveday [Lucchesi 2008: 194-6]. At that distance, family visits were out of the question. Joe, his constitution further shaken by the journey, had to undergo surgery in the camp hospital. He was to get back home in January 1944, a broken man [Lucchesi 2008: 196, 198].

Life writing as argument

"The internment practices should be understood as an extension of Australia's defence policies and security concerns … inextricably linked to the White Australia policy" [Alcorso and Alcorso 1992: 29-30]. Let us take this proposition as a starting point in taking stock of the Italian Australian discourse on internment. Hostilities between Italy and Australia act as a trigger for the internment of

Australia's Italians, defining them as enemy aliens, but the extent and manner of it is predicated on an exclusive, and singular, definition of Australian identity as British. Ethnic identity – nationality of origin as opposed to acquired nationality – overrides the legal naturalisation process and determines what rights the subject does or does not have and how far due judicial process obtains in the individual case.

The subjects of the four life histories we have scanned, while not forgoing their Italian identity, identify themselves as Australian prior to their internment: in Alcorso's case, by volunteering for the RAAF; in Dalseno/Delano's case, by upbringing; in Maffina's and Bonutto's case, by naturalisation. Subsequent to their internment they also claim Australian identity by the identity-performative act of writing about themselves in English (or, in Maffina's case, his daughter does this for him, and her testimony is first published in Italian translation). They are double subjects. However, the state of war between Italy and Australia (as part of the British Empire) determines the stripping of legal rights from ethnic Italians in Australia. (This applies to Germans also, and to home-grown Australian Fascists.) The exclusion and reclusion of internment presents to the writers of these life narratives the bitter irony of captivity by their own side, with attendant stigma. By depriving them of citizenship, it challenges their status as subjects.

The life narratives we have considered constitute an argument retrospectively denouncing the stripping of Australian identity and attendant rights. The argument is conducted at various levels of discourse: not only at the level of ethical and juridical rationality (although this is prominent in all four cases), but also at the level of language (the style and idiom of Australian English selected and, even more intriguingly, via the Italian of Lucchesi's translation of Elsie Enright's English-language record of her father Joe Maffina's experience). The texts deploy a novelistic rhetoric involving a complex articulation of narrative time, an intermeshing of private history and public history, characterisation and dramatisation, memorial introspection and reflection – all strongly referential in the sense of affirming and relying on the experiential reality of the people and things referred to, starting with the narrating subjects themselves.

This reality is narratively (re)constructed at the discursive level and socially constructed at the experiential level. "Italian" identity, for the subjects of these life narratives, is ascriptive, not elective: it is the complex of experiences and social networks internalised while living in the *paese* or town or area (singular or plural) in Italy or among co-nationals of varying degrees of closeness (familial or of neighbouring origin) in places outside Italy, such as Australia. This means there is no unique or uniform Italian identity. Origin from the Valtellina Alpine valleys (Maffina), the urban Veneto (Dalseno and Bonutto), or Rome (Alcorso), and different social classes, produces heterogeneous "Italian" identities which are treated as homogeneous under the political process of internment.

Australianness, for the immigrant, is elective. It, too, is constituted by experiences and social networks internalised while living in Australia, but it depends also on choice, on commitment. Eva C. Karpinski, discussing multinational immigrant autobiography in North America, takes up from Paula M. L. Moya a slightly different distinction between "ascriptive" and "subjective" identity, and continues:

> People neither are wholly determined by social categories through which they are identified, nor can they be wholly free from them. There is a close connection between how society is organized, what social categories are available, and what subjectivities are possible in a particular historical time, place, and situation. [Karpinski 22]

The choice of Australianness by immigrants from Italy is invisibly marked by a silence. The process of acculturation as Australians is taken for granted, the costs of divestment as Italians and investment as Australians are played down, the subjects concerned do not present themselves as having been "lost in translation", in the words of the title of Eva Hoffman's Polish-American autobiography, though Dalseno's Peter Delano does squirm occasionally between his double identities [Dalseno 1994: 70], and we have seen Rino Baggio refusing to fake Australianness. Baggio's and Dalseno's greater resistance to being integrally translated into the host culture has its linguistic and literary correlative in their slightly idiosyncratic English: while

Elsie Enright, Claudio Alcorso and Osvaldo Bonutto display a high degree of limpidity in their English, writing with an ease that eschews almost every trace of strangeness, Baggio and Dalseno (both schooled in Australia) display a certain amount of turbidity. Their writing is inventive, idiosyncratic, transgressive, improper in a way which opens up a linguistic "third space" (to use Homi Bhabha's phrase), moving beyond conventional or idiomatic English but not towards Italian. The transparency of language is challenged. The opacity of their English draws attention to itself, and therefore to the conventional nature of language as such, and therefore of Australian English also. In this respect, at least, and to a certain (limited) extent, Baggio's and Dalseno's writing challenges and stretches Australianness in a way in which smoother writing does not. Karpinski pursues these linguistic issues to impressive effect in her study of North American immigrant autobiographies, *Borrowed Tongues*, analysing them in terms of translation.

Sequential chronology rules these internment narratives. Alcorso does, indeed, put his chapter on internment first, out of its chronological sequence, but this is a strictly limited operation of expository rhetoric and not a cognitive upheaval: the before and after are promptly and precisely reinstated. Sequential chronology is typically at home in life writing, given the usual developmental and documentary presumptions that inform life writing. The documentary imperative is very strong in these internment narratives, but the developmental model also obtains, though in markedly different ways. Alcorso's internment experience, despite his fleeting references to "fear" and "hatred" and "squalor", comes across as a rite of passage into mature manhood, as he reaches age thirty in 1943. It entails a discovery of the world, humanity, nature, creativity, and a protracted epiphany, an enchantment, engendered by enforced (but in large part uplifting) community, revealing positive values despite the prevailing negativity: values which will be pursued or at least posited in his ensuing life as recounted in the following chapters.

For Dalseno's Peter Delano, who is some six years Alcorso's junior, the considerably briefer internment is also a rite of passage, but one of disenchantment: though Dalseno/Delano is much readier than

Alcorso to excuse the injustice of his internment as a by-product of war, the internment experience appears to confirm a darkly humorous sense of human irrationality and meanness which makes little distinction between ethnicities or nationalities. Although Peter Delano is only twenty-three years old at the end of his internment, his story ends there; internment is not so much a negative epiphany as a culmination and a confirmation of the story so far – that is, leading up to internment. Resolution comes after the end of internment with his acceptance as an Australian, a "mate". The fifty years of middle-class normality, prosperity and multi-ethnic intermarriage glancingly alluded to in his conclusion are the tacit response by this Candide to the nightmarish and the uncanny of life – his dubious philosophy of "cultivating his own garden". Maffina's story also ends when his internment ends: as the climax of a life-time's series of hard knocks which he has stoically survived, though he will live many more years of a premature old age in retirement. Bonutto, younger than Maffina, still has some distance to run after internment, and devotes a further chapter to a redemptive post-war episode at Gympie, where he survives an attempted boycott of his hotel by his (Australian) competitors thanks to the support of the local (Australian) public. Alcorso presents internment as the beginning of his story, while for the others, who had spent the better part of their lives in Australia, it was the end.

How widely are these life histories read? And by whom? Editions are tiny. Alcorso's book has had two editions, and much of his chapter on internment has appeared in a scholarly work both in Australia and in Italy [Alcorso and Alcorso 1992]. Bonutto's book has had two editions some thirty years apart, and Dalseno's only one. Lucchesi's work on Joe Maffina is a special case, since it is used as an Italian university text on Italian migration to Australia. It has been through several editions, and has also been published in English translation. Circulation of these texts in Australia would be hard to trace, but may be partly guessed at: Queensland Italians for Bonutto and Dalseno and Western Australian Italians for Lucchesi's life history of Maffina, cultural and business elites for Alcorso, and for all of them a sprinkling of students of Australian multiculturalism and of its Italian component in particular, of people interested in Australian society generally over the last century – teachers and social workers and public servants. Hardly enough to jog the Australian psyche.

The argument I have just advanced is predicated on the personal and social trauma occasioned by the internment of Italian Australians as "enemy aliens", but it might also be extrapolated to cover less conspicuous traumas. Rosa Cappiello's quasi-autobiographical *Paese fortunato*, based on a year's experience of Sydney's sweat-shops and multi-ethnic proletariat, challenges Italian norms of language and representation, as its translation by Gaetano Rando, *Oh, Lucky Country*, challenges Australian norms of expression [Maher 2011: 21-49, 164]. However, of the more straightforwardly autobiographical or biographical literature about Australia's Italians, few works can make similar claims. One is Cristina's memoir of childhood sexual abuse, *Secrets of a Broken Heart*, published in both English and Italian versions, and two others are, in their different ways, Fernando Basili's account of his alleged victimisation, *Vita vissuta,* and Helen Garner's inquiry into an apparent failure of justice in a Canberra chronicle of a death foretold, *Joe Cinque's Consolation. Secrets of a Broken Heart* and Basili's *Vita vissuta* will be discussed in the following chapter. But the most radical case of discursive disruption is Fosco Antonio's *My Reality*, to which I devote a separate chapter. Before moving on to discuss a fuller array of texts dealing with trauma and grievance, those of Alcorso and Dalseno deserve to have more said about them beyond their presentation of the internment experience.

Life outside internment: Alcorso and Dalseno

As we have seen, Peter Dalseno's communally autobiographical third-person narrative *Sugar, Tears and Eyeties* ends, and Claudio Alcorso's more self-centredly autobiographical first-person narrative, *The Wind you Say*, opens, with the internment experience. Dalseno's story of Peter Delano ends with his finding his identity and acceptance as an Australian and a "mate" at the age of twenty-three, while Alcorso's story of identity-formation begins at the age of twenty-nine as he emerges from internment. Alcorso had come to Australia as an adventurer, intent on making his own destiny rather than having it made for him by his father:

I cannot recall melancholic thoughts on the ship that took us to Australia, the *Strathallan*. I was looking forward to the new life, to the realization of something which *I* had conceived of and which had not been made by my father. … Dominant was the desire for independence. I was arrogant in my self-confidence. This would be my own venture and I had no doubts about its success. [Alcorso 1993: 57; original emphasis]

The author's emphasis on *I* extends to his making virtually no mention of his younger brother, who also went to Australia with him and shared the experience of internment. Claudio says lightly that upon arrival in Australia "I had no feeling of estrangement. Migrants often mention the difficulties of adjusting, the many habits they had to forgo, but the only two things I can remember missing were fresh bread and coffee" [Alcorso 1993: 68]. His struggles were of a different kind. One, unsuccessful, was the attempt to introduce brightly coloured and patterned textile prints into Australian homes before Australians were ready for them. This, and related enterprises, are narrated in lovingly intricate detail, both as regards the technical and the business processes, in his fourth chapter, while subsequent chapters focus with equal resolution on his other, and more successful, life enterprises – the silk trade with China, the Sydney Opera House and the Elizabethan Theatre Trust, and, in his home State of Tasmania, the Wild River conservation campaign and his own Roman villa and vineyard.

These represent Alcorso's defining endeavours and achievements as an Australian citizen and as an individual interacting collaboratively with his fellow citizens across a multiplicity of different fields – industrial and social, cultural and environmental – as well as in the domestic sphere. Yet in his conclusion to *The Wind You Say* Alcorso is driven to ask "Who am I?" [Alcorso 1993: 167] and to lament that his emotions have been left out of his life-narrative [Alcorso 1993: 168]. The salience he gives to the trauma of internment contradicts this but, that apart, there is little in the way of soul-searching, and it comes as a shock when he remarks, in passing, "Following my son Adrian's tragic death, I was in a black hole" [Alcorso 1993: 91]. He is laconic about his estrangement from his first wife, but markedly less so about his warm feelings for his second wife, Lesley. He succinctly relates a mystical experience one evening in a quiet side-street of ancient Beijing: "Suddenly something happened: I was no longer myself. I was pervaded by a warm feeling of belonging, of being at home, in peace and harmony" [Alcorso 1993: 106]. He speculates that it might have been triggered by a subliminal boyhood memory of Rome. He recalls another mystical feeling of belonging connected to the birth of his daughter Caroline in the same year as the planting of the Moorilla vineyard [Alcorso 1993: 153-4].

Alcorso's longitudinal search for the self as largely self-made by "the choices we make" [Alcorso 1993: 167] approximates to one model of autobiography. In Dalseno's *Sugar, Tears and Eyeties* it is harder to judge whether the young Peter Delano makes his own choice or has it made for him. As a work of social realist docufiction or reportage – a collective narrative of the Italians of the Herbert River sugar-cane area around Ingham in northern Queensland from the 1920s until internment in the 1940s – the book has its merits, despite its ungainly English and its heterogeneous sprinkling of Italian expressions. It dramatises interconnected scenes and characters, vividly documenting hardships, the often primitive, squalid or sordid living conditions and family and social relations, discriminatory practices, floods and epidemics, thus capturing a mimesis of a significant Italian-centred, but remarkably objective, slice of Australian history with a critical eye and pen. The historical details and issues which the author Peter Dalseno and his autobiographical alter ego Peter Delano were too young to fully grasp at the time when they unfolded are well researched and well integrated into the narrative.

But if *Sugar, Tears and Eyeties* is already impressive as docufiction, it is even more so if viewed as autobiography. Perhaps uniquely in autobiographical narrative, the collective drama is functional to the individual destiny, and a fine balance is maintained between Peter Delano's personal story and that of his social group. He arrives in Queensland in 1923 as the infant Pierino. His mother has eloped from her patrician Venetian family with a cheese salesman, who takes mother and child to the cane fields of Queensland as to a land of opportunity, only to find the living and working conditions unbearable, and to declare that he is going back to the wife and three children he has left in Italy, suggesting that little Pierino be consigned to an orphanage. Pierino, left with his mother, grows up in close proximity to the seamy side of the social and sexual mores of the local Italian community, complicated by friction between northerners and southerners. His own mother has children by two more different partners, and then a scissors abortion, and father-child incest also occurs. The overall picture is unsavoury, so Pierino's removal to the St Therese convent boarding school for boys and his translation into Peter and into an Irish-inclined and strongly Catholic Australian, though traumatic, represents escape.

This narrative structure is sturdy, and makes up for the awkward handling of the narrative moment when the young boy's mother leaves him at the convent:

> Pierino witnessed the edifice that gave him birth, the warmth that spawned his survival, the only being in existence that gave him the sense of 'belonging' [i.e., his mother] was gradually retreating from his view, leaving in the vacuum a feeling of abandonment, a feeling of loss.
>
> …
>
> He stood there, a pathetic little creature, conscious, yes, of the lump in his throat and the tears that welled in his eyes. [Dalseno 1994: 66]

So ends the book's sixth chapter, and the seventh opens mapping the boy's change of identity with his change of environment:

> … the more he dwelt on the subject, the more confusing it became. Experiences and events of yesteryear – Italian in thought and in words – he found himself transcribing them into the English language. He saw himself recalling 'Italian' experiences and interpreting them in English. [Dalseno 1994: 70]

When, at the age of thirteen, the time comes for Peter to leave the convent, he has internalised his Australian identity, and the trauma is renewed: "He felt the old nagging feeling of abandonment. The cry of restlessness – an urgency for tranquillity and peace. This was one memory he wished never to retain." This trauma is renewed yet again a few years and chapters later, after he has left school, with the outbreak of war against Italy, when he is identified as Italian and interned, and the trauma is not overcome until his internment with his fellow Italians is over. The internment experience reiterates Delano's confinement within a community whose limitations he desperately wanted to overcome or escape.

Never give in: anti-Fascism in Australia

Giorgio Venturini, the author of *Never Give In: Three Italian anti-Fascist exiles in Australia* [2007], declares in his Preface that he is "not a historian, or a political scientist," and that "he makes no pretence to write as such. He comes from the law and has improved on it by re-dedicating himself to justice and liberty – rather to *Giustizia e Libertà*, which was the name taken up by the earliest partisan formations in the fight against the Fascists and their final masters, the Nazis" [Venturini 2007: vi]. His disclaimer at first sight seems strange, given that much of this massive book is given over to panoramic sweeps and targeted local reconnaissances of both Italian and Australian history, and that another large proportion of *Never Give In* consists of verbatim reproduction of voluminous archival material relating to two of Venturini's three biographical subjects: police and consular reports and ministerial notes and other official documents from both the Australian and the Italian side. But Venturini's title is the clue: it translates the watchword, "*Non mollare*", of the anti-Fascist *Giustizia e Libertà* movement, and Venturini sees his role not as a neutral academic but as a barrister pleading a cause from *parti pris*.

Venturini's third man, Massimo Montagnana, cannot be considered to have lived an Italian Australian life. Born in Turin in 1903 of a well-established Jewish family committed to Communism, he left Italy for Australia in 1940 after the passing of the Race Laws and returned to Italy as soon as he was able in 1948. During those eight years he was instrumental in setting up the anti-Fascist organisation

Italia Libera in 1943 and subsequently its newspaper *Il Risveglio* (The Reawakening). In Venturini's book, Montagnana's personality comes into focus within the frame of the mobilisation of anti-Fascist militancy, particularly in Melbourne.

The other two main biographical subjects of Venturini's book share with Montagnana this predominantly one-dimensional profile, dictated by the focus on anti-Fascism, but also by the nature of the archival material on the two men. Their very different family origins and upbringing are viewed in terms of their relation to the respective local economy and the experiences that radicalised them. Both arrived in Australia in 1924, in the wake of the murder of the courageously outspoken socialist member of the Italian Parliament, Giacomo Matteotti.

The older of the two, Omero Schiassi, had been born in 1877 in the little township of San Giorgio di Piano, near Bologna, of lower middle-class parents – his father a local administrator, an anti-clerical and atheist, who was the first to have a non-Church funeral in the local cemetery, and his mother a school-teacher who embraced the socialist cause. The young Schiassi got drawn in to the growing peasant agitation from the 1890s, and graduated at Bologna in law, playing an important part in organising agrarian socialism over the next quarter of a century. With the rise of Fascism in the early 1920s, he was repeatedly targeted by Fascist thuggery and twice had his legal practice burned out, prompting his escape to Australia. His personal trajectory is consistently presented within the Italian historical narrative.

This is compounded by the Australian dimension upon Schiassi's arrival in the new continent. Venturini gives an account of the Australian racist extreme right and of forces within Australia sympathetic to Italian Fascism and to related interests, prominent among them the Catholic establishment. The attempts by the Italian Consul-General, Grossardi, to silence Schiassi and to deny him academic employment are amply documented, as are Schiassi's own endeavours to make the anti-Fascist voice to be heard in Australia through the Matteotti Club in Melbourne and associated activities and through direct political lobbying, and to maintain world-wide co-ordination between anti-Fascist exiles. Schiassi's activities in sending relief to war-torn Italy, and then in remonstrating to the Australian government, in 1952, over the treatment of Italian immigrants held for months at the Bonegilla reception camp, are also documented.

Schiassi's profile as an indomitable and indefatigable defender of Italian workers' interests right up to his death in 1956, little short of eighty years of age, emerges through the welter of documentation. Other aspects of his personality – generosity, courtesy, hospitality, frugality – are attested mostly from tributes penned by Schiassi's friend and supporter, Melbourne University's Professor Chisholm and quoted by Venturini. Schiassi's eloquence as an orator on political matters is exemplified in several excerpts quoted from his speeches, but shows no particular individuality. His thousand and over sheets of notes from his studies of Dante's *Divina Commedia* and his lectures on that subject as part of his teaching at Melbourne University remain a closed book, despite his considerable reputation in this field. The biographical portrait remains that of the political activist.

Francesco Fantin, born in 1901 at San Vito di Leguzzano, near Schio in the Venetian province of Vicenza, figures in Venturini's book on account of his death in the Loveday 14D internment camp in November 1942, apparently by the hand of a Fascist sympathiser. The archival record of the coronial and judicial proceedings covering his death is amply quoted in *Never Give In*, with disproportionately little biographical advantage, though the impression of Fascist intimidation within the camp is overwhelming. Fantin's adolescence near the front line during the First World War, with the exemplary execution of servicemen on grounds of indiscipline [Venturini 2007: 97-8], and the experience of worker exploitation in the nearby textile factory [Venturini 2007: 101-2], is scanned for clues of how he was attracted towards anarchism, to which he adhered for the rest of his life, and Fantin's role in the founding of Melbourne's Matteotti Club in 1927 is highlighted. However, in Fantin's case, the narrowly political profile is augmented by the inclusion of an appendix containing the English translation of his "Pensieri e ricordi" [Venturini 2007:

442-50], of which the Italian original has been lost. In this apparent mixture of verse and poetic prose, the political and the personal come together in acute anguish, with clear forebodings of violent death.

Chapter 3

Trauma and Grievance

Kinds of trauma

Internment as an alien – indeed, an enemy alien – was clearly a traumatic experience for many Italians who had made Australia their home; and, as we have seen also, even those who were not interned were affected. This is eloquently attested by Rino Baggio and is darkly alluded to in Maria Triaca's *Amelia, a Long Journey*. Some autobiographies and biographies of Australia's Italians have thus been prompted, at least in large part, by the desire to have that wrong morally righted and that hurt healed.

But internment is only the most prominent instance of discrimination, hostility and xenophobia with which Italian immigrants have often been received by some Australians at various levels and in various sectors of society: attitudes which are also well attested in the texts that address the experience of internment. And though overall, and in the long run, Australians have proved hospitable to the new arrivals, the mere fact of moving from one social culture and language environment somewhere in Italy to a very different one in Australia can itself prove traumatic, as is attested by the number of Italian migrants who have returned to Italy and of those who wish they had.

These lives do not get written or published and have not been much researched, but occasionally one comes across significant anecdotal evidence. One such instance is that with which I open this book, about the Italian worker in Canberra in the 1950s who, in his exasperation at being taunted and humiliated by the Australian-born, and at his inability to respond because of his lack of English, put his arm under a circular saw. Though that was an individual instance, it was clearly not isolated, but a symptom of systematic societal discrimination amounting to persecution.

An even clearer instance of collective discrimination and resultant trauma appears incidentally in a 1996 Melbourne University PhD thesis on attitudes to home ownership by Italian immigrants in Victoria. The researcher, Mariastella Pulvirenti, encountered extreme difficulty in finding informants. Visiting a club in the Melbourne suburb of Brunswick whose membership, typically, was composed of immigrants originating from one particular locality in Italy, Pulvirenti thought she had gained an entry thanks to the support of the club's president.

However, neither the women, playing tombola (bingo) in one room, nor the men, playing a card game in another room, were disposed to be interviewed, and all of them pointedly ignored the researcher. Eventually, one of the men expostulated, "'You could write my story in one word – HELL! It was hell'" [Pulvirenti 1996: 75]. Another man weighed in: "'I'm sure if you asked everyone their story it'd be the same …'" and referred to the experience of the immigrant reception camp at Bonegilla (near Victoria's north-eastern border with New South Wales). The other men present confirmed this: "'We all went through the same thing … it was awful.'" At this point, the club's president also chimed in: "'You didn't have to be at *Bonegilla* to suffer! We *all* suffered!'"

Pulvirenti comments: "I wondered whether this wasn't an old argument, something used as a rebellion against his [the president's] authority or a class issue that separated him from the others." The treasurer, who had led the remonstration, commented, "'See, we all have the same story.'" Pulvirenti's final comment is: "Not only was I astounded at the response and the rowdy atmosphere that had been created, but also at the sense of defiance against him [the president]" [Pulvirenti 1996: 76].

These are first-generation Italian Australians who do not share their lives in print either with other Italians or with other Australians, but shut themselves off among their fellow *paesani*, people from the same locality or birthplace, in a virtual ghetto, leaving it to their children, the second generation of Italian Australians, to merge into the broader Australian community. There is no knowing how many other Italian Australian micro-communities replicate the experience and attitude of this micro-community visited by Pulvirenti.

That the negative experience was quite widespread is evidenced on a collective scale, both as regards Bonegilla and as regards working and living conditions, discrimination and financial stringency, in Battiston's account of the Italian immigrant organisation, FILEF [Battiston 2012: 19-21, 29-34], while on an individual level Borghese's *Appunti di un emigrante* [1996] (discussed in a later chapter), presents a very circumstantial picture which is borne out by several other Italian Australian life histories.

Pulvirenti's final recollection of her visit to that Brunswick club graphically clinches the point: "… the grass clippings I inadvertently brought into the club rooms on the soles of my shoes were pointedly vacuumed from under my feet at the end of the meeting. As the vacuum cleaner nozzle pushed me out of the way, I recall thinking that every trace of me, my questions and the memories they evoked were being extinguished and made untraceable" [Pulvirenti, personal communication, 2011].

This anecdote encapsulates the attitude of a group or groups that actively resist telling their story or having it told, except possibly in a closed circle amongst themselves. It graphically pits the social or communal perspective of lived experience against the individual perspective.

There is a hidden converse to this. The often painful, and not always successful, effort at acculturation by Italians into Anglo-Celtic Australia masks the dispossession and quasi-genocidal marginalisation in their own homeland of Australian Aborigines, which has arguably resulted in their societal traumatisation. This historical injustice receives virtually no attention in Italian Australian life writing. However, in 2012 there appeared the autobiography of Chris Sarra, *Good morning, Mr Sarra*, authored by an Aboriginal activist whose educational leadership had transformed the school of the Cherbourg district of south-west Queensland by emphasising Aboriginal self-esteem and capacity to achieve. Sarra was himself one of several children of an Aboriginal mother. Their father was an

Italian immigrant from Abruzzo who had come over in the 1950s, and who had supported their mother in instilling Aboriginal pride and self-reliance in her children. He had left behind in Italy three other children from a previous relationship, and encouraged contact and comradeship between his two families, to the extent that Chris visited his half-siblings in Italy in his twenties and took pride in his dual ethnicity.

A life story published as recently as 2012 may fittingly inaugurate this chapter's survey of narratives of trauma and grievance. Meticulously researched, it reconstructs the life of Francesco Sceusa, who was born in Trapani, near the westernmost tip of Sicily, in 1851, escaped political persecution by emigrating to Sydney in 1877, and returned to Trapani with his Australian wife, Louisa Swan, in 1908, a broken, disappointed and poverty-stricken man, after having devoted his whole life, first in Italy and then in New South Wales, to the cause of Socialism and internationalism, representing the Social Democratic Federation of Australasia at the Zürich Congress of the Socialist International in 1893. The title of Gianfranco Cresciani's biography of Sceusa pointedly avoids an individualistic perspective: "'Socialismo per la generazione presente': Rifugiati politici italiani e movimento socialista australiano." [Socialism for the current generation: Italian political refugees and the Australian Socialist movement.] But, Socialist though he was, Sceusa stands out as an individual, sacrificing his middle-class privileges for the cause. Cresciani follows his political activities and choices with analytical finesse and with human sympathy, recording Sceusa's initial enthusiasm on finding Australian democracy and working-class rights more securely established and taken for granted than in Europe, and his subsequent dismay at the Australian labour movement's inward-looking and xenophobic discrimination against the few Italians and other non-British immigrants. Other Italian radicals in Australia discussed in Cresciani's account were far less consistent and steadfast than Sceusa in their political commitment.

Traumatic experience varies enormously in kind and degree, and its nature and symptoms are notoriously hard to define and classify. Clinical analysis cannot be the aim of my presentation. The anecdotes I have cited are a clue to traumas untold and unwritten. Kinds of trauma emerge from the texts themselves.

The most extreme forms of trauma are rare: Italian emigrants to Australia have not faced anything as terrible as the Holocaust, but some have had experiences of war or have had family members who have had such experiences. None of the life histories discussed exhibit the psychopathology of post-traumatic stress disorder, with the probable exception of Cristina's *Secrets of a Broken Heart*, which will be examined shortly.

I canvas trauma and grievance as threats, varying in kind and intensity, to the existential project, or sense of self, perceived by the person concerned – the autobiographical or biographical subject – whether this is explicitly stated or implicitly conveyed by the text. The published life stories which I discuss in this book are undoubtedly selective as regards the painful experiences on which they dwell.

Broadly speaking, trauma and grievance are more openly addressed in the more straightforwardly autobiographical works. Of the biographies, Helen Garner's *Joe Cinque's Consolation*, discussed in chapter 1 above, is one that most closely addresses trauma and grievance, first in the parents' grief over the loss of their son and secondly in their indignation at what they perceive as the failure of justice; while another is Flavio Lucchesi's chronicle of the repeated persecution of Joe Maffina, culminating in his internment, discussed in the first two chapters of this book. However, all the books discussed in chapter 1, with the exceptions of B. A. Santamaria's autobiography, Judith Armstrong's biography of the De Pieri brothers and Piero Genovesi's biography of the Pitruzzellos, and possibly the life story of Carlo Zaccariotto, address major hardship, grievance or trauma.

A variety of other texts approach the trials of migration and a variety of other ordeals in a variety of ways. Marie Alafaci's *Savage Cows and Cabbage Leaves: An Italian life* [1999] is a minutely detailed – often minute-by-minute – recreation of the immigration experience of the Calabrian Carmela Barbaro, who arrives at Victoria Dock in Melbourne as a four-year-old with her mother in March 1927. The strangeness of the new environment, the struggle with a new language, the initial lostness in a new school system in which no one knows Italian, let alone Calabrian, the only language which Carmela knows, are deftly conveyed as experienced by the little girl.

The language divide confronts the reader in frequent snatches of Calabrian intercalated in the lively English narrative, with footnoted English translations. Stressful experiences arising from the immigrants' lack of English and cultural differences between Calabria and Victoria are re-enacted in the writing. Carmela's mother, Maria, gives birth to her son in an impersonal hospital where she is denied visits by her family, and has to fight to avoid having her baby taken away from her by the obstetrician [Alafaci 1999: 40-8]. On her first day at school, Carmela, the only Italian pupil, has her gold earrings taken away from her by a fellow pupil, their cultural significance being lost on the school authorities [Alafaci 1999: 54-60]. The Barbaros' boarding house, which houses several Calabrian non-union wharf-side labourers, is bombed and gutted, though, miraculously, no one is seriously injured [Alafaci 1999: 62-75]. And, generally, the family have a life of hard toil trying to make ends meet during the Depression years, with a devoted father, though one who too readily resorts to the strap.

But this is not a whingeing narrative; stoicism is garnished with good humour and the will to live and to enjoy life, and projected within a broad socio-historical perspective, with numerous newspaper clippings of the period. The subtitle, *An Italian life*, accurately suggests that this is a fairly average and typical story and, being in English, that it is an Australian Italian story. Grievance, stress, trauma, in undefinable but manageable proportions, thus figure within a tale of survival and gradually improving security and prospects of social promotion for the younger generation.

Many Italians, of course, came to Australia in a spirit of adventure and in search of opportunity, and their life narratives may thus have a celebratory air. This is the case with Desmond O'Grady's finely crafted life of Raffaello Carboni, who spent a year in Victoria during the 1850s gold rush and left the most coherent eye-witness account of the Eureka Stockade uprising. It is also the case with Daniela Volpe's less intimate, more distant account of the achievements of three other well-educated nineteenth-century Italian immigrants, the Tuscans, Pietro Baracchi, Carlo Catani and Ettore Checchi, who integrated seamlessly into the upper echelons of Victorian society. More recently, the Pitruzzellos' migratory enterprise has been described as an adventure, and immigrants as different from one another as Ivo Vellar and Franco Lugarini, among others, use the same word.

The surgeon Ivo Vellar, who arrived in Melbourne in 1938 at the age of four with his family from the Germanic Cimbro-speaking village of Camporovere near Asiago in the Dolomites in northern Italy, was the first Italian Australian in his field, and enjoyed an outstanding educational and professional career, so that his 2008 autobiography could be deemed to belong to the celebratory mode. To pigeon-hole it as such, however, would be altogether too simple, as its title, *Adventures in Two Worlds: My battles with the D word*, indicates. The adventures include dramatic or suspenseful episodes of various kinds – near-death experiences, professional achievements and vicissitudes and also four public confrontations involving the D word, *dago*, a term of vilification once widely used in Australia to taunt and humiliate immigrants from Mediterranean countries, most especially from Italy.

Given that the four instances of confrontation recounted in his autobiography do not acquire great prominence among the medley of other incidents narrated, Vellar justifies his choice of subtitle by devoting the fourteen pages of his final chapter to "Racism and the D word" [Vellar 2008a: 165-78]. With historical penetration and humane conviction, he points up the repeated recrudescence of racism directed by some – too many – Australians against the currently most recent wave of new immigrants, and passionately argues against such discrimination. "It was episodes such as this," he comments on one occasion, "that made me feel apprehensive and on guard, so to speak, whenever I found myself in a large gathering of Australians" [Vellar 2008a: 134].

This grievance, however, does not dominate his main narrative, which constitutes a signal contribution to the autoethnography of Italian Australians, with an impressively numerous cast of individuals – members of an extremely extended family, boyhood friends and schoolmates, teachers and mentors, and professional colleagues – and with a particularly detailed and concrete description of domestic life in the "Little Italy" that was the Melbourne suburb of Carlton in the 1950s, as well as of several hospitals in Melbourne and in England and of a multiplicity of technically detailed surgical operations – all with prolific photographic illustration. Vellar also published *From Camporovere to Carlton: The story of five families*, as well as the biographies of the eminent pioneering surgeons, Thomas Peel Dunhill and the remarkable and spectacularly adventurous half Italian and half English Thomas Henry Fiaschi (1853-1927), *Italo-Australian Patriot, Surgeon, Soldier and Pioneer Vigneron*.

As for the globetrotting Franco Lugarini, the title of his autobiography says it all: *Mio padre mi chiamava zingaro* (My father used to call me a gypsy). Lugarini spent some time in Brazil, before settling down in Melbourne as a fashionable women's hair stylist. He was a left-wing activist and rose to prominence and official recognition as a spokesperson for Italian working people in Australia and, more broadly, for migrants of varied ethnic background. Lugarini also gives an interesting account of his adolescent experiences trying to survive in various small towns in the Roman region of Lazio during the 1940s under an increasingly obnoxious Fascist regime and through the frightful military conflict in that area between the Axis and the Allied forces. Lugarini attributes his restless wanderlust to this unsettling experience.

My next chapter will look at life narratives that are couched as success stories (though many of them also confront frustration, struggle and grief) and will discuss their features and implications. This chapter is devoted to examining life stories that foreground various kinds of traumatic experience, including some others that involve mixed identity as a factor in the experience of trauma.

Two such cases are autobiographical accounts by non-Italian wives of Italian Australian husbands. Zelda D'Aprano, of an East European Jewish immigrant family, describes, in her 1977 autobiography (republished in a revised edition in 1995 as *Zelda: The becoming of a woman*) how, when, at the age of sixteen, she married Tony D'Aprano in 1944 in Melbourne, both the bride's and the bridegroom's fathers refused to attend the wedding, as both objected to the transethnic match [Zelda D'Aprano 1995: 30]. Tony suddenly left, twenty-one years later, depriving Zelda of emotional security [Zelda D'Aprano 1995: 142], but her text makes no mention of her personal relations with Tony, either from an ethnic or any other point of view, except to report on the involvement of both of them in left-wing trade-unionism, before Zelda committed herself to militant feminism, of which her autobiography is a prime Australian document, at once illuminating and eloquent.

Vivien Stewart's account of her marriage to Eliseo Achia, *Marrying Italian: When love is not enough* [2013], is unique in being the only account by an Anglo-Australian woman of her marriage to an Italian husband, and thus presents a unique interest, shedding a strong light on both the attractions and the barriers of such a match. Deep love on both sides proves unable to overcome contrary forces. Is it on account of an incompatibility between the two partners' respective social cultures and behavioural codes? Or is it due to idiosyncratic characteristics of either or both of the individuals concerned? Or to traumatic life-experiences undergone by Eliseo as a youth in war-torn Italy?

Vivien's account gives much to ponder over. It presents a vivid chronicle of a 1950s Victorian country girlhood followed by a 1960s Melbourne young womanhood, at once individual and yet typically and recognisably Australian, which gives the reader a good idea of who the woman is who will fall in love with the much older Eliseo. Eliseo represents Italian style at its most dazzling. A bricklayer by profession, in company he dresses immaculately, and he provides excellent cuisine. We see Vivien drawn into his lifestyle and into his social group, to find, upon becoming his wife, that a lot more is expected of her than she bargained for, and that her best efforts are often treated with scorn. A prolonged visit to Eliseo's family of origin in the countryside outside Rome sees her enthusiastically plunging into the Italian way of life and becoming one of the family.

Nevertheless, mutual attachment does not save the relationship from becoming unsustainable, and this is aggravated by physical and financial setbacks, leading to Eliseo's gradual decline and eventual death. Vivien's book is an attempt to make sense of this love-tragedy and is in itself a loving gesture towards Eliseo, ending with his final message of love for her. Her second visit to Eliseo's family in Italy, undertaken after his death, constitutes a pledge that the link between them will not be broken, and this extends to Vivien's renewed commitment to Victoria's Italian community and its heritage. She remains a bridge between Anglo-Celtic and Italian Australia.

Grievance and trauma may of course have causes unconnected with nationality or ethnic origin, cultural cleavage or the experience of immigration as such, and some Italian Australian life narratives do not particularly dwell on issues of sociocultural identity in facing trauma and aggrievement.

The author of the extraordinary *Secrets of a Broken Heart*, published in 2003 simultaneously with its Italian version, *Segreti di un cuore spezzato*, is named simply as Cristina.[21] Unlike almost every other life narrative discussed in this volume, this has no illustrations except two miniature frontispiece photographs of a little girl and a crude drawing of a broken heart on the front cover with "Shame Guilt Grief Loss Tears Pain Hate Fear Incest" engraved on its shards, and on the back cover, "Love Truth Hope Joy Faith Grace Spirit Peace Love Of God". Substantial Biblical quotations fill every available space and abound throughout the text, taken prevalently from the exilic books (*Lamentations*, Isaiah, Jeremiah, Hosea), but also from the *Psalms*, and from the New Testament, especially Paul. There are also some incantatory pieces of Cristina's own composition, one of which, almost a page long, opens: "If I had a dream to dream let it be real, so I can dream for evermore this dream" [*Secrets*: 87]. This torrent of quotations is itself a component of the book's own anguished, overwhelming, torrential discourse. A postscript by the publisher/editor, Luigi (Jim) Scarano, to the Italian version of Cristina's book reveals that the linguistically assured and idiomatic English version passed through at least three pairs of hands, and the more uneven

---

21 Cristina, *Secrets of a Broken Heart*, published simultaneously with its Italian version, *Segreti di un cuore spezzato*, Thornleigh, NSW: Bridge to Peace Publications. 2003.

Italian version through at least five [*Segreti* 202-3]. Presumably, Cristina, who says she was born in a South Italian village [*Secrets*: 13], was not fully proficient in either standard Italian or standard English. The complex language mediation process does not seem to have impaired the book's expressive power, especially in the English version.

Uniquely, among the several dozen texts discussed in this volume, Cristina's is a religious work. God is invoked emotionally in Olga D'Albero Giuliani's autobiography, discussed in chapter 1 above, but is not a prominent presence. Religion is a central concern in Fosco Antonio's *My Reality*, discussed in chapter 6 below, and death-of-God theology haunts the text. But, even in life narratives centred on practising Catholics, such as Angela Napolitano's *Liborio: My Great Love* (to be discussed shortly), religious belief and practice do not prominently enter the discourse of Italian Australian life writing. This remains a secular pursuit: religious experience, if any, appears to be kept a private matter. In *Secrets of a Broken Heart*, on the other hand, God figures centrally, and is on occasion directly addressed, in worship or in prayer, Cristina affirming her faith or imploring salvation. Religious faith (Christian, but of no identifiable denomination) is central to her struggle to exorcise her resurgent horrific memories of childhood sexual abuse.

Secrets of a Broken Heart is not a narrative autobiography, but a spiritual exercise, a writing therapy, and a testament. However, it depends on memory flashbacks recovered through counselling [*Secrets*: 14] and psychotherapy when Cristina is already in her forties. The flashbacks start when she is nursing her father until he dies of a brain tumour, aged 72. "How could anyone believe what I was seeing and saying?" She, and everyone around her, thinks she is going mad [*Secrets*: 11]. As a result of her resurgent memories, at the age of forty-three, she says: "I left my marriage of 27 years, which for many years had already been dead" [*Secrets*: 11]. It is implied that her own children, whom she dearly loved, abandoned her for the same reason [*Secrets*: 138].

Cristina's flashbacks are intermittently and disconnectedly mentioned in her text. She more than once reports a distinct memory from the age of three of her father first lavishing on her affectionate love and endearments and then forcing himself sexually upon her [*Secrets*: 111]. She claims to have given birth before the age of nine:

> I am Cristina, the nine year old who had a child, and I say that this is not good enough for me and I promised myself as that child, that one day I would tell the world what my father did to me. [*Secrets*: 139]

> I never held my child. I never shared his love. I never saw him grow up, but I feel love for my son. [*Secrets*: 148]

One of her memories is of a shining statue of the Virgin holding out her hands to Cristina [*Secrets*: 16-17]. Her visionary memories link sexual abuse with "a city in the sky":

> I saw myself and my mother being abused from inside the womb and after my birth the abuse continued. At 10 days old the abuse was so horrific I had, what I now know and believe was a near death experience. I saw myself in a city in the sky where I could hear music. I saw harps and could feel what the other people there were feeling and thinking. [*Secrets*: 13]

This city in the sky is later explicitly identified as Heaven [*Secrets*: 83], and in turn identifies the entire universe with Cristina's restored individual identity, an identity of the individual with the totality predicated on a love that is distinct from sexuality:

> In my city in the sky I saw, felt and knew everyone else. It was like a single thought which everyone shared with one mind. With a thought I could be anywhere, see anything and hear all. The peace and love that I felt there, no words could describe … It was a feeling of oneness with God, the creator of heaven and earth, to feel and see his love without seeing Him, to know He was there all around like breath itself, life itself. [*Secrets*: 84]

Isolated from her own family and from all but a handful of newfound supportive friends, Cristina finds in writing her book her "lifeline to God" [*Secrets*: 119] and says: "The writing of this book is a way to honour God, myself and my descendants" [*Secrets*: 122]. It is a recovery of her self, with and through God, from the "self-made prison" of "co-dependency" (or, simply, dependency) on others: "We all live in a self-made prison and we don't know how to open the jailer's door" [*Secrets*: 125]. "All my life," she writes, "I have been someone's daughter, wife, mother, but I never became Me. ... My self-worth was only in what I did for others. I was of no value to myself and I don't believe others thought I was of any value" [*Secrets*: 122]. She invokes the only non-Biblical authority mentioned in the book, Melody Beattie, a critic of "co-dependency" [*Secrets*: 123] and announces that her quest is a "search for *me*" [*Secrets*: 126-7].

Cristina's text is thus an explicit assertion of individual agency and identity construction, fraught with doubt: "Many times I doubt that this is from God" [*Secrets*: 133]. "Am I giving my power away to someone else? Am I still doing that?" [*Secrets*: 134]. This is soon answered by a ringing affirmative: "I have found my identity. I know who *I* am" [*Secrets*: 149], but the book necessarily remains open-ended, an exemplar of what we may call conative autobiography, the striving to affirm selfhood. (This can be related to the *conatus* – the effort of each individual being to sustain itself, as posited in Spinoza's *Ethics* and as applied to the maintenance of individual selfhood, in the face of the threat of effacement, by Antonio R. Damasio [see Damasio 2003: 36, 269]).

Cristina's text neither constitutes forensic evidence of incestuous childhood abuse, nor admits rejection as a product of false memory syndrome, but has to be taken as an autobiographical self-portrait, expressing anguish really experienced. As such, it exceeds what Leigh Gilmore calls the "limits of autobiography", that is, of canonical autobiography, limits which presume the possibility of objective verification.[22] Trauma here produces testimony of a different kind, which could not improperly be called testament.

The conative character of Cristina's *Secrets of a Broken Heart* – its explicit striving to achieve selfhood and autonomy – appears closely linked to its under-developed narrativity. A story which for over forty

---

22 Leigh Gilmore, *The Limits of Autobiography: Trauma and testimony*. Ithaca and London: Cornell University Press, 2001.

years could not be told struggles to emerge, revealing itself bit by bit amid a welter of agonised discourse and ardent invocation.

This is a striking instance of how self-identity and narrative are in reciprocal relationship with one another (an issue dealt with in depth in the volume *Narrative and Identity: Studies in autobiography, self and culture*, edited by Jens Brockmeier and Donal Corbaugh [2001].) So we will see in Fosco Antonio's *My Reality* that where there is no coherent self there is no coherent story, but miscellaneous fragments of story. This applies in biography as well as in autobiography: the many biographies treated in this book that construct or reconstruct a coherent self do so by means of a coherent narrative, while Helen Garner's quest to reconstruct the personality of the murdered Joe Cinque remains fragmentary, as the narrative of her quest, itself coherent, does not result in a coherent narrative of Joe Cinque.

Giuliano Montagna's autobiography opens with an ending: "I've come back home in pursuit of a hope: that of becoming who I am." [My translation from Montagna's Italian: "Sono tornato a casa inseguendo una speranza: diventare la persona che sono." Montagna 2004: 5]. The explanation of this paradoxical sally starts with the book's title, *Mio padre Giovannino Guareschi: dal Po all'Australia inseguendo un sogno* [My father Giovanni Guareschi: from the Po to Australia in pursuit of a dream.] Home is Parma and its rural hinterland in the Po valley. The dream includes the author's wish to have his real name – Giuliano Guareschi – engraved on his tombstone [Montagna 6]. Like Cristina's book, the elderly Montagna's is also a coming-out text.

Giovanni Guareschi was world-famous during the third quarter of the last century for his Don Camillo stories which humorously defused the political strife between Catholics and Communists in Italy, with the figure of Christ gently showing the parish priest Don Camillo that his antagonist, the Communist local mayor, Peppone, was his brother beneath the skin. Within Italy, Giovanni (Giovannino, to his friends) was also prominent as a political journalist of Catholic populist hue. Fathering a son out of wedlock could cause someone in his position more than a little embarrassment if it were known [Montagna 54], so Giuliano was kept secret, not recognised as his father's son, until this coming-out late in the son's own life. Limited throughout his life to relatively few, intermittent, brief and non-committal meetings with his father, the unacknowledged son nevertheless worshipped his "paper father" (as he came to think of him, since he came to know him through his writings and through what others wrote about him) and he took him as his role model. He dreamed of following his father in a journalistic career, though without any ambition to vie with him. An audio-cassette recording of his father addressing him, sent to Giuliano the year before his father's death in 1968, remains his constant companion through all the years after that event [Montagna 114-15]. As Montagna feels his own end approaching, the imperative to reveal the truth, to claim his legitimacy, to assert his identity, finds expression in this book.

Montagna's book is bifocal in more ways than one. The clandestine father-son relationship itself determines a double focus, the son's identity being constantly defined in relation to the father's, and modelled on it. Although the elder Guareschi appears here in the third person, the sustained pathos of frustrated longing in the narrative makes of him a virtual second person.

This is in turn translated into the book's double focus on Italy and Australia: the antipodean remove, placing an ocean between, paradoxically brings father and son closer together. The hurt of paternal non-recognition makes *Mio padre Giovannino Guareschi*, of all the Italian Australian life narratives which I have read, the one in which the identity of origin remains strongest, though attachment to Australia is not in question. Italian is the language of this autobiography not only because it remains Montagna's dominant language, the language in which he could but is too modest to claim literary proficiency, and the language of his journalism for the Sydney newspaper *La Fiamma*, but because his essential dialogue is with his father, who was an Italian writer of note, who had his own distinctive way with the Italian language, and, through his father, his dialogue is, arguably, with Italy itself, whose parental relationship to its offspring has not been straightforward or wholehearted.

The double focus makes explicit the deep structure of every autobiographical narrative: the duality of the now of writing and the then of living, the latter as reconstructed by memory or by investigation. Starting, as often in life narratives, at a point after the narrative ends, in what is in effect a preface, the book makes a second start with a second ending – the news of Giovanni Guareschi's death in 1968 reaching his son Giuliano Montagna in the Sydney newspaper offices of *La Fiamma*, of which he is editor, and where no one knows of his parentage. This is the narrative trigger that sets off the following retrospective and chronologically consecutive chapters on the youthful liaison between Giovanni and Giuliano's mother, Luisa, on key family members, on Giuliano's boyhood and then his first meetings with his father, on his employment in various unsatisfactory situations in and around Parma, and then his emigration to Australia in1961, first to work in a pasta factory in Adelaide, and finally, in 1963, for *La Fiamma* in Sydney. This sequence is interspersed with criss-crossings between then and now and with various return visits to a Parma increasingly remote from that of Giuliano's memories and attachments. The word "adventure" appears several times, indicating something which the autobiographer sees as characteristic of himself and also of his move to Australia, and the text itself comes across as an adventure in narrative, an adventure which further relates the son Giuliano to his famed storytelling father.

The problematical father is again in large part responsible for the move to Australia in Liliana Belardinelli's 2002 *Liliana Lucia: Destination Australia*. The book is precisely titled, in that it does not describe the experience of living in Australia or becoming Australian, but the shocks that drove the author to this continent. Born before the Second World War of a Maltese mother and an Italian father, she describes her earliest years growing up in Malta until her father, a fervent Fascist, was imprisoned in Malta on a charge of military espionage, and then deported. Then follow her primary school years in Tripoli, Libya, where her father was consul, and her secondary school years living with her mother and brother in her grandparents' house in Rome, through the Second World War, while her father travelled round Italy and beyond on secret work. All these recollections are richly detailed, with lively mediation between the reminiscing elderly autobiographer and her former adolescent self, and between that self and the various historic milieux through which she passed. Belardinelli then gives fascinating accounts of herself and her mother lying low in German-occupied Italy and getting through thanks to her mother's resourcefulness. She also describes the sixteen-year-old Liliana travelling unaccompanied from Rome to Verona through the chaos of war-ravaged Italy as soon as hostilities had ceased, to learn, through snooping into police records, that her father had been sentenced to death *in absentia* for crimes committed under the Fascist regime [142-5]. At her father's next visit home in Rome, an altercation between him and her mother leads to her father advancing threateningly on Liliana, who strikes him with a saucepan of hot milk [149]. A penitent Liliana's Catholicism implodes when a priest treats her confession as an opportunity for lewd sexual self-gratification [150-1].

As if this were not enough, in the course of a few years working first with the Allies in Rome, then in Malta and in England, the great love of her life ("Yes, I remember my first love; he is vivid and alive, always young in my memory" [152]), an English serviceman, who apparently fully reciprocated her feelings, unaccountably dropped out of the picture, being last heard from on his way to the Persian Gulf [155]. The young man, Ted Shore, a sergeant in the Royal Signals corps, had kindled Liliana's enthusiasm for them both to emigrate to Australia. The Australian continent becomes the destination where the emotions undisclosed in the course of Liliana's narration of her experiences and adventures remain undisclosed. Australia is a silence, a question that cannot be asked, let alone answered, an escape from an unacceptable reality, a liberation. Liliana writes: "I was seventeen years old, and I already considered my life to be concluded, that is, my real life inside me. The rest of me would go on living, acting out a life that from now on would not be 'for real'" [156]. But she asserts her still on-going "search for the self" [157]. The book's closing remark is: "This is far from being a conclusion – it is the end that marks a beginning." This is Italian Australian autobiography at its most oblique in relation to Australia.

Two highly literate men of working-class origin bring traumas of very different kinds into their autobiographical writing, experiences that threaten their sense of self and their hold on life. Luigi Strano, born at Galimi di Castellace in Calabria in 1913, goes to Sydney in 1930 to join his father, who had abandoned his family years before, and now leeches on his son all he can. So this is yet another case of fatherhood deficit. But that is not all that Luigi had to face, and not for nothing does he title his autobiography *Rocciosa è la via* (Rocky is the path).[23] He is surprised to find worse hardship in Australia in the Great Depression than in Italy [L. Strano 74], and is tempted to commit suicide [L. Strano 44-5]. But, young as he is, he has to support the family, and he goes through a multitude of occupations, including office-boy, language teacher, farmer, estate agent, charcoal-burner (under a wartime scheme to harness the labour of "enemy aliens"), poet and amateur scholar.

The episodic (but not the thematic) structure of the book is picaresque, recounting a succession of vicissitudes, endeavours, adventures and encounters, including several with Calabrian criminality among his own relatives and acquaintances. It is an engaging ramble through remarkable reminiscences, reflections, comments, *professions de foi*. The connecting thread of his life story is his passion for literature. His one consolation for having to ship to Australia is that he would learn English and read Shakespeare in the original [L. Strano 28]. Baulked by circumstances of the opportunity of a university education, he gives himself a broad literary and intellectual education not only in Italian, but also in Latin, Greek, English and German, familiarising himself with the Italian literary classics from Dante to Alfieri and beyond, and reading the works of thinkers as varied as Schopenhauer and Malinovsky. He establishes a reputation as one of the leading Italian Australian poets and is at last rewarded with a Sydney university degree *honoris causa*, all of which is touched upon with the same unassuming modesty as that which characterises the style and language of the book as a whole. Endurance is not merely a passive virtue in Luigi Strano's life and life writing; it is the fulfilment of a meaningful vocation vigorously pursued. The rural Australian landscape and lifestyle is the correlative to the bucolic

---

23 There is a French, but not an English, translation of this work.

poetry of the ancients and of Strano's own poetry.

Fernando Basili, who was born in the Tuscan town of Pistoia in 1930 and migrated to Sydney in 1960, has, like Luigi Strano, an intellectual vocation. Unlike Strano, he has a strong bond with his father, and Fernando's account of his last visit home to see his aging father, followed shortly after by the latter's death, though laconically narrated, is the most moving thing in his book, *Esperienze di un emigrato* [2004], translated by the author as *A Migrant's Experience* [2006]. Also unlike Strano, Basili has no less than eight tertiary qualifications, six of them from Australia, including two Master's degrees and a doctoral degree. Yet he finds himself all his life discriminated against by the Italian consular authorities who, he claims, repeatedly deny him Italian study bursaries, and by the Italian Department of Sydney University during the 1960s and early 1970s, which he accuses of blocking his academic career prospects, particularly under the leadership of Professor Frederick May, of whom Basili is scathingly critical. Basili's book is subtitled *"Perché?" – "Perché!"* ("Why?" – "Because!"), implying gratuitous and arbitrary class prejudice and antagonism which, in his Postface, he regards as systemic.

Basili, then, writes not only on his own behalf, but on behalf of socially disadvantaged Italian immigrants generally, documenting his case as evidence of widespread discrimination. His book is remarkable for its combination of minutely detailed and documented circumstantial accounts of alleged malpractice with a sustained verbal energy and impact for over 280 large-format pages, accompanied by 140 pages of photocopied documentation, ranging from certificates and official records to press cuttings, letters, Futurist graphics and examination question papers. The linguistic verve of the Italian version is matched by that of the almost flawless English version. Though this is not the story of a life, it is powerful autobiography in that it conveys the meaning which his life has for the author, and may also be called autoethnography in that it offers testimony on behalf of a social group, that of underprivileged Italian migrants.

Social and moral redress is powerfully claimed by Angela Napolitano's 2006 *Liborio: My Great Love*. This is a husband-and-wife autobiography, drafted by the wife, Angela, predominantly about her husband, Liborio, but also telling her own story and that of their family. The book is centred, however, on the couple's apparently hopeless, but eventually successful, lawsuit against the owners of the Wittenoom blue asbestos mine in the north of Western Australia, where Liborio had worked before the marriage, and where he had contracted the deadly asbestos-related lung condition, meso-thelioma, and consequential depression. The depression severely impaired Liborio's employability and the mesothelioma caused his early death. The progress of the lawsuit chapter by chapter supplies the consecutive longitudinal narrative element in Napolitano's book, but this is ably spliced, chapter by chapter, with consecutive narra-tive segments on the origins of both spouses, their early lives, their meeting and courtship, their work experiences up to the time of their marriage and subsequently, the birth of their children and family life. The legal proceedings and courtroom hearings and the points at issue are described in detail and are used to connect with the flashbacks of their life histories, the two narratives – that of the lawsuit and that of the family's life histories – gradually converging and coinciding at the endpoint.

This unostentatiously sophisticated narrative structure gives Napolitano's story a concentrated impact. The writer, born in Sicily but raised in Western Australia, couches her narrative in an idiom that includes the precision of medical and legal terminology but is dominated by the style of popular romance (as signalled in the title), with tragic and heroic overtones relating to Liborio's early death but also to both spouses' resolute perseverance in pursuing justice. Remarkably, uplift is the consistent effect of what might seem to be a grim tale ending in a painful and untimely death. It takes the reader from Liborio's origins in Vasto, on the Abruzzo coast, and his youthful years, the adventure of his move to Australia in early manhood, his charismatic personality within the Italian community in Western Australia and then to his coming forward as a suitor for Angelina's hand.

A joyful, loving relationship between the couple and between them and their children is conveyed throughout the narrative. This is all the more striking in that Liborio's mesothelioma is not the only life-threatening condition that enters the narrative. The couple's first son, Cesario, is born with biliary atresia, an incurable condition which no child had been known to survive beyond the age of seven [Napolitano 92]. Yet the narrative never falters in conveying the loving relationship between parents and child and the child's own zest for life, which carried him to the age of seventeen instead of the predicted seven. One of the milestones in baby Cesario's condition comes when he is only four months old. An operation which has apparently been unsuccessful belatedly turns out to have been a success, but this hardly relieves the parents' anguish:

> As the weeks went by, a healthy glow replaced the sickly yellow tinge in Cesario's cheeks. But despite the slight improvement, the anguish and anxiety still took its toll on both of us. Liborio lost his hair by the handful and I became terribly thin and pale. We both became objects of pity, and cruel remarks were overheard, "Looks like the mother will die before the son," and, "she looks terribly thin." [Napolitano 94]

The doctor urges the despairing and unreceptive Angela to have a second child as the only way to avoid a nervous breakdown. When she reports this to Liborio, her husband puts his arm round her, saying, "We must have faith in God. He will give us strength," and persuading her that her husband and infant child need her to be well and happy. He offers to be her doctor who will give her an injection that will cure everything. "In the midst of tears," Angela recounts, "we laughed for the first time in months." She gets rid of all her tranquillisers and starts to think positively. Little Cesario gains strength: "Our baby was a fighter and we were determined to fight with him" [Napolitano 94-5]. So, against all expectations, this protest and testimony against the pernicious evil of asbestos mining, this confronting of trauma, turns out to be life writing of a celebratory kind, though in no self-congratulatory way.

This is true of several of the texts that have already been examined which tell tales of hardship, suffering and loss, yet show a zest for life. Many of these have been put into words by someone other than the subject of the work – we may think of Maria Triaca's *Amelia:*

A long journey, Emma Ciccotosto's *Emma: A recipe for life*, drafted by Michal Bosworth. *Nicolina's Story: A woman of the land* by La Contadina Nicolina (Nicolina the peasant woman), but penned by D. A. Davies, is another case in point, not only in the general sense of celebrating a hard-working life and a loving family, but more particularly in that, like Angela Napolitano's *Liborio*, it includes a child with a congenital and lethal defect, Nicolina's daughter, Grace, who was born with a hole in her heart but, against all expectations, lived a joyous life till the age of eighteen.

In these life stories, dual cultural identity is not an issue, as it is in some of the texts discussed elsewhere in this book, but appears to be taken for granted as no different from any other normality. Consciously or unconsciously on the part of either author or subject (and possibly both, if they are different), these life narratives approximate to the model of the "Aussie battler", a tale of survival and endurance, gilding it with the aura of a life well lived and a life worth living, implicitly claiming a dignity and an achievement, even without any social distinction or recognition beyond that of the life narrative itself: democracy in print.

Numerous Italian Australian life narratives exhibit this quality. This presentation may be influenced by Australian culture, especially where the scribe of the autobiography is an Australian, as in the stories of Emma and Nicolina, or a third-generation Italian Australian, as in the story of Amelia, but there is ample evidence that stoical perseverance and cheerful endurance are not an Australian monopoly and that many Italian immigrants, whether of peasant origin like Adele Bentley or of the urban middle class like Osvaldo Bonutto, brought these qualities with them.

In the case of Franca Arena's 2002 *Franca: My story*, it is well-nigh impossible to separate the life from the telling of it, so much is the telling a part, and a continuation, of the life, a life lived very largely in public even before its publication in print. Her book is a full-length narrative self-portrait giving in-depth coverage of the social milieux she found herself in – her native city (the international seaport of Genoa), England (where she paid a long visit during her late teens), and Sydney (where she emigrated in 1959). Uniquely, she was an unaccompanied young woman of twenty-one, emigrating on a ten-pound assisted passage, for whom the occupational category of "assistant interpreter" had to be invented [Arena 32].

Right from the start, during that outward voyage, Franca describes herself as being propelled into mediating between English-speaking Australia and immigrants from Italy. In what, to the reader, may look like an ineluctable process, on arrival in Sydney she is drawn into the Italian-language and bilingual (Italian and English) media, taking over the Mamma Lena agony aunt column and some reportage magazine services in the newspapers *La Fiamma* and *La Croce del Sud* and on radio stations. However, she is far from being a passive subject: she seizes opportunities and takes initiatives, and she recounts how her experience of teaching English to Italian and other immigrants leads her to champion their cause in combating disadvantage and discrimination, especially in so far as these affect women. She gets an intimate insight into the hostility encountered by Italians in Sydney through the Sicilian family of the man who is to be her husband, the architect Joe Arena. Racism plays a part in Anglo-Australian competition with his father's fruit shop; at school flavoursome Italian sandwiches and Italian mothers "all dressed in black and with big gold necklaces" are the object of mockery on the part of the Anglo-Australian schoolchildren [Arena 58-9]. (Such behaviour is widely reported both in the life stories studied in this book and anecdotally in the oral culture of Australia's Italians.)

An energetic participant in Australian civil society, Franca is active in promoting a great variety of initiatives: an Inner City Education Centre, the Italian Welfare Committee, ethnic radio, Workers' Educational Association courses on India and China, the Australia-China Friendship Society, and, later, Citizens for Democracy and the Australian Republican Movement. She titles her fifth chapter "Making a Contribution" and declares: "I wanted to show all those Australians who thought that we immigrants were second-class, that we were valuable citizens" [Arena 103].

By the late 1970s Franca has become a prominent public figure, quickly achieves high public honours from both the Commonwealth of Australia and the Italian Republic and is elected in 1981 to a Labor seat in the Upper House of the New South Wales Parliament. Here, though always inexplicably feeling herself to be an outsider [Arena 159-60], she continues to be an outspoken advocate of immigrants' and women's rights, constitutional reform, the fight against AIDS, child protection and other issues.

During the 1990s, however, Franca suffers two devastating blows. The first falls when she is embattled with the gay community over the allocation of resources for medically acquired AIDS (as opposed to transmission via sexual intercourse or sharing of needles), and it is discovered that both her twin sons (her only children) are gay [Arena 202-9]. Though opposed to homophobia, Franca cannot bear the shock, including the realisation that she will never have grand-children. Overwhelmed by circumstances which she describes in detail, and by her own emotions, she attempts suicide [Arena 207]. Family bonds are thus a life-and-death matter for Franca, whose mother had deserted her family when Franca was little [Arena 12, 18-20], and whose father was autocratic and repressive. The title of this chapter, "Unconditional Love", gives a meaning to this episode, reaffirming her commitment to her two sons.

The second blow may be said to provide the essential *raison d'être* for the autobiography as a whole, the overarching trauma or grievance which it sets out to redress. The ministry which the Labor Premier, Bob Carr, promises her in 1991 is denied her [Arena 215, 230-1] and she feels sidelined by her male Labor fellow-parliamen-tarians [222-3]. Things gets even worse when Franca takes up the cause of child protection and pursues evidence of paedophilia and of cover-ups in high places, and, on 17 September 1997, goes as far as naming names in a speech in the Upper House of the New South Wales Parliament. An uproar ensues, as she is accused of abusing parliamentary privilege, and Bob Carr tries to have her expelled from the parliament. She fails to be re-elected to the NSW Senate in the 1999 State elections but, though exhausted by electioneering and costly and stressful litigation, she stands by her actions and her com-mitment to combat paedophilia, and repeatedly appeals for future researchers to investigate the allegations which she has made.

Franca's story is thus a plea for historical justice and truth-finding and an attempted self-vindication by Franca in the face of her father's conviction of her worthlessness and of Anglo-Australians' low opinion of migrants. She closes her book quoting Edmund Burke: "All it takes for evil to prosper is for people of good will to do nothing."

A different case of career vindication is that of Domenico Cacciola. Domenico Cacciola, known as Mick, in his autobiographical *The Second Father: An insider's story of cops, crime and corruption* (co-written in demotic Australian English with Carmelo Cacciola and Ben Robertson), is concerned to put the record straight as regards his life's work in the Queensland police, both under cover and in uniform, fighting criminal gambling, sly-grogging and prostitution, and corruption within the police force itself. His autobiography is embattled on two fronts. One is that of some of his fellow-Italians, whose criminal practices he was instrumental in exposing: "Some Italians," he writes, "remain bitter, believing I betrayed our community through my detection and undercover work" [Cacciola 1]. Another front is that of the Queensland police and civil society, in the eyes of whom his long involvement in the fight against police corruption left him compromised. "Reliving buried memories for this book was traumatic," he continues. "My hair has fallen out and my health has suffered" [Cacciola 1]. But he feels the battle with memory has to be fought, now that the colleagues he had worked with are all dead: "I'm the only one left from the infamous Southport SP Betting Case, the one still burdened with the truth" [Cacciola 91]. The trauma of writing the autobiography echoes that of living the life: "I can't make up for the lost years or the pain and misery that my family suffered while I was blinded by the heat of battle to clear my name" [Cacciola 212].

Cacciola's, then, is a testimonial autobiography, richly circumstantial and full of narrative zest, motivated by the need to vindicate his choice of vocation and his integrity in fulfilling it. His Sicilian origins might seem incidental to this issue, but in fact intermesh with it in various ways. The "second father" of the book's title, Cacciola explains, refers to the Sicilian tradition that the eldest son in the family should act as a father towards his younger siblings and should carry on the paternal authority and way of life into the next generation. That was Domenico Cacciola's situation. Born in Sicily in 1945, he moved to Brisbane with his family in 1954 and had to surmount the linguistic, cultural and social divide, largely by dint of physical courage and prowess. Cacciola's is one of the most vivid, and most perceptive, recollections of growing up as a recently arrived Italian Australian: "It was hard to keep remembering which life you were living: the Australian one at school, with all these slang words and strange expressions, or the traditional one at home. My brain got all muddled up. Was I speaking Sicilian or English?" [Cacciola 14].

The Sicilian second father role did not fit easily in the new environment and its new horizons, and, like so many young Italian Australians, Domenico found himself at loggerheads with his father, who had destined him to succeed him in his greengrocery business and could not understand or accept his son's determination to enter the police force. Once within the police force, Domenico's Sicilian origin was used against him in an effort to draw him into the network of corruption. His "Prologue" foregrounds the memory of his first confrontation, when a fellow officer points his gun at him in the presence of other colleagues and Domenico turns the tables on him. "Go back to Italy, wog! That's what the cops loyal to the bagman Jack Herbert used to leave on a page in my typewriter" [Cacciola 3-5]. Ethnic integration and ethical integrity are held together in a life narrative in which the forceful agency of the individual is never in doubt.

Another Mick (Dominic or Domenico) is the symmetrical opposite of Mick, or Dominic, Cacciola. Mick Gatto was born in Melbourne in 1955 of Calabrian parents, his father having migrated in the 1920s [Gatto 2009: 6-7]. A ne'er-do-well from his earliest years, he comes across as a lovable villain, or perhaps not as a villain at all, but as an honourable man by his own lights, and not guilty of the charge of murder. His co-authored autobiography, *I, Mick Gatto*, must be one of the most widely read of any written by an Italian Australian, as Gatto had leapt into prominence in connection with the gangland warfare and associated killings that troubled Melbourne in the early 2000s and inspired the television dramatisation *Underbelly*. In fact, his book opens with the most explicit declaration of the compensatory function of a published autobiography, in view of the possibility of a movie of unreliable truthfulness being made out of his life story:

> This is the book I never wanted to write. But in the end, I had little choice.
>
> The underworld, by its very definition, is a hidden world. And for most of my life, that's where I've made my living: out of the spotlight, under the radar, quietly doing my own little thing. But in 2008, the *Underbelly* television series propelled me into the limelight. [Gatto 2009: ix]

Gatto makes no bones about his rough do-it-yourself justice (he had a short, and not unsuccessful, career as a youthful heavyweight boxer, being once billed as "the Italian stallion" [Gatto 2009: 41]). One typical instance, dating back to his teens, is a remarkable illustration of ethnic integration. An older and bigger Anglo-Australian teenage tough addresses Mick, and the Anglo-Australian girl he is with, with ritual ethnic abuse: "How are you going, you fucking wog? … Do you know he's a fucking wog?" [Gatto 2009: 21]. Mick wins the ensuing fight, and next time the two boys meet they are mates [Gatto 2009: 22]. The Australian "mateship" theme is consistently sounded in Gatto's account. No other Italian Australian life history that I have read deploys such a wide and strong and supportive friendship network, with loyalty and trust to the fore and uncompromising contempt for their opposites.

The Italian theme is very lightly touched on. Many of Mick's mates and contacts are of course Italian, especially Calabrians, and Calabrians from the Melbourne markets throng his boxing performances [Gatto 2009: 41]. Huge Italian weddings and family get-togethers are occasionally referred to. His mother at first objects to his wanting to marry a non-Italian wife, "But it didn't take Mum long to fall in love with Cheryle too" [Gatto 2009: 36]. All this must partly reflect the fact that ethnicity was not a problematical issue for Gatto, and especially that Italianness was not a problematical issue for Melbourne at the time of writing. Italian identity had been accommodated within a multicultural Australian identity.

What matters to Gatto is to clear his name, and this is

foregrounded by the terse first chapter which opens the book with his account of how he killed Andrew "Benji" Veniamin in self-defence in 2004, the very first sentence being: "My life changed forever the day I shot dead Australia's busiest hit man" [Gatto 2009: 1]. From then on a crisp no-nonsense linear narrative documents Gatto's life from infancy to grandfatherhood, including his lifelong compulsive gambling, his brief career as burglar and safe-breaker and his much longer career in running illegal gambling outfits, until the opening of Melbourne's Crown Casino in 1994 put an end to the illegal business, following which he was highly successful as a behind-the-scenes mediator in industrial disputes between employers and trade unions. The not-guilty verdict at Gatto's trial for Veniamin's murder is not enough for Gatto: the tribunal of public discourse must also recognise his self-vindication not only by the narrative of his life but also by his determination to have it published. Mick Cacciola and Mick Gatto, for all the differences between them, appeal to the same tribunal and make not dissimilar claims of integrity.

The classic paradigm of the migrant Italian Australian life story is most visible in Diana Ruzzene Grollo's 1997 *Growing Through the Brick Floor*, and is explicit in the title of the 1999 Italian version by Piero Genovesi, *Noi gente d'emigrazione* (We emigrants). The book's chapter headings, many of them in Italian even in the English version, articulate this paradigm still more explicitly, starting with "Geography and history of Mure" (the place of origin, a rural village near Treviso in the Veneto), and continuing with "La famiglia Ruzzene" and "La famiglia Claut" (genealogy), "Veneto Region in the First World War", and on in strict genealogical and historical sequence through the catastrophe of the Second World War.

The author is a history graduate and relates history from above to history from below, history as experienced and suffered by ordinary people, like her own family of humble peasants. Her father, Giovanni Ruzzene, sent off to fight in Russia, manages to find his way back from the rout of the Axis forces to Italy, and, "like many other men, in silent protest, he emigrated" [Ruzzene Grollo 1997: 104; 1999: 128-9], moving to Melbourne in 1951, his wife and six children following him in 1955, at which time his daughter Diana was aged seven. The newly arrived Ruzzene children find their father a stranger, not having seen him for four years [Ruzzene Grollo 1997: 146; 1999: 181]. Personal and family history as part and parcel of world history, and individual experience as part of a collective experience – these are, in varying degrees, implicit but fairly conscious assumptions in almost the entire literature of Italian Australian life writing, and they are asserted and reflected upon in *Growing Through the Brick Floor* and manifested in the very structure and terms of the narrative and in the style in which the story is told.

This is, therefore, like several other works, autobiography both in the singular and in the plural, family autobiography. The book opens with a bleak overview: "In those early years in Australia we suffered humiliation, racism, and far greater deprivation than we had in Italy. This experience has left me scarred for ever" [Ruzzene Grollo 1997: 2; 1999: 4]. Small incidents weigh heavily. As the immigrants from Italy land in Melbourne, an immigration official snatches an orange out of the hands of a small boy; the official is applying Australia's (or Victoria's) strict quarantine regulations, but the rough gesture leaves an indelible mark [Ruzzene Grollo 1997: 146; 1999: 181].

The rudimentary living conditions experienced in an outer Melbourne suburb during the first several years after arrival are described in detail, and so is the hostility and discrimination shown by some of the previously settled residents and authorities. These negative experiences of the host country are usually glossed over or passed over completely in the life narratives written by or about Italian Australians, with few exceptions. Apart from *Growing Through the Brick Floor*, the texts that do express the immigrant's grievance (those by Baggio, Bonutto and Lucchesi) do so in close proximity, as we have seen, to the issue of wartime internment. Marie Alafaci's *Savage Cows and Cabbage Leaves*, discussed above, is another exception.

A theme which almost invariably, but often rather fleetingly, surfaces in Italian Australian life writing texts, is the problem of facing a new language, English, especially for immigrants who have at best limited literacy or even oral proficiency in standard Italian, being speakers of one of Italy's regional languages, commonly referred to as dialects. This becomes a major theme in *Growing Through the Brick*

Floor, within the broader theme of the overlapping culture differences that include education and Catholicism. Diana Ruzzene Grollo dwells on the deep cleavage between home life, where only Veneto is spoken [Ruzzene Grollo 1997: 169; 1999: 206-7], and school, where only English is spoken, and no provision is made for children from other language backgrounds [Ruzzene Grollo 1997: 172-3; 1999: 211]. The language barrier is a painful problem even when Diana's mother is in hospital dying of cancer [Ruzzene Grollo 1997: 220-1: 1999: 275-6]. One of Diana's most bitter memories is that of being publicly accused by the Mother Superior of her school of cheating in an English examination for which she had prepared long and hard and thus obtained a good result [Ruzzene Grollo 1997: 179; 1999: 220].

Diana is writing of the period before multiculturalism became official Australian policy in the 1970s, when Anglicisation and assimilation were the norm [Ruzzene Grollo 1997: 217-18; 1999: 272]. Even Catholicism was practised differently from Italy in Australia's Irish-dominated church [Ruzzene Grollo 1997: 183-4; 1999: 226]. The result was that she, like others in her condition, found herself condemned to a life of manual labour as factory fodder, in the words of one of her chapter titles.

She recounts the revelation experienced in revisiting Italy long after as an adult and her feeling of belonging in Venice and its surrounding region [Ruzzene Grollo 1997: 228; 1999: 286]. This belonging manifests itself in the book in ways which include the use of Venetian proverbs as epigraphs to each chapter, as well as the details of the narrative. Diana becomes increasingly aware of the glass ceiling above which certain immigrants, and women, cannot hope to rise [Ruzzene Grollo 1997: 229-300; 1999: 288], and the book's concluding chapters turn into the story of her struggle to rise out of the underclass, to which she feels condemned, by dint of following evening classes [Ruzzene Grollo 1997: 216; 1999: 271] and eventually undertaking a first and then a second university degree. This equips her to write her life story and that of her family and people with its own inbuilt sociohistorical commentary and analysis, marrying the experiential with the dissertational.

Migration as a traumatic process in itself therefore finds manifold expression in Ruzzene Grollo's account. There is first of all the double trauma of an entire peasant class in Italy being faced first with economic deprivation and then with the calamity of war, its menfolk being conscripted in military service in theatres as distant and inhospitable as Russia. There is the separation from the father of the family, who moves out to a distant continent years ahead of the rest of his family. There is the shock of having to settle into a socially and economically isolated and materially deprived habitation in an area speaking a different language and practising a markedly different material culture. And there is the children's struggle with a foreign educational system.

These traumatic factors are endured to a greater or lesser degree and in varying combinations by all the less privileged Italian immigrants to Australia, constituting the overwhelming majority. In this and in previous chapters, we have also encountered other traumatic factors: more or less delinquent fathers, ethnic hostility, exploitation by employers and exposure to life-threatening health hazards, tragic illness and death in the family. Except in Cristina's *Secrets of a Broken Heart*, these traumas have not usually been of the kind (typically, experiences of war and genocide) that result in post-traumatic stress disorder, and that have baffled and blurred boundaries between various therapeutic and knowledge disciplines [Caruth 1995: 3-12, 151-7]. Rather, they are less catastrophic but long-drawn-out experiences of suffering and grievance that have found release and some redress through expression and public recognition.

There is one autobiography, however, that does not fit comfortably within this general picture: this is *An Italian Down Under: A migrant woman's tale*, by Cloris De Matteis, self-published in 2008. It is one of the longest and most comprehensive Italian Australian autobiographies, running to 472 large format pages, without any illustrative material. Cloris is literate and comes to Australia as a married woman and a mother, endures an increasingly negative relationship first with her husband and then with other male partners, including a second husband, and suffers neglect or worse from her own family of origin, but is resourceful in sustaining herself and her sons, eventually asserting her autonomy as a person and as a woman by writing her life experience.

Cloris comes from an entrepreneurial middle-class family from the affluent North-West of Italy – specifically from Stresa, on Lago Maggiore – while her husband is a successful architect (which does not prevent the couple from availing themselves of an assisted passage to Sydney). They migrate in 1969, at the end of the great wave of migration from Italy to Australia which lasted through the 1950s and 1960s, and the narrative begins with the move to Australia, the preceding period of Cloris' life being the subject of only a few brief flashbacks.

Cloris writes her autobiography in fluent English, yet ends by shaking the dust of Australia off her feet and heading back, when nearing sixty, "to [her] new life in [her] native country" [De Matteis 2008: 472], even though her experiences of Italians, both in Italy and in Australia, have been as appalling as her experiences of Australians of many generations' standing or of various ethnic origin. The back cover blurb in her book reveals that "after spending six years in Italy in self-imposed exile to write her book" she has returned to Australia as to her home. A prefatory note explains that "All the names of people in this book have been altered to protect their true identities, including myself." She assures the reader, in a quaintly archaic Italian expression, "However, it is all the sacrosanct truth."

This "sacrosanct truth" is the longitudinal account of her life starting from the sea-voyage out to Australia and the encounter with an as yet unrefined Australian material and social culture, followed by life in Sydney and the Blue Mountains in New South Wales with first one and then another Italian husband both of whom, in very different ways, did all the taking and no giving (as did also several non-Italian partners), accompanied by various employment experiences, mostly fulfilling, and then the running of a very successful restaurant. Pet cats also figure in the narrative.

Things deteriorate catastrophically when Cloris, virtually the single parent of two adolescent sons, moves to Noosa, on Queensland's Sunshine Coast, to find herself repeatedly short-changed and finally entangled in an inextricable living and business relationship at Noosa with an Australian builder, who is here called Jeremy. All along, various visits back to her family of origin in Italy reiterate the persecution she suffers especially at the hands of her father and her sister, and subsequently also of her brother.

Cloris' narrative verve and moral indignation carry the reader along on a wave of existential suspense with an inexorable focus and a remarkable power of recall or reconstruction, scene by scene, of an unfolding nightmarish drama that trumps soap opera. Concrete minutiae of milieu and repartee are brought onto the page, and financial details of sums owed or misspent or misappropriated are consistently recorded. The final disastrous episode of the relationship with Jeremy, the builder at Noosa, extends for two hundred pages. A hundred pages describe in agonising detail – including lengthy verbatim courtroom exchanges [De Matteis 2008: 371-405] – the legal saga of action and counter-action between Cloris and Jeremy and the American couple who have invested in their development project, ending in Cloris' giving up the Australian (or Queensland) legal system and its magistrates as worthless, and returning to Italy.

An Italian Down Under therefore reads in large part as the protagonist's bid to vindicate her righteousness and get her own back at Jeremy and others. "I wondered what fatal attraction I had for people who came into my life and made things more difficult for me," she remarks, a little before Jeremy comes on the scene [De Matteis 2008: 238]. She recurrently attributes her misfortunes with male partners to the contempt with which she had always been treated by her father. She records, a little after her meeting with Jeremy, a repressed memory of attempted sexual abuse by her father when she was aged seventeen [De Matteis 2008: 322-4] (though she has mentioned that she had suffered from her father's attitude towards her before that). Her father emerges from this book as a compulsive womaniser and predator on young girls, increasingly from poverty-stricken strata of developing countries. She thus also vindicates her righteousness against her father, her sister, her brother and at least the second of her two Italian husbands. As noted, the story continues after the end of the book, with the blurb announcing her return to Australia, having realised that "there were too many Italians in Italy for my liking".

The ethical perspective which presents Cloris as a woman of goodwill giving of her best but being systematically exploited financially and otherwise by two husbands and several sexual partners, as well as by her own family members, is unprovable, but on the whole persuasive. There is some equivocation between the blurb, which claims that her first husband, Pierantonio, "convinced her to migrate to Australia", and the main text, which avers "Australia seemed a better place to us and to me especially, being far away from my family" [De Matteis 2008: 68]. And Cloris' ethical perspective appears high-handed on one occasion, when she throws in a job which she has hitherto enjoyed on the grounds that her new boss is a "slime ball", for which she offers no evidence other than a generic accusation of incompetence.

The migrant experience as such, with the interplay between two ethnic identities, and with Cloris' shuttling between Italy and Australia, plays a significant part in her autobiography, but not a dominant part. The interplay between gender issues and financial interests – including work roles, domestic responsibilities and property rights – looms larger in this life story, which is one of the rare instances which delves into the existential experiences of middle-class Italian migrants to Australia. Here, the family is still the central institution, yet appears to play a largely negative role. In this sense, De Matteis' book also has considerable ethnographic interest for both Italian and Australian society, appearing to belong transnationally to both and to neither.

Chapter 4

Celebrating Italian Australian Lives

1. Piero Genovesi's *Sebastiano Pitruzzello: l'uomo – la famiglia – l'industria* (Sebastiano Pitruzzello: the man – his family – his company)[24]

On one evening in 2005 I had what was for me a novel experience, though I daresay it was an experience which would not have been unfamiliar to some readers of this piece. It was a book launch, but of a rather unusual kind. It was held at the Sortino Social Club which is to be found in a nondescript part of North Fitzroy, an inner Melbourne suburb, and whose neon sign stood out brightly in the rather dimly lit street. As I went through the doorway, I was struck by such a spacious interior for a community originating from such a small place. Sortino's population has been reduced by emigration to just 7,000. Many of those who had emigrated were present in the club that evening. One hundred and eighty guests were accommodated around dining tables in front of the podium from which the speakers were to address them. Very few of the guests appeared to be under thirty years of age.

Amid that company I was probably the most complete outsider, though my birthplace, the island of Malta, lies only about 150 kilometres to the south of the small inland township of Sortino in the

---

24 Piero Genovesi, *Sebastiano Pitruzzello: l'uomo – la famiglia – l'industria*, Thomastown (Victoria): Pantalica Pty Ltd, 2003; 2nd ed. 2004. English translation by Walter Musolino, *Sebastiano Pitruzzello: the man – his family – his company*, Thomastown (Victoria): Pantalica Pty Ltd, 2003. The Italian and English versions are otherwise identical in cover design, pagination and illustrations. Page references shown here within the text therefore refer to both versions.

province of Siracusa, within the southern corner of Sicily. I was there at the Sortino Social Club in my capacity as a university professor of Italian and an associate of the Italian Australian Institute to lend an academic aura to the occasion. The aura was enhanced by the presence of others from outside Sortino and outside Sicily – the Italian Consul-General, a Neapolitan, and the Director of the Italian Institute of Culture, from the North of Italy, as was also the author of the book to be launched, my colleague Piero Genovesi.

Every guest was presented with a copy of Piero Genovesi's biography of Sebastiano Pitruzzello, either in the original Italian or in Walter Musolino's exactly matching English translation, its glossy cover illustrated with colour photographs; and then came the speeches – an introduction by the master of ceremonies, an unaffectedly warm and modest welcome and thank-you by Sebastiano Pitruzzello, then the characteristically witty and entertaining presentation by the author Piero Genovesi himself. This was interrupted by what was for me the most novel part of the evening: a telephone call direct from Sortino, from the town's mayor, in fact, which was relayed to the assembled audience over the loudspeaker system. The Sortino diaspora – *i sortinesi nel mondo* – were wedding the global and the local, thanks to today's technology, and giving official sanction to the civic celebration of their collective identity, as well as of an individual's success, through instant communication.

The specifics of the celebratory mode as they are encoded in Genovesi's biography of Pitruzzello and his family are the subject of this section. The semiosis, or generation of meanings, of the life – *bios* – is translated into the semiosis of the text – *graphia* – and it is only the meanings transmitted by the latter that I can deal with, while bearing in mind that the meanings of the life itself are subject to a myriad possible alternative or complementary or supplementary writings.

The biographer in question, Piero Genovesi, shows a sophisticated awareness of this in his opening metabiographical reflections and disclaimers:

> Recounting all this in story form meant going constantly
> from what seemed easy to the impossible, pushing

language to its limits. This is another reason why I felt obliged to choose the type of narrative I did, looking for the most direct method based on the interview as opposed to the more anonymous form of narration by a third person. In this way I left it up to the reader to make connections and judgements, which otherwise, as I see it, would have limited the natural flow of the narrative if they had been made by the editor, according to his or her personal taste. [8-9][25]

I quote here from Walter Musolino's resourceful translation which mediates the interviews and surrounding narrative for a primarily Australian readership more at home in English than in standard Italian. This English version is part of the complex inter-lingual presentation of the experience of a Sicilian-speaking family which has already been transmitted or translated via Italian. I'll give just one example of how different the resulting perspectives may be: Genovesi, implicitly quoting the Sicilian Pitruzzello, describes the latter's wife as "la donna 'veramente donna'"– "a real woman". This comes out in the English version as "a woman who is 'like women used to be'" [195], converting a cultural distance into a historical distance. (My next section contains a study of Musolino's translation and the issues it raises.) This is clearly a matter of interpretation, and in the passage I have quoted it was interpretation that Genovesi was explicitly concerned with, not "taste": by basing his account mainly on interviews, he is bringing his reader into as direct a relationship as possible with his subjects – Pitruzzello and his family –, relaying what they (and others) say as a collective, and moderately multi-voiced, quasi-autobiography and thus shifting the responsibility for

---

25 In the original Italian: "Mettere tutto questo su pagine significa passare costantemente dal facile all'impossibile, vivere i limiti della parola. Anche per questo motivo le scelte relative allo stile della narrazione mi sono apparse quasi obbligate facendomi privilegiare la forma più diretta, quella dell'intervista, al più anonimo narrato in terza persona lasciando in tal modo a chi legge il compito di realizzare quelle connessioni e quei parametri critici che altrimenti, a mio avviso, avrebbero in un certo modo limitato le naturali espansioni del narrato circoscrivendole alle interpretazioni personali del redattore."

interpretation as much as possible away from himself as biographer and on to the reader.

In particular, Genovesi is at pains to avoid discussing Pitruzzello's life in terms of social class [8]. This is of course one of its most striking aspects, since the book is the frank celebration of a success story, a story of social promotion from industrial shop-floor worker to industrial entrepreneur and head of a flourishing family business. Genovesi prefers to insert this individual story within the community paradigm of the migrant's story, of which it is at once characteristic and yet distinctive [8], and the rhetorical strategy of the whole book and of its component voices, Genovesi's and those of Pitruzzello and his family and supporters, is to subsume Pitruzzello's success story as the success story of Sortino's diaspora – *i sortinesi nel mondo*. As such, it prompts analysis, and rewards us with some surprises.

The main outline fits the expected paradigm well enough: migration from rural Sicily to Melbourne in the early 1960s; the long sea journey; nine years of long hours of wage labour and careful saving accompanied by the stubborn pursuit of a dream; the difficulties of getting past Victoria's industrial gate-keepers until a lucky break brings the support of an influential insider; the tough beginnings in producing for a niche market overcome by dogged persistence and the patient pursuit of quality; then take-off and the rapid rise to dominance of that niche market in Italian cheeses and *ricotta* both within Australia and in expanding exports.

In this whole endeavour the supportive socioeconomic network of the migrant group is paramount. I shrink from calling this the "ethnic" network, as we are all ethnic, whether we belong to a minority or to a majority group, and an "Anglo-Celtic" Australian is as ethnic as anyone anywhere. But certainly, a whole system of networks is shown as being crucial to Pitruzzello's success: family and relatives; the *sortinesi* at large; wider Sicilian and Italian networks; kindred migrant groups, especially those from the Mediterranean area – my own Maltese, Greeks, Lebanese, Southern Slavs; and migrant groups from further afield. The text invokes all these connections. In particular, Sebastiano Pitruzzello played a key role in setting up and sustaining the Sortino Social Club, and we could invoke the Italian term *campanilismo* – attachment to the local village belfry as the symbol of group belonging – to denote this powerful category of Italian social bonding. Baldassar's adoption of this term in the context of migration studies has an interesting bearing on Pitruzzello's case, in which the transnational interaction between Sortino and its diaspora is constantly in evidence, both in the semiosis of the man's life and in that of the writing of his life [Baldassar 1994: 44-5; and 2001: 110-17].

But contacts within the homegrown Australian society also play a part and are invoked – the Catholic priest [93-8], the Victorian State Parliament independent MP [106-7] and the Speaker of the same Parliament [107-12]. The successful migrant's stronghold is his community niche, both narrowly and broadly defined, but he is not confined to that niche, and his success depends in large part, and very crucially, on links established with the host society. And, after all, the niche market for ricotta and mozzarella and pecorino does not only comprise the Italians and other Mediterraneans, but includes all those within the broader Australian community who have developed a taste for pizza and tortellini and other cheesy Italian dishes. So we see mainstream Australian society and culture evolving under the influence of other cultures which subsist in relative independence. Culinary and gastronomical interaction between groups is also sociocultural and socioeconomic interaction between those same groups. The Sortino contribution is integrated into the broader Australia, but not assimilated into it; it is the next generation of Pitruzzellos that moves closer to assimilation, as they achieve asymmetrical bilingualism in Sicilian and English rather than Italian and feel more at home in Australia than in Italy [154-5].

All this, I have suggested, fits within an expected paradigm, and does not differ fundamentally, but only in degree, from more familiar, and mostly unwritten, success stories and stories of acculturation and social integration among ethnic minority groups involving relatively small businesses in the food and catering sector, such as pizzerias and restaurants. Where, then, are the surprises?

The surprises are there at the very start, and show that a paradigm is not the same thing as a stereotype. If our stereotype of mass immigration to Australia from southern Italy and Sicily during the 1950s and 1960s is one of illiterate, poverty-stricken and backward-looking or tradition-bound peasants, then the story of the Pitruzzellos, as told in this biography, presents a subtle and creative dialectic.

Neither Sebastiano Pitruzzello nor his future wife Lucia came from a low socio-economic group. Lucia had a secondary education in a boarding school away from her native Sortino and had then trained as a seamstress and dressmaker [60-2], while Sebastiano's family were small landowners and lease-holders who practised traditional mixed farming [27]. The extension of free market economics to Italy in the early 1960s spelled the rapid decline of the mixed farmers, but that in itself did not determine Sebastiano's migration. In fact, he had completed the full five years of primary school, had served an apprenticeship as a welder and fitter and was in a relatively well-paid job as a metal-worker in a local factory [34-7]. Going to Australia was not Sebastiano's idea or initiative at all, but Lucia's [56-7].

We are used to the sociological norm for south Italian emigration of the male going out first and then sending for his bride (sometimes not personally known to him but introduced by mail and photo). Lucia Mandragona, however, decided on her own to take the opportunity to migrate (temporarily, as she thought) to Australia with some relatives. That her parents agreed to this suggests a freedom of movement not usually associated with unmarried young south-Italian women at the time. The reasons Lucia gives for her desire to go so far from home are vague – the appeal of that distant land as reported by her relatives there, the chance to save up some money, to build a future [63]. Adventure and escape seem to be part of it, and Lucia mentions her distress at returning home from boarding school at the age of fifteen [62], but the book does not venture deep into the private sphere. The text speaks clearly enough, however, on the facts, though without drawing attention to how we might interpret them: Lucia took the initiative of going to Australia, persuading her suitor to follow her, which he was able to do some eighteen months later. During that time she worked in Melbourne to save up money for their wedding and to set up home, while living with her relatives

[70-4]. For the early 1960s that represents quite an interesting degree of female autonomy and innovation within the traditional familial and matrimonial dispensation. This is certainly not straightforward patriarchal control, but a creative dialectic negotiating between tradition and modernity, between security and opportunity. The interaction between Sicily and Australia produces a new reality.

Something analogous applies to Sebastiano himself. As the fourth brother in the family, Sicilian custom ordained that he could not marry until all his elder brothers had married. Australia offered a pragmatic way out of his impasse, enabling him to sidestep Sicily's social norms with his family's approval, marrying ahead of his elder brothers well out of the way in Australia, while remaining within the familial and matrimonial dispensation [81-2]. The interaction between the local and the global again allows the negotiation of societal norms, adapting them, bending them, but not breaking them.

The Pitruzzellos' entry into Australia is thus not a simple encounter between tradition on one side (Sicily) and modernity on the other (Australia). The Sicilian social culture harbours tendencies towards change within which Australia acts as catalyst. But the presence of the Pitruzzellos in Australia itself acts as a catalyst to precipitate change in Australia, change which also points in the direction of modernity.

One minor but intriguing instance of this regards the arrangements for their church wedding, which in itself represents a reaffirmation of tradition. It is precisely out of respect for tradition that the Pitruzzellos insist on a modernistic invasion of the Catholic Church. In order to reassure the folks back home in Sortino that they are actually getting respectably married, they insisted on having the marriage ceremony filmed, and consequently had some difficulty in finding a parish priest willing to agree to this [93-5]. This was something of a novelty for the year 1963, uncannily in step with the innovations brought about in the Catholic Church by the Second Vatican Council under the leadership of Pope John XXIII, who died in that same year.

The major instance of the interaction between tradition and modernity in the story of Sebastiano Pitruzzello is of course his production on an industrial scale of traditional cheeses (and subsequently the development of new ones) [117-23]. This is the success story which has made the fortune of the Pitruzzello family and of which the biography is a celebration. This is the dream that Pitruzzello brings with him to Australia, that he pursues for nine years in his shed every evening after he comes home from working overtime as a fitter at General Motors [101]. This is what provides the heroic epic of individual endeavour that sustains every success story, and which is inlaid within the collective epic of transoceanic migration. This epic resonance is consistently amplified by the narrative voice-over of the biography, its style and rhythms throwing into relief the unassuming *pietas*, the stubborn sense of purpose, the devotion to inherited values of Sebastiano Pitruzzello himself, and the equally unassuming matter-of-factness of the members of his family, who have all contributed massively to the success of the family enterprise, again combining traditional familism with up-to-the-minute skills in electronics, information technology, financial planning and marketing.

The modernity of mass production of cheese, however, is not an Australian prerogative, but part of a world-wide industrialisation. Australia provides the opportunity, and not a very obvious opportunity, since the cheeses that in Sicily or Italy would be staple items would in Melbourne represent a niche market, though an increasingly substantial one. Pitruzzello more than once talks of his life in terms of destiny.[26] This is perhaps a self-deprecatory trope, a secular version of Providence, a protestation that circumstances, a higher power, has determined the individual achievement, and yet at the same time

---

26 See pp. 9 and 82; while on the other hand, we hear Sebastiano saying "I knew what I wanted" [37], and he refers to his "dream" [40] and his "certainty" [75] (which of course does not contradict the notion of destiny). The determinations of the will and the part they play in life writing are discussed in Richard Freadman's *Threads of Life: Autobiography and the will*, Chicago and London: University of Chicago Press, 2001. See esp., for general considerations, pp. 11-83. In Pitruzzello's account as relayed by Genovesi, the amount of detail and the depth of introspection are too slight to be productively discussed, but it is nevertheless interesting that an achievement as single-mindedly willed as Pitruzzello's is felt by him to have been wrought by destiny.

it paradoxically serves to heighten the epic overtones. A rhetoric of understatement plays counterpoint to the celebratory mode. That protestation cannot cancel the account of persistent and tenacious effort, in which even the decisive stroke of luck, in the shape of the support of the then Speaker of the Victorian Parliament, had been earned by Pitruzzello's intervention to prevent an attempted act of industrial sabotage at General Motors [108-9]. It acknowledges, however, both the importance of fortuitous coincidence and its virtual inevitability, for which Gyorgy Lukács argued in a not unrelated context.[27]

These coincidences which are not really coincidences but are over-determined by a complex of factors of social history include, at the personal level, Lucia Mandragona's initiative in bringing Sebastiano to Australia and, at the historical level, mass migration from Sicily and southern Italy to Australia, making it inevitable that sooner or later someone or other would be mass-producing *ricotta* and other Italian cheeses in Australia. Sebastiano Pitruzzello's "destiny" is history itself, which made him as he helped to make it. And there is a suggestion also that "destiny" is a personal compulsion, an irresistible drive, a drive which is, in a sense, beyond the individual's own choice. This is the area of personal psychology into which this biography, or quasi-autobiography, does not delve too deeply. We might be tempted to surmise that the young Pitruzzello was driven to overcome or, better, to get astride, the historical determinism that had made his father's mixed farming business obsolete, and with it much of the small-scale agriculture typical of Sortino and similar areas. This is what is commonly called moving with the times, but in Pitruzzello's case, and no doubt in most cases, it involves something more besides. The young man may have seen personal success from the first in terms of a come-back, of the economic revival of his family and community; he may have dreamt of the transition from mixed farming to agribusiness as an endeavour of historical *pietas*. Personal destiny is conceived as part of a larger group destiny. This is not

---

27 Lukács argues that historical inevitability and novelistic coincidence are one and the same with regard to Tolstoy's novel *Resurrection* [Lukács 1980: 58-9].

explicitly stated in the biography, but appears to be its inherent logic, the consciousness on the part of individuals that they are players in a world history.

This historically rooted *pietas*, with its sense of destiny, is certainly the dominant semiosis of the book, its central system of signification. The colour photograph which forms the book's front cover shows a portrait of Sebastiano Pitruzzello in close conjunction with the white statue of the emigrant from Sortino which he had recently financed for a new *piazza* in his native town [172-81]. The back cover has two colour photographs, the lower one showing Sebastiano and Lucia with their children, daughters-in-law, son-in-law and grandchildren, celebrating the familial *pietas*, while the upper picture shows the firm's new factory building, sporting the Italian and Australian flags on either side of the firm's logo. This latter has the words *Pantalica Cheese Co.* circling a medallion which bears the heraldic emblem of the town of Sortino, with the Latin motto *universitas obedientissima Sortini*, "the most obedient community of Sortino".

The affective link with the place of origin is reiterated throughout the text, whose first four chapters are wholly devoted to it. The first indeed traces Sortino's origins to a period preceding the ancient Greeks and Romans, when Sicily was inhabited by peoples we know as Sicans and Sikels, and the second chapter dwells on the haunting ruins of the ancient Greek settlement of Pantalica, now overgrown by a pastoral wilderness, where the boy Sebastiano found his still-remembered freedom and whose name he has given to his company.

Like so many successful colonists, Sebastiano Pitruzzello thus brings a mythic dimension to recreating his place of origin in his new homeland, but the recreation cannot be a restoration. His rural estate and olive plantation adjacent to the newly built sumptuous and ultra-modern Villa Lucia in rural Victoria may be something that takes him back to his boyhood, it reinstates the traditional technology of the olive press, but is a new creation, a blend of Sicily and Australia [193-201]. It is commemoration and celebration, as is also Pitruzzello's decoration with one of the highest honours of the Italian Republic, the title of *Commendatore*, or Knight Commander [182-9]. This officially sanctions Pitruzzello's individual and family achievement as an achievement of a group wider than that of the people of Sortino, entrepreneurialism as a national virtue. The celebration in print in the shape of this book published in two languages enshrines it within a transnational epic, the epic of the bourgeoisie, with a global piquancy that links the classical memories of the Sicilian countryside with the relatively recent European settlement of Victoria's rural Gippsland and metropolitan Melbourne.

2. Translating an Italian Australian life

Voices

Piero Genovesi's biography of Sebastiano Pitruzzello and his family, immigrants from Sicily into Australia, and Walter Musolino's translation of the work into English present an opportunity to study cultural translation and the effects of different languages on the presentation of a life story. The linguistic and discursive transactions of the texts are here examined as part of an enquiry into the writing of life histories of a linguistic and cultural (or "ethnic") minority. Who is being addressed? What strategy of identity construction is being sought – assimilation? integration? dissociation? Most cultures are themselves heterogeneous, so that translation may operate between different sectors of what is commonly supposed to be a single culture. Using the concepts of translation norms and of a cultural filter in translation, this enquiry suggests that even a translator who is bicultural and an insider to both the source and the target cultures and languages (respectively, Italian and Anglo-Australian) subtly but quite pervasively subordinates the former to the latter by eliding some of the experiential and discursive values of the source text at all levels of language. The comparison between the two versions of the life history of the Pitruzzello family shows the specific differences between the two dominant cultures perhaps all the more precisely thanks to the close literal correspondence between those versions.

Genovesi's *Sebastiano Pitruzzello: l'uomo – la famiglia – l'industria* and its English translation by Musolino, *Sebastiano Pitruzzello: The man – his family – his company*,[28] from the outset present themselves

---

28 The Italian and English versions are identical in cover design and illustrations,

as a medley of voices. The opening "Nota" [7-9] by the author, Genovesi, an Italian literary academic trained in Milan who has been working for over thirty years at universities in Melbourne, immediately establishes the biographer's voice in a way which cannot comfortably be replicated in English. The biographer as person and textual author is first grammatically deleted by the consistent use of the Italian impersonal *si* (or *si passivante*), which can roughly be compared to the English passive as used, for instance, in reporting scientific procedures or experiments. [29] This self-effacement is then prolonged by referring to the writer generically (*chi scrive*) [7].

The second page introduces a testimonial first-person plural ("quella che per noi è eccezione" / "what we might think is exceptional"; "nel nostro viaggio alla ricerca del 'vero' volto di questa nostra gente" [in our quest for the "real" countenance of these people of ours] "as we pursue the truth about these migrant people of ours" [8]) which associates the writer with his unspecified readership, presumably a generic Italian readership distinct from the people he is writing about.

From the third paragraph, the remaining two pages of the author's "Nota" descend to the engagingly familiar first person, appropriately to recall his relationship with his main subject, Sebastiano Pitruzzello himself, and his family and friends. Throughout the body of the book, however, Genovesi the biographer, on the relatively rare

---

and virtually identical in pagination. Page references shown within the text of this section therefore refer to both versions but, where they differ, reference to the original Italian appears first. Musolino's renderings are shown in quotation marks alongside Genovesi's text. On Genovesi's biography of Pitruzzello, see the preceding section of this chapter.

29 The text opens thus: "Scrivere la biografia di una persona può sembrare, all'apparenza, cosa abbastanza facile: incontri, interviste, altri incontri. Si studia l'ambiente, si studiano i tanti e vari personaggi ..." (Writing a person's biography might seem, apparently, quite an easy matter: meetings, interviews, more meetings. The ambience is to be studied, the many and varied personalities are to be studied ...) Here, and generally in this section, the English version shown without quotation marks is my own relatively literal approximation to the Italian.

occasions when he has to refer to himself, does so self-effacingly in the first-person plural, grammatically equivalent to the English *we*. This would sound pompous or odd in English, but in Italian is a modest rather than a majestic plural, again, testimonial in import. Pronouns apart, the biographer's presence in the biography remains, of course, perceptible as manager of the narrative and as a voice, or rather, as a variety of "voices".

The translator, Musolino, is also perceptible as a voice, or set of voices, but less obviously, or more, to use Venuti's term, "invisibly" [Venuti: 1995]. It is this invisibility that is the object of my enquiry, and it is marked, or unmarked, by the fact that the "Author's Note" is not accompanied by a "Translator's Note". In that "Author's Note", Musolino more than competently renders Genovesi's impersonals with approximately equivalent English devices ("There is a whole world to become familiar with, there are so many different and varied people to get to know" [7]),[30] in preference to a possible alternative: "You make yourself familiar …"), and in the biography proper uses *I* when the biographer is referring to himself. This already reduces the psychological distance between narrator and reader in English compared to the Italian, making for a slightly greater degree of intimacy which, as I hope to show, is also in some other respects a fairly consistent difference between the English version and the Italian original. Since Sebastiano Pitruzzello's success story is consist-ently presented as a successful case of integration of a Sicilian Italian immigrant family into Australian society,[31] its English translation by a highly cultured, Australian-educated, fully bilingual Italian Australian like Musolino presents an illustration of the terms and degree of transethnic integration in this particular case.

The delicacy of the translator's role is evident in that unresolved first person plural: "as we pursue the truth about these migrant people

---

30 For the original Italian text, see footnote 29 above.

31 Sebastiano Pitruzzello followed his future wife to Melbourne from Sortino in Sicily in 1963, when he was aged 23. After nine years as a metalworker in a factory, he started mass-producing Italian-type cheeses and proved very successful.

of ours". Whereas for Genovesi and his readership *we* (and *ours*) in Italian unequivocally includes Italians as a national and ethnic group, in the English version it might mean "we English-speaking Australians of Italian origin or descent" or, less clearly, it might mean "we Australians" in general or simply the *we* constituted in the compact between writer and reader in the act of reading. The phrase "these migrant people of ours" becomes particularly challenging. What readership, what social or ethnic constituency, what "imagined community" in the making confronts us here? [Anderson 1983] The in-between or transethnic subject position could not be more self-evidently unlocatable. This key phrase signals the welcoming absorption of Italian origins into an Australian dispensation that to some extent discounts those origins. What is at stake is the inclusiveness of the "mainstream" which absorbs those foreign origins and the extent to which it allows itself to be modified by them. How much "Italianness" is admitted into "Australianness"?

In his "Nota", Genovesi talks of his difficulty in tackling his biographical task: "Mettere tutto questo su pagine significa passare costantemente dal facile all'impossibile, vivere i limiti della parola" [7]. (Putting all this down on paper means going constantly from the easy to the impossible, living the limits of the word.) Or, in Musolino's English: "Recounting all this in story form meant going constantly from what seemed easy to the impossible, pushing language to its limits" [7-8]. This "limit" of linguistic representation is explained by Genovesi precisely in terms of balancing the voices concerned – the biographer's, on the one hand, and those of his subjects and informants on the other hand:

> … le scelte relative allo stile della narrazione mi sono apparse quasi obbligate facendomi privilegiare la forma più diretta, quella dell'intervista, al più anonimo narrato in terza persona lasciando in tal modo a chi legge il compito di realizzare quelle connessioni e quei parametri critici che altrimenti, a mio avviso, avrebbero in un certo qual modo limitato le naturali espansioni del narrato circoscrivendole alle interpretazioni personali del redattore.

> ... I felt obliged to choose the type of narrative ... based
> around the interview as opposed to the more anonymous
> form of narration by a third person. In this way I left it up
> to the reader to make connections and judgements, which
> otherwise, as I see it, would have limited the natural flow
> of the narrative if they had been made by an editor [*i.e.,*
> *biographer*], according to his or her personal taste. [9]

The biographer here announces his self-denying ordinance, his
intention of restraining himself from imposing his own voice on
those of his subjects, from imposing his own interpretations on their
story. Genovesi uses the word *interpretazioni*, which the translator
has here rendered as *taste*.[32] Thus the translator himself at this point
and at some other points in the text, invisibly (except to someone
comparing both versions) substitutes his own voice, his own interpretation, his own taste for those of the biographer or of one or other
of his subjects [Hermans 2002].

We have, then, a transmission of voices, inevitably configured in
a discursive hierarchy determined by the homogenising tendency of
the print medium. The Pitruzzello family's first language is Sicilian.
Sebastiano and his wife have learned Italian at school in Italy, but
their three children have grown up with English. Some other informants are Sicilians with a highly educated command of Italian. The
discourse of all these informants is relayed in Sicilian-inflected Italian
or (in the case of the young Pitruzzellos) in Australian English, to the
biographer, who converts it into fluent standard Italian. Quite a lot of
translation has therefore already taken place before the English translator mediates between Genovesi's standard Italian and a primarily
Australian English-language readership.[33] The interviews with the

---

32 Perhaps in order to avoid repetition, as he has used the word *interpretation*
    to render the Italian *aspetto*: but this highlights a weakness of lexico-semantic
    coherence in this area of the translation.

33 This complex of mediations is not usually emphasised but implied by Genovesi,
    who shows quotation marks without indicating what language is being used:
    "Ascoltando le sue parole." / "As I listen ..." [31]; "come traducendo dal suo
    dialetto, lingua famigliare" / "as though he is translating from his dialect, the
    language he is most comfortable with" [179]. The younger Pitruzzellos refer

younger Pitruzzellos were rendered from English (intermingled with some Italian and Sicilian) into Italian by Genovesi and retranslated back into English by Musolino.[34] The voices of Pitruzzello and the other informants are therefore primary as the source of the story (*histoire*), but the discursive hierarchy of the text (*récit*) is ultimately controlled by its final redactor – Genovesi in the case of the Italian, Musolino for the English.

Interpretation

The translator's intervention is most marked, yet invisible, in the blurb, on the book's back cover, where "la fedeltà alla cultura d'origine ed a quella della patria d'adozione" (loyalty to one's origins and to one's adopted country) elusively becomes "belief in a certain past, belief in the present". Similarly elusive, in the body of the text, is the English version of a remark by Sebastiano's son Silvio, referring to his own generation of Italian Australians: "There are times when even we use some Italian but it's more an expression of our heritage than anything else." *Heritage*, in Genovesi's version, was "il sapore delle parole" (the flavour of the words) [154], conveying an experiential intimacy. Analogously, "the simple things of country living" enjoyed in Sicily by the boy Pitruzzello are "things that are so precious to his understanding of himself" rather than "necessarie come l'aria che respira" (as necessary to him as the air he breathes) [29-30].

What I think we can see here in the translation is an elision, a blurring of difference, a hesitancy in interpretation which interprets itself as a matter of "taste", an uncertainty between different experiential worlds (Sicilian and Australian) and their related hermeneutical grids, which may be viewed from the perspective of the impossibility, of the kind addressed by Gadamer, of either transcending both these worlds within a "universal" perspective or of fusing the two seamlessly together. The interethnic or multicultural pact, the "third space" hypothesised by Homi Bhabha [cf. Rutherford, 207-21] is by its nature unstable, precarious. But we do not have to see this

---

to their varied language competences [142, 151, 154].

34 Personal communication by Piero Genovesi, 31 August, 2005.

negatively (as Bhabha does not). Rather, mobility and dynamism can be seen as evidence of societal health and vitality, and the function of an enquiry such as this can be seen as that of investigating the force-field and the influence of vectors within it making for increase or decrease of societal dynamism or entropy. The resultant awareness may in turn influence the orientation of subsequent cultural interventions – such as life writings or translations of life writings – so as to maximise the dynamic rather than the entropic possibilities of the given situation, pushing towards the fullest possible fusion of horizons.

Returning now to Musolino's translation, we can already perceive in the instance just examined a discernible Australian "interpretation" or model of the integration of immigrants from an "other" (and this is itself a construct that can only be arbitrarily defined) ethnic origin. The elsewhere of origin becomes "past" to the "present" of Australia, a "heritage" rather than an immediately experienced "flavour", something precious to the immigrant's self-understanding rather than as necessary to him as the air he breathes. The immigrant's formative experience is thus conceptualised as being absorbed, integrated, perhaps superseded by the new Australian reality. If we wish to adopt the slippery but inescapable notion of "translation norms", possibly in the guise of a "cultural filter",[35] we could talk here of an "integrative" translation norm and cultural filter. The value of these terms is in reinforcing the sense that the individual translator is not operating in a social vacuum, but negotiating a position within a force-field.

Syntax

Though language and culture are inseparable elements of the same force-field and cannot be peeled apart, some features of the holistic language-culture complex manifest themselves specifically at the level of language. This applies to syntactic cohesion: the construction of discourse at sentence and paragraph level. The English language in all its geographical varieties including the Australian variety favours

---

35 Translation norms, first mooted by Jiří Levý, are discussed by Toury [1995] and in Snel Trampus [2002]. Translation norms and the cultural filter are discussed in House [2002].

asyndeton and paratactic structures (with relatively few degrees of subordination and with relatively short sentences), so that cohesion operates very largely between sentences at paragraph level, rather than within individual sentences as in Italian. This makes for a relatively staccato prosody and corresponding mental processing as compared to Italian, which cultivates comparatively more hypotaxis or degrees of subordination and longer sentences involving more sustained intonation and mental processing and more complex cohesion at sentence level. Put simply, the English language tends to press upon the translator a translation norm calling for shorter sentences in English than in Italian, and Musolino's translation generally does this, substituting an English prosody at sentence and paragraph level for Genovesi's Italian prosody. In this respect also, then, this translation is, to use Venuti's terms, a domesticating or naturalising translation rather than a "foreignising" one [Venuti 1995], in keeping with Musolino's tendency to apply what I have called an "integrative" cultural filter.

Musolino does this with great skill, often having to radically reconstruct an entire paragraph, sometimes a whole page, in order to retain all the information while preserving cohesion. One example will have to suffice. This passage grades from the biographer's paraphrase of Sebastiano Pitruzzello's own words to the biographer's own eloquent authorial reflection. I give the original Italian, followed by my own unreconstructed approximation and then by Musolino's rendering:

> Ma se potenti erano le ragioni del cuore, dall'altra parte poco lo legava più alla sua amata Sortino. Il lavoro in fabbrica non era per lui. L'aveva provato, aveva cercato, aveva tenuto duro … ma non era per lui. Il suo sogno rimaneva quello di creare qualcosa di solido, qualcosa di duraturo a cui legare il proprio nome, quello della futura famiglia e quello dei luoghi che si vedeva costretto ad abbandonare per poter riuscire, per potersi creare quella vita, quel futuro che sapeva con certezza lo attendeva al di là degli oceani.
>
> Persa la possibilità di dedicarsi a quei lavori che da sempre erano stati per lui il bene della sua terra, viste vendute

mandrie ed armenti, terminata la piccola ma promettente industria famigliare, era tempo per lui di andare avanti, di guardare ad altri orizzonti. Tempo di partire.

E partire non fu facile, così come non era stato facile per i tanti prima di lui, ma la gente legata alla propria terra, la gente nata sulla terra e vissuta al ritmo delle stagioni, reca in sé l'atavico coraggio del camminatore, una consapevolezza delle proprie forze che pochi altri possiedono. Prima di Sebastiano avevano dato prova di questo quei milioni di anime che erano andate a dar forma, fra gli anni Cinquanta e Sessanta, al popolo dell'esodo, a quelle pagine di storia patria che restano fra le più drammatiche del Secondo Dopoguerra e, al tempo stesso, fra le più ricche di vissuta umanità. [Genovesi, 82; suspension marks in the original]

(But powerful as the reasons of the heart may have been, little else bound him still to his beloved Sortino. Factory work wasn't for him. He had tried it, he had striven, he had stood fast ... but it wasn't for him. His dream was still that of creating something solid, something that would last, which would bear his name, that of his future family, and that of the places which he found himself forced to leave so as to be able to succeed, so as to be able to make that life for himself, that future which he knew for certain awaited him beyond the oceans.

Having lost any chance of devoting himself to those labours which had always been for him the joy of his land, having seen flocks and herds sold off, having seen the end of the small but promising family business, it was time for him to move on, to seek new horizons. Time to leave.

And leaving wasn't easy, just as it hadn't been easy for all those before him, but the folk who were attached to their land, the folk born on the land, who lived their lives according to the rhythm of the seasons, bear within themselves the ancestral courage of the wayfarer, an awareness of their own strength which few others possess.

Before Sebastiano, this had been proved by those millions of souls who had gone to make up, in the fifties and the sixties, the people of the exodus, giving those pages of national history which remain amongst the most dramatic of that post-war period and, at the same time, among the richest in human life-experience.)
[Gatt-Rutter, rough direct translation]

But if his heart seemed to be ruling his brain, on the other hand there was little that still tied Sebastiano to his beloved Sortino. Factory work was not for him. He had given it a go, he had really tried, had persevered … but it was just not for him. He still held on to his dream of creating something of substance, something enduring to put his name to, his family's name to. And it would bear the name of the places he would have to leave behind in order to make a go of things, in order to create that life, that future which he was convinced lay ahead of him, beyond the oceans.

Now, the chance of continuing to do the type of work he was used to and which was the best part of being on the land was gone. He had seen flocks and herds sold. The small but promising family business had come to an end. It was time for him to go forward, to look further afield. Time to leave.

But leaving was not easy, just as it had not been easy for so many others before him. Still, people connected to the land, the people who have been born on the land and used to the cycle of the seasons, seem to have inherited the courageous spirit of the wanderer, they seem to have an awareness of their strength that few others possess. This is what millions of souls, the people of the great exodus of the '50s and '60s who preceded Sebastiano, had given proof of. They contributed some of the most dramatic pages to the history of a nation in the post-World War Two period, a history though rich with common human experience. [Musolino, 82]

Musolino makes that sound so natural in English, the rhythms sound so spontaneous, belying the amount of reworking that has gone into this one translated passage. And the transformation, the naturalisation into English does not by any means involve only the phonic level – rhythm and prosody – but also the turns of phrase and idiom: all that may be subsumed within the area of discourse labelled "register", "tenor" and "style" [Halliday, 222; Gregory and Carroll, 53].

Idiom

Let us turn then to the verbal level of the translation – lexis, idiom, metaphor and suchlike. The integrative tendency to naturalise the Italian into English, absorbing or effacing difference, is widespread throughout the volume, but with some curious exceptions. Leaving the contrary instances till later, let me first expand on the dominant register. It is this that constitutes the integrative cultural filter which presents reality in Australian terms – easy-going and matey.

The indulgently colloquial Italian "il birichino" (the naughty one) becomes "the cheeky one" [29] and the drier "coetanei" (age-mates) becomes "mates" [30], but in the following passage there is a shift from the more expressive Italian: "forse qui in Australia tutti sono più tranquilli perché si vive 'a pancia piena' mentre ai miei tempi, al paese, si era spesso 'a pancia vuota' e allora si andava in cerca di qualcosa da mettere sotto i denti" (perhaps here in Australia everybody's more relaxed because they live "with a full belly" while in my time, in my home town, people often had "an empty belly" and so they went around looking for something to get between their teeth), to a more neutral: "maybe here, in Australia, they're more relaxed because people can feed their cravings while in my day, back in our town, we were often starved and so we went around looking for something to eat" [30]. This takes the verbal edge off those hunger pangs of the young Sebastiano in Sicily, perhaps also distancing the folk memory of hunger in the years of the Great Depression in Australia.

A proverbial phrase in Italian becomes a familiar but slightly different English expression: "da una giornata di sole può nascere una notte di temporale" (a sunny day can lead to a stormy night), turning into: "there were clouds looming on the horizon" [34].

Mostly, expressions take on an intimately English / Australian feel: "si sapeva tutto gli uni degli altri" (everybody knew everything about one another) – "We lived in each other's pockets" [43]; "orto" (kitchen garden, fruit and vegetable garden) – "vegie garden" [44]; "il pensiero di separarci ci tormentava" – "The idea of being separated was killing us" [for "tormenting", 63]; "più coraggioso" – "gutsier" [76/75]; "non sarei partito così, all'avventura" (I wouldn't leave just like that, on an adventure / happy-go-lucky) – "I wasn't leaving on a wing and a prayer" [64]; "ci si capiva bene" (we understood each other well) – "we had a terrific understanding" [105]; "fatte le sue brave domande, se le vide regolarmente rifiutare" (having made his fine applications, he saw them regularly rejected) – "application after application regularly got knocked back" [105]; "il tortuoso svolgersi" (the tortuous winding) – "the twisting and turning" [117]; "consuma la bellezza di duemila" (consumes the beauty of two thousand) – "consumes a ripping two thousand" [138]; "Costruire oggi per un più tranquillo domani" (Build up today for a more tranquil tomorrow) – "Work hard for a worry-free future" [159/8]; "la tensione" (her tension) – "her raw energy" [161]; "la decisone del fare" (her decisiveness in doing) – "her determination to get results" [162]; "quel filo di selvaggio" (that thread of wildness) – "that little touch of wildness" [162]; "Lungo il cammino dei ricordi" – "Down Memory Lane" [171]; "comunità viva" (live community) – "vibrant community" [181]; "qualcuno si è mosso" (someone got moving) – "someone started the ball rolling"; "È stato come toccare il cielo con un dito" (It was like touching the sky with my finger [i.e., I felt elated]) – "I was on top of the world" [188]; "(il) mio paese d'origine e mai dimenticato, Sortino" (my town of origin, never forgotten, Sortino) – "my home town, the Sortino I hold so dear" [188]; "la casa è lo specchio delle persone che la abitano" (a home is a mirror to the people who dwell in it) – "a house tells us a lot about its owner" [193]; "si aprono nuove avventure" (new adventures unfold) – "there are new adventures in the pipeline" [197]; "comincio ad avere i miei anni" (I'm beginning to have my years [i.e., getting old]) – "I'm getting on" [200].

An aspect of this Australianisation of the register, in keeping with the shift in prosody and idiom, is the tendency to lower the tenor of the Italian from a relatively abstract, high-sounding, and intellectual level to a display of down-to-earth, no-nonsense Australian practicality. So, in the metabiographical introductory "Author's Note", "testo" (text) becomes "story" [7], "approfondirne la genesi" (exploring its origins) becomes "to understand how things began", "quel mondo contadino che gode di una propria universalità di valori" (that peasant world that enjoys its own universality of values) – "that peasant world that may be found anywhere, whose values …" [8], and "nel contesto di una indifferenziata quotidianità" (in the context of an undifferentiated quotidian existence) – "while enduring a life of mundane activity" [9].

Throughout the book it is, likewise, mainly (but not only) the biographer's voice-over that is translated down-register: "urbanistica dettata dall'umano" (urban layout dictated by the human) – "unregulated urban growth" [13]; "con i coetanei … a contatto con la natura" (with his age-mates in touch with nature) – "with his mates out in the countryside" [30]; "il fine del percorso esistenziale che si era prefisso" (the goal of the existential path he had set himself) – "the point of what he had set out to accomplish" [100]; "filosofia esistenziale" (a philosophy of existence) – "attitude to life" [153]; "Si riceve in base alla quantità e qualità del lavoro che si fa" (One receives on the basis of the quantity and quality of the work one does) – "You get out of it what you put in" [153]; "dandoci quelle soddisfazioni" (giving us those satisfactions) – "he has made us happy in many ways" [155]; "avevo appreso un bagaglio di nozioni teoriche" (I had acquired theoretical baggage) – "I'd learnt so much" [165]; "operare scelte proprie" (carry out her own choices) – "stand on her own two feet" [166]; "un'esperienza sia teorica che pratica che si traduceva …" (both theoretical and practical experience that translated …) – "new ideas and work practices that meant …" [166]; "fa sì che certi aspetti della nostra personalità a tratti prendano il sopravvento" (makes certain aspects of our personalities sometimes get the upper hand) – "means that sometimes one of us tries to dominate the other" [166]; "efficiente nell'esprimere quel tutto che è diventato se stessa" (effective in expressing that whole that she has become) – "serves to reveal the sort of person she has become" [168]; "vigili ad intervenire" (watching out to intervene) – "very hands-on" [174]; "realizzare la loro avventura esistenziale" (fulfil their existential adventure) – "fulfil their lives" [179]; "dialogo" (dialogue, i.e., sociability) – "chatting endlessly" [196]; "la logica gastronomica di oggi" (today's gastronomical logic, i.e., eating habits) – "the logical requirements for good eating" [200].

Resonant phrases by two Italian politicians likewise come down to earth: "la significativa realtà istituzionale australiana" (Australia's significant institutional reality) becomes "the country at all levels" [173]; and "ferrea operosità" (iron-hard industriousness) comes out as "fearsome appetite for hard work" [212]. The specifically Australian reality is invoked when a technical college is called a TAFE (Technical and Further Education) [153] and a *tuttofare* Pitruzzello is called "Mr Fixit" [155], while the Sortino boys in the 1950s "barrack" for their cycling heroes [171].

Asymmetrical effects

The dominant "integrative" translation effects I have listed above are of course not uniform either in the strength or in the manner of their integrative thrust. A variety of other effects of Musolino's translation lend themselves even less to easy classification, but some can loosely be grouped together as "non-integrative effects" and others as "anti-integrative effects". As a non-integrative effect we may consider a short passage where the Italian adopts a dramatic, or perhaps an evocatively lyrical, exclamatory, nominal style: "E poi le rocce, le caverne in cui passava le notti … Dormire sulla terra, ascoltarne l'immensa voce …" As an unreconstructed gloss of this I offer: "And then the rocks, the caverns in which he spent the nights … Sleeping on the ground, listening to its immense voice." Whereas Musolino has: "And then among rocks and in caves, he spent nights … He slept on the bare earth, listened to all its sounds …" [22]. We may feel here that something of the sublimity attached to the memory, the sense of a privileged Sicilian existence, has been occluded.

A similar occlusion, if not of the sublime, of an existential extreme, may be sensed in the rendering of: "Quando uno è giovane è sempre pronto a prendere il cielo a pugni" (When one is young he's always ready to come to blows with heaven) by "When you're young, nothing seems beyond you" [79]. In these cases, it does not seem to be a matter of a pre-existing incommensurability between cultures and languages in construing existential experiences, but rather of a cultural filter intervening to create a gap, or to understate an alternative (non-Australian) fount of value.

A different and unique, perhaps extraordinary, case is the gnomic: "… il sudore della fronte è l'unica cosa che non lascia macchie", which glosses straightforwardly as "the sweat of one's brow is the only thing that leaves no stains". For this memorable phrase, Musolino produces the even more memorable, and monumentally enigmatic: "a brow wet with honest sweat owes not any man" [81]. Isolated as this instance is, it can only hint at an invisible dimension that haunts the Italian and the English versions of the biography of Pitruzzello, an inkling of the "pure" language beyond or before or between languages posited by Benjamin.

Sometimes, however, the Italian and the English are estranged: "coronare il proprio sogno d'amore" (to crown his dream of love) – "to satisfy his love's ambition" [81]; "il proprio essere" (their own being) – "their own humanity" [87]; "e qui la lingua batte dove il dente duole" (here the tongue pokes at the aching tooth [meaning: this is a sore point]) – "And this is a topic close to my heart" [99/100].

At other times, very untypically, the Italian shows through the English, or disturbs its otherwise generally smooth surface. This effect may be barely visible, as in: "conquistando nuovi mercati" / "conquer new markets" (where "win" would be the unmarked English translation) [174]. Or it may be slightly more visible, as in: "sparsi come i figli delle quaglie" (scattered like quail fledglings) "scattered all over the place like baby quail" [100] (whereas "baby" quail might fall out of the nest, but cannot take flight). "Un po' dappertutto" (here, there and everywhere), gives "a bit everywhere" [138/137] as an exact phrasal equivalent, a bit of "translationese" rippling that smooth surface of the English as if hankering to rise to the challenge proposed by Sturrock.

This is foregrounded in the chapter title "An Odyssey called a

Licence", for the Italian "Un'odissea chiamata 'licenza'" (which, in idiomatic English, could be The Licence Saga) [103]. But two isolated perturbations cannot subvert the overwhelming transparency. (Such transparency is perhaps bound to dominate the translation contract relating to an immigrant's success story.) The same applies to a rendering that is not translationese of a phrase describing the two lovers vowing themselves to their joint adventure, "occhi negli occhi" (eye to eye; i.e., looking each other in the eye) – "staring into each other's eyes" [82]. This is momentarily disconcerting, but neither does it disrupt the Australianness, nor does it hint at Italianness.

Other traces of his presence left by the translator of the Pitruzzello biography are no more likely to challenge the cultural filter of Australianness. The omission of a paragraph containing Pitruzzello's boyhood recollections of the Allied bombings and invasion of Sicily in 1943 [29] appears to be inadvertent, as the discursive continuity is fractured at that point, and may possibly constitute a case of censorship on the part of the "translator's unconscious", censoring out a historical memory of hostilities between Italy and Australia that might interfere with the project, shared by both the subject of the biography and its translator, of a seamless integration of the Italian and the Australian experience [L. Venuti, 2002]. (Other omissions are less visible, but may also be unconsciously motivated, as when Lucia's account, "it'd been decided at home that once I turned eighteen I was going to Australia for a year or two", loses the phrase "dietro mia insistenza" (at my insistence) [63]).

There are visible parapraxes: Sortino's Chiesa Madre is mentioned first as the biggest and then as the second biggest church in town [13], B.C. becomes A.D., the Siculi are confused with the Sicani [17], and a car becomes a motorbike [41]. Testing some equipment ("collaudare un macchinario") becomes incomprehensible in context as "train a machinist" [108], and quantities become progressively more improbable as a hundred or so sheep ("un centinaio") become "a few hundred" and 2000 kilos of *ricotta* a week become an unimaginable and "ripping" 2000 tonnes [138/137]. The translator also shows himself nodding when "le notizie che avevano avuto" (the news they'd heard) comes out mystifyingly as "the news we'd received" [184] and the Pitruzzellos' conservatory ("serra-veranda") appears as an "observatory" [196].

But these are instances in which the translator finds himself caught out in the open, it seems, involuntarily and accidentally, rather than showing himself boldly so as to challenge the hegemonising and homogenising reflex which tends to be spontaneous in the receiving culture and which, as has already in part been seen, is to some extent internalised by the translator himself. It is a different matter when Italian cultural icons are transferred without explanation into the English text: Pascoli, a poet not known among non-Italians [21]; Guareschi, once rather well-known in the English-speaking world as the creator of *The Little World of Don Camillo*, and his other main character, the lovable Communist mayor of a country town, Peppone, but neither of them introduced as such [30/29]. Film actors and actresses and film titles, mixing Cinecittà with Hollywood, many of the Italian ones internationally famous, fit into a more intelligible context, but film titles given in Italian untranslated [47], like the unexplained authors, point to an unfamiliar culture out there, remote from English-speaking Australia. Likewise, when mentioning that the successful Sebastiano Pitruzzello has instituted a prize called the *Pungiglione d'Argento* for the annual bicycle race held in his native Sortino, not to say that this is a Silver Bee-Sting is to deny the English-language reader of the biography of Pitruzzello an insight into the humorous connection between cycling and bee-keeping in that corner of the Sicilian countryside – in fact, to deny that reader any insight whatsoever. From being wholly transparent, the translation at this point becomes fully opaque. Is this a challenge to the situationally advantaged Australian society and its culture? or resignation to the hopelessness of the task of a complete mediation between cultures? or an outright rejection of such an enterprise? At these points, Italy remains a closed book, and this is another way in which its meanings are occluded.

Spoken in another tongue

To the extent that, as theorists from Heidegger to Lacan and after have claimed, we are spoken by language, then the translator, in shifting from being spoken in one language to being spoken in another, has illustrious predecessors, including the Bengali poet Rabindranath Tagore, who won the 1913 Nobel Prize for literature largely on the basis of his own English translations of his Bengali poems pitched in such a way as to fulfil the English reader's expectations of the "Oriental" poet. To invoke a colonial or First World-Third World relationship is not wholly inappropriate in our present case, as Sengupta, in discussing Tagore's case of self-translation, refers back to the more general relationship between situationally advantaged and disadvantaged languages and cultures as traced by André Lefevere. Immigrants of different language from that of the host country indeed find themselves in many ways disadvantaged and subordinated (we might even use the Gramscian term "subaltern"). The extent to which this relationship of subordination is spoken by language is highlighted by the Australian use of the word "migrant" where other Englishes (and other European languages including Italian) generally distinguish between "immigrant" and "emigrant". Historically derived from the sporadic phenomenon of temporary or shifting migration, the Australian word "migrant" implies impermanence, and this word is, perhaps inevitably, used on the book's back cover to describe its biographical subject, Pitruzzello.[36]

I take this as a cue to trace further the extent to which Musolino's translation goes beyond "naturalising" or "domesticating" the biography of Pitruzzello as an "Australian" text and occludes some of its "Italianness" and its existential or experiential distinctiveness. Some of the traces of this process are delicate to the point of evanescence. Take the "white ships" (*navi bianche*) which brought the "migrants" to Australia and are a key image in the folk memory or social symbolic of Italian Australians, who also refer to them as the "Last Fleet", in clear contradistinction to the First Fleet which inaugurated British settlement of the continent in 1788 and which is itself a key image in the Australian social symbolic. These images are invoked

---

36 For similar objections to the Australian use of the word "migrant", see Gunew 1994: 4, 7, 11-12, 23, 116. Gunew further points out that "the term 'migrant' camouflages a hidden distinction between Anglo-Celtic and non Anglo-Celtic writing" [116].

by Genovesi's text ("due continenti legati fra loro dal sottile filo di quelle navi bianche, di quella 'ultima flotta' che col suo carico di angosce e di speranze umane è valsa a plasmare il volto e le fortune dell'Australia di oggi") and translated fairly closely by Musolino: "two continents that are connected by the thin thread of white ships, of the 'last fleet' that carried its cargo of anguish and human hope, and helped to shape the face and fortunes of today's Australia" [8; see also 86-7]. That is understated in English, whereas in the Italian version the historical self-awareness of the Italian or migrant Other has been effectively foregrounded: those two continents "bound together", in Italian, by such a slender thread, call for "those" white ships, and "that" last fleet which, in their passage from the Italian to the English, have lost their deictics (markers of the dialogic relation between the source of the utterance and its addressee – in this case, the deictics are the demonstrative adjectives "those" and "that") and, with them, some of their affective and symbolic or mythic valence.

Certain words in a given language are affective signifiers whose dictionary equivalents in another language cannot convey their value-laden affective associations, or do so in a distorting form. *Paese*, in the sense of one's own small country town associated with a traditional rural way of life, is one such word which is central to Pitruzzello's life-story. The unavoidable English translations, "town" or "home town", evoke, for the Australian reader (and also, to varying extents, for other English-language readers), sprawling low-slung rural townships very different from the densely clustered and more intimate stone-built South Italian towns, often perched on hilltops. Even the rendering "home town" does not carry with it that sense of belonging which attaches to the Italian *paese* and infuses the personal nouns *paesano* and *compaesano*, which approximate to the Australian use of *mate*. Analogously, *cuore* ("heart") occupies a more prominent place in Italians' discourse about their feelings than in contemporary English, where it quickly slips into sentimentality. Musolino consequently drops the term discreetly from time to time. Let one instance suffice. On page 82, *cuore* comes up twice in the Italian. Its first occurrence is retained in the English: "Ma se potenti erano le ragioni del cuore ..." (But strong as were the reasons of the heart ... – "But if his heart seemed to be ruling his brain …"). The second time, the heart remains implied. In Italian: "… il cuore torna a respirare aria di casa …" (his heart once again breathes his native air); and, in Musolino's English: "Is he taking in the sweet air of home once more?"

Some words or expressions sometimes assume thematic prominence in a given discourse which is not easily transferable into another language. The mercurial Sebastiano Pitruzzello is consistently characterised (first and foremost by himself) in the Italian as having quicksilver in his veins, so that, like the Mad Hatter, he is forever restless and cannot sit still: "'Ero sempre in movimento' ricorda Sebastiano 'tanto che si diceva che sul mio naso una mosca non si posava. Avevo l'argento vivo addosso.'" ("I was always in motion," recalls Sebastiano, "so much so that people said that on my nose no fly settled. I had quicksilver in me.") Musolino has: "'I couldn't keep still', recalls Sebastiano, 'and so much so that they used to say flies couldn't land on my nose. I was like quicksilver'" [30]. But the mercury level, or rather, frequency, gets too high for translation, and the Italian idiom is sometimes re-interpreted: "con l'argento vivo addosso" (with quicksilver inside him) – "who couldn't keep still" [87]; "con l'argento vivo addosso" – "who was as fast as quicksilver" [123].Where repetition is a stylistic signature of the original, avoidance of repetition is that of the translation.

In this particular instance, however, the terms of discourse are not as significantly affected as in other cases. Two other key thematic words carry experiential resonance in the Italian, *avventura* (adventure), and *vivere* (to live) and its derivatives, and in fact refer to experience as such. *Avventura* gets caught in the integrative cultural filter, and its frequency is less in the English version than in the Italian. The word is thematic to the text as it defines the Pitruzzellos' act of migration to Australia and Sebastiano's risk-taking entrepreneurialism. The translator de-emphasises the adventurousness of both the migratory and the business initiative by reducing the frequency of the word. Is this because Australian identity is too serious a business to be reduced to something as capricious, perhaps even frivolous, as an "adventure"? Or because it conceives "migrants" as coming to the Island Continent in a more respectful and beholden spirit? If we cannot explain the phenomenon on such slender evidence, we can at least observe it. Here are some instances: "la sua avventura australiana" / "his time in Australia" [40]; "non sarei partito così, all'avventura" (I wouldn't leave just like that, on an adventure / happy-go-lucky) – "I wasn't leaving on a wing and a prayer" [64]; "il tempo del cuore non portava ad avventure ma al sacramento del matrimonio" (the season of the heart led not to adventures but to the sacrament of matrimony) – "love was not an excuse for an affair but a reason for marriage" [83]; "mi piace l'avventura" / "I like excitement" [169]; the politician Mezzio's phrase, "avventura australiana", is retained as "Australian adventures" [174]; "realizzare la loro avventura esistenziale" (realise the adventure of their existence) – "fulfil their lives" ("fulfilment" being an equally resonant but differently oriented term in the post-Second World War English-speaking democratic cultures); Sebastiano is quoted as saying "si aprono nuove avventure" (new adventures unfold) – "there are new adventures in the pipeline" [197].

Avventura is semantically linked to the word *vivere*, as adventure is, *par excellence*, what is *lived*, in the sense of experienced or felt keenly and intensely, meaningfully. This is regularly expressed lexically by *vivere* in the Italian, but is de-lexicalised, and thus made less visible, in the English. Thus (to pick only on these intensive uses of the verb *vivere*) "vita di lavoro vissuta giorno per giorno" (life of toil lived out day by day) becomes "whose life of daily toil went on" [8]; "vivere i limiti della parola" (living the limits of the word) – "pushing language to its limits" [8/9]; "tutto era … più vissuto" (everything was … more [immediately] lived) – "more meaningful" [45]; "ricca di vissuta umanità" (rich in lived humanity) – "rich with common human experience" [82]; "rivivere le nostre tradizioni" (relive our traditions) – "recreate something of home" [98]; "rivissuta riunione con la loro gente" – "exciting [relived] reunion with their own people" [179/180]. These intensive uses of *vivere* stand out almost rhetorically in Italian and might have provided an opportunity for the translator to intercalate an Italian dimension within the Australian discursive space.

Generational shift

The Italian itself offers an open dimension which may be seen in the variation between two similar phrases. I was led to writing this present piece by stumbling, in my first reading of the Pitruzzello biography, on the phrase "donna 'veramente donna'" (woman "truly woman", i.e., real woman) [193]. Struck by the enigmatic nature of this semantically undefined but socioculturally determined phrase, I looked at Musolin's rendering, and found "A woman who is 'as women used to be'": this defines a sociocultural distance in chronological terms, but still does not specify its nature. Had the translator perhaps, applying an integrative cultural filter, identified Australia and Australian women with modernity and Sicily and Sicilian women with the past?

In fact, I discovered, Sebastiano himself had set up an opposition, not between Sicily and Australia as such, but between the women of a past era, whether Sicilian or Australian, and those of the present. Early in the biography, introducing the subject of his engagement to Lucia Mondragona, he is quoted as saying:

> ... a quei tempi non era come oggi che i giovani si incontrano, vanno insieme, si lasciano e così via. No, ai miei tempi era un'altra cosa. L'amore era una cosa seria e le donne erano veramente donne, non come adesso che tutto è facile, superficiale, e non era facile avvicinarle se uno non aveva intenzioni serie.

Musolino has:

> ... in those times things weren't like they are today when young people meet, go out together, leave each other and so on. No, in my day it was completely different. Being in love was a serious matter, and women were really women, not like now when everything's so easy, shallow, and it wasn't easy getting to know them if your intentions weren't honourable. [51]

"Go out together" is even more delicately put than "vanno insieme", but Musolino, in translating "A woman who is 'as women used to be'" towards the end of the book, has clearly remembered

Pitruzzello's earlier remark couched in the same words, as Genovesi also must have done. Musolino has taken Pitruzzello at his word, and gone further, implicitly placing the accent on Australian modernity where Pitruzzello honours the Sicilian tradition.

Venuti's argument for "foreignising" translation as a challenge to hegemonising and homogenising forces within the receiving language culture is applied to classical or canonical, or, alternatively, avant-garde, literary texts which are quite different in character and purpose from Genovesi's biography of the Pitruzzello family.[37] This biography does not remotely propose to challenge either the Italian or the Anglophone/Australian value-system. It has no overt ideological or cultural axe to grind, except – and it is a large except – to celebrate the "self-made" achievement of an individual and his family in their adopted land. Privately distributed, the text has no ambitions to circulate either in Italian or Australian literary milieux,[38] though it clearly has literary merits within the conventional limits of its well-defined genre. Without straying outside these limits, an intermediate space was available for the translation to position itself, relatively speaking, closer to Australianness or to Italianness. In tracing how Musolino's translation has, more or less consistently, inclined towards Australianness, we have explored, at the level of discourse in the print medium, what makes Australianness and what makes Italianness and what characterises each in terms of the other.

The past figures in the construction of Italy (or Sicily) both in the Italian and in the Australian discourse, but is perceived in Italian existentially in terms of identity and of its continuity into the present, as something "lived" and adventurous, while in the Australian discourse it is perceived as "heritage" or "memory". More generally,

---

37 Lawrence Venuti [1998: 124-57], however, effectively exposes the systematic sanitising for US consumption of texts apparently as innocuous ideologically as Guareschi's "Don Camillo" books, which suggests that an "uncensored" translation of even such anti-Communist works of popular literature was expected to have a destabilising effect in a society officially committed to the view that decent human beings cannot be Communists (or vice-versa).

38 It is, however, used in Sicily as a school text on emigration. (Personal communication by Piero Genovesi, 14.10.2005.)

the Australian translation de-emphasises the "lived" nature of Italian experience, from work to company to literary representation itself, as it de-emphasises the role of the heart, and the spirit of adventure (especially when applied to migration into Australia itself), and existential self-awareness, as also historical self-awareness in relation to that same epic phenomenon of mass emigration from Italy. Italian experience is welcomingly Australianised but somewhat muted in this translation. The mainstream Australian discourse could have been broadened and strengthened by more visibly accommodating a distinctive Italian discourse as one of its components. The issue, then, is whether mainstream Australia needs to be continually defined and defended in terms of Anglophone purity, or whether it can harmonise other discourses within it.

3 Making good: success stories

The section of this book devoted to the life story of Sebastiano Pitruzzello and his family presents a paradigmatic case of the celebratory mode of life writing, a classic instance of the self-made man. The life writing text – the biography or autobiography – is a monument to a socially recognised achievement which is often, as in Pitruzzello's case, marked by high official honours. As in Pitruzzello's case, the achievement may be industrial or commercial, bringing with it significant financial and social advancement, while in other cases it may be of a professional or vocational kind, involving a particular career, or of a more nebulous kind. The autobiography of Claudio Alcorso, which has also been discussed above, approaches this latter paradigm: Alcorso, having endured the ordeal and stigma of internment as an "enemy alien", and vicissitudes in the textile industry, achieves notable successes both in that industry, and in the trade with China, as well as in his public-spirited work for the Elizabethan Theatre Trust and in the Sydney Opera House enterprise, in environmental and pro-Aboriginal activism and in introducing the wine industry into Tasmania, yet his life history and quest for self-definition remains largely interrogative rather than affirmative.

Genovesi's presentation of the Pitruzzellos sets their life story in the context of the mass migration from Italy to Australia during the

1950s and 1960s, as one tessera in the complex mosaic of an epic demographic movement. This is often implicit in Italian Australian life writing (as in Ruzzene Grollo's books) and explicit in the socio-historical literature on the phenomenon (as in the title of Ivano Ercole's *Un'infinità di esperienze: un'unica storia* – "An infinity of experiences: a single [hi]story"). While Genovesi's book emphasises the Pitruzzellos' Italian (and, more strictly, Sicilian) identity, the majority of Italian Australian life writing texts – biographies and autobiographies – stress the *duality* of Italian and Australian affiliation, sometimes more, sometimes less, problematically.

The title of Robert Pascoe's life of the brilliant engineer, Natale Bonacci – *Nat Bonacci: No ordinary Australian* [2012] – strikes a different note. Whilst, like the Pitruzzello biography, it gives full weight to the place of origin (in this case, the rural conurbation of Decollatura in Calabria), and to Natale's marriage to a girl from that same location – though he was brought up on a tobacco farm in Myrtleford, near Victoria's eastern border, while she grew up in a Melbourne suburb – the main thrust of the book consists in a close-grained study of the various Australian milieux – educational, social and occupational, but emphatically including the respective built environments – which formed Natale and within which his life's achievement was defined. The concrete technicalities both of tobacco farming and of the civil engineering aspects of very tall buildings are gone into in detail, as are the remarks of numerous friends, colleagues and acquaintances or contemporaries of Bonacci's in the various spheres in which he moved, as well, of course, as family members. Although the precise nature of Bonacci's contribution to the spectacular development of civil engineering in Australia towards and beyond the turn of the second millennium remains hard to define (a strong preference for concrete structures rather than steel, the patenting of the "Bonacci Beam"), Pascoe's book has an epic ethnographic sweep of a different kind to Genovesi's account of the Pitruzzellos, telling an Australian rather than an Italian story, but without occluding its Italian dimension.

We have already seen cases where the clash of ethnic identities has involved serious trauma or grievance, and where writing the life story constituted an endeavour to overcome that hurt, and in that respect constituted an achievement in itself. Likewise, we have seen life writing grappling with other major traumas. Coming now to celebratory life histories of successful careers, we find that they, too, involve painful experiences – tensions between generations, especially across the migratory divide, or major disappointments or sorrows.

Carlo Zaccariotto's *"Me ricorde ..."* ("I remember") opens with a brief section explaining the motivation for writing the book, mostly for the benefit of his children and grandchildren. The cue comes from the scribe, Pino Bosi's, visit to the Koala Club leisure centre, which Zaccariotto had donated to his birthplace, the village of Gaiarine near Treviso in the Veneto [Zaccariotto 4], a benefaction which the people and authorities of Gaiarine did not appear to greatly appreciate [Zaccariotto 106]. This lack of recognition by the place of origin was not outweighed by the official honours received by Zaccariotto from the Italian Republic in recognition of his munificence towards the Italian immigrant community in Sydney and New South Wales and his generous donations for earthquake and flood relief in Italy, as well as his civic commitment to Australia's multiethnic development. Zaccariotto, who migrated to Australia after having been a prisoner of war in the 1940s, recalls with gratitude and affection the helpers, both Italian and Australian, who enabled him to find his feet in his first difficult years in Australia.

Another Veneto, Sir James Gobbo, born in 1931 in the Melbourne suburb of Carlton of recent immigrants from Cittadella, near Padua, has written a classic memoir, the stylishly produced *Something to Declare* [2010], about his illustrious career in the legal profession and as a member of many public bodies, which culminated with his appointment as Governor of the State of Victoria. All this is narrated with unassuming matter-of-factness, and his elevation to a knighthood in 1982 is only fleetingly mentioned [Gobbo 235, 291], much more space being devoted to his presidency of the Oxford University Boat Club and his captaincy of the crew that won the historic 100th boat race against Cambridge [Gobbo 57-8].

Self-aggrandisement is not the something this book has to declare, though the author is at pains to set on record his experience of events and institutions and his perspective on them. People he has known and worked with throng this book, constituting citizenship and service as a collaborative and convivial enterprise. The individual and the social intermesh. And the issues, many of them controversial, in which he was involved in various capacities – schoolboy or schoolteacher, undergraduate, barrister, committee worker or chairman, State Governor – are concretely presented. The lived and the written life is a contribution to the history of Australia's civic development from the 1960s into the beginning of the Third Millennium in terms of immigration policy, the arts, multiculturalism, welfare services for Victoria's Italian community and economic, artistic, educational and technical cooperation between Italy and Australia.

Assured of his Australian identity, Gobbo displays pride in his Italian, especially Venetian, heritage and connections. The one disappointment, painfully and honestly acknowledged, that mars the glitter of existence at the top of Australia's establishment is that a change in the government of the State of Victoria results in his appointment as Governor not being extended [Gobbo 264-78]. Nevertheless, Gobbo's life story is a powerful message of how someone born in Australia of Italian parents with no particular privileges or advantages (they were small shopkeepers) and growing up in the 1940s, when Australia and Italy were at war with one another, could climb unimpeded up the educational and institutional ladder and achieve the highest honours.

"Gold and a dream of becoming rich in a new world brought the young adventurer to Melbourne." These words open Geoff Easdown's *Gualtiero Vaccari: A man of quality* [2006] and pick up Vaccari's own assertion, shortly before his death, that his move to Australia was prompted by "a spirit of adventure" [Easdown 156], a note often sounded in the life narratives of Australia's Italians, but rarely in Australian accounts of migration from Italy and elsewhere. Vaccari (1894-1978), was a generation older than Zaccariotto and nearly two generations older than Gobbo, and came to Melbourne from Sant'Agostino in Emilia-Romagna in 1912. As with so many Italian Australian success stories, tribute is paid to Australian helpers, particularly to the Irish-born Irene Major, who advanced the young

Gualtiero the very substantial sum of money which started him off on the road to becoming by far the largest importer of Italian products into the State of Victoria [Easdown 8]. A letter from Gualtiero's father after her death is quoted: "she was like a sister to you. When you were poor, alone, with limited knowledge of the language, your existence in Australia would have been vastly more sorrowful if you had not had her friendship" [Easdown 10].

Large-scale philanthropy both in Italy, via Sant'Agostino, and in Victoria, in the areas of social welfare and health care, education and the teaching of Italian in schools and universities, features largely, and in considerable detail, in this life story of Vaccari as a public figure in increasingly difficult times as Mussolini's Italy during the later 1930s entered into imperial rivalry, and then into outright war, with the British Empire, and, consequently, with Australia. Easdown talks of Vaccari's walking "a veritable tightrope" [49], having naturalised as a British subject in July of 1939 and then mediating between Italian Australians and Australian authorities through the war years. His dealings with the Casa d'Italia or Club Cavour, according to Easdown, brought Vaccari under fire from both sides, pro- and anti-Fascist [Easdown 38]. Much space is devoted to Vaccari's efforts, in concert with other influential figures of both Italian and non-Italian provenance, to minimise the internment of Italians in Victoria and to mitigate its effects [Easdown 59-95] and, likewise, to ensure the welfare of Italian prisoners of war being held in Australia [Easdown 96-105]. Easdown's biography is thus a vindication of Vaccari's integrity and of his role in Australian history, and particularly in the history of the Italians in Victoria. This role is continued in the post-war years with Vaccari's advocacy in favour of immigration from Italy [Easdown 106-17] and the endowment for provision of age-care facilities for Victoria's Italians and for Italian studies at university level.

A success story with a difference is the 1986 life of Ezio Luisini, *Luck Without Joy: A portrayal of a migrant*, by Alfredo Strano (translated into English by Elizabeth P. Burrows), whose title is pointed, but slightly misleading. The Italian *fortuna* does not necessarily mean *luck*, and in this case is closer to *success*. Luisini, a Tuscan, from desperately luckless beginnings, joins his irresponsible and long-absent father in Western Australia between the two world wars, only to find him in penury. The young Luisini is lucky enough to get some support from his Australian employer, but it is his own thrift and enterprise and business sense that enable him to build up a successful drapery business in Perth, which becomes a focal point for newly arrived immigrants from Italy from the 1930s to the 1960s, and then to diversify into agricultural property, crop farming and viticulture. He becomes a rich man, and this is his "success" or "fortune", rather than "luck", but it proves joyless through his obsession with accumulating wealth and his inability to create a loving family or a close circle of friends.

Strano points to a factor unnoticed by historians: the different expectations of immigrants arriving up to the Second World War compared to those arriving after. This corresponded to a generational change and inter-generational friction, which can be noted in several Italian Australian autobiographies. Strano [1986: 94] remarks: "An ignorance of the history of the immigrants, history which will not be found written in books, was one of the causes of the disagreement between the old and the new migrants, between fathers and sons and it made life difficult, often unbearable." Luisini, of course, belonged to the earlier generation of Italian migrants, but Strano adds another observation: "One thing distinguished him, however, from both the old and new migrants: he was totally immune to the dreaded disease, homesickness. For him, Australia swiftly became the land of his dreams and he never showed any desire to return to his homeland" [1986: 96]. *Luck Without Joy*, pieced together mainly from conversations between Strano and Luisini and between Strano and his own father, a friend of Luisini's, is thus far from a celebratory life history, ironically presenting apparent success as failure.

Alfredo Strano had a literary education in Italy and was a writer, mainly journalistic, by profession, some of whose writings were collected in the 2001 volume, *Lo sguardo e la memoria: diario di un emigrato in Australia* (The gaze and memory: diary of an emigrant to Australia). The title seems promisingly autobiographical, but the observing gaze and memory are directed outwards, not towards the author's own life experience. He had earlier, however, produced an autobiographical text, one in which Australia plays no part, though it indicates what personal baggage an Italian immigrant to Australia can carry with him. This is the engaging and humane prisoner-of-war narrative, *Prigioniero in Germania: (settembre 1943 – luglio 1945)*, published in Italy in 1973, in which the narrator, some thirty years after the events narrated, recounts how his eighteen-to-twenty-year-old self managed to survive, yet avoid being either brutalised or corrupted or embittered.

Damian Tripodi's bilingual *Parole di mio padre: Il sogno di un emigrante / Words of my Father: A migrant's dream* (2003) is a testimony and a testament to his two cultures, having come from Calabria to Australia as a small child after the Second World War. It is also a troubled tribute to his father, who brought his family to an ultimately more prosperous life in Australia, but could not reconcile himself to the inevitable difference in social culture and, like the traditional peasant *padre padrone* patriarch, still sought to impose his authority on his family [Tripodi 48/127-8]. Tripodi is in effect, corroborating two of the points made in Alfredo Strano's biography of Luisini. He is confirming the clash between generations and the initial hardship of newly arrived immigrants having to face harsh conditions as well as linguistic, cultural and social disadvantage. For the younger generation, caught between two languages and two social orders, developing a balanced competency in both could be a painful undertaking [Tripodi 40-1/118-20]. The main narrative focuses on how the author persevered in this undertaking and succeeded in entering the educational system in the field of vocational training and of Italian linguistic and cultural maintenance and development in the Gippsland area of south-east Victoria, for which he has received high official recognition.

Tripodi's volume is in handsome large format with pictorial collage backgrounds as well as a central photographical section dividing the Italian text from the English text. Des Tobin's 2009 *Michael Tricarico: The journey not the destination*, a collaborative biography involving the author with his subject, is even more striking visually and even more impressive in format. With few exceptions, the life histories – biographies or autobiographies – of Australia's Italians are lavishly illustrated with photographs, both places, and faces, staring straight at the reader and into eternity. Tobin's book takes the pictorial dimension to new levels, making it all-enveloping. Magnificent panoramas provide the backdrop to pages of text, the photographic portraits are dynamic, the pictorial montage extends to full-page images of agricultural equipment or racecourse spectacles, and there is a colourful pull-out complex family tree.

Yet this celebratory biography has many surprises. Though the title names an individual, this book embraces a complex family history, stretching back two or three generations into the peasant community of San Marco in Lamis, near Foggia, in Puglia. And this is no family utopia: malfunctions abound – father-son conflict, in-law feuds, misfits, infant mortality, a failed marriage. The book is, of course, also, like all the other texts considered in the present volume, a migration history, with the Tricarico family joining the father, Giuseppe, in Victoria's agricultural Gippsland in 1930 and the young Michael growing up through the Depression and war.

The approach, comparable to that of Ruzzene Grollo's *Growing Through the Brick Floor*, is in large part that of social history and ethnography, with social relations and material conditions and practices described in lively detail. Here, too, as in Tripodi's volume, we have a *padre padrone* and intergenerational tensions with Italian peasant parents finding it hard to adapt to a different society and cope with the language barrier and having to face discrimination, hostility and marginalisation. The children traverse a crisis of identity. Tobin quotes Michael Tricarico: "We didn't know who we were. On one level we were clearly Italian. We spoke Italian [presumably meaning Pugliese], ate Italian food and in some ways lived like Italian peasants in San Marco. But we knew our future was in Australia and could see the need to be Australian … In a sense I was an Australian trapped in an Italian body and environment from which I struggled to be free" [Tobin 63]. It is not until a visit "home" to San Marco in Lamis in 1971 when, aged 40, he has already achieved success in the agricultural equipment business, that "he began to understand how it was to feel and be Italian. He became aware of an overwhelming sense of feeling at home and 'with a right to belong', in this obscure, impoverished village" [Tobin 161]. His Australian identity, conversely, seems assured in such terms as his 17-hectare home at Harkaway [Tobin 119] and his Valentine's Day present to his wife of a thoroughbred racehorse [Tobin 134].

Carmelo Caruso's life is multiply celebrated, first by his own intimate autobiography published in 1998 and 1999 in two extremely handsome and very substantial matching volumes, one in English, drafted by Gaetano Rando and Janine Dickinson, *Under Another Sky: The life and sentiments of an Italian emigrant*, and a version in Italian by Pina Catania, *Sotto un altro cielo: vita e sentimento di un emigrante*; then, in 2008, in the more detached biography by Irene Sampognaro, *Carmelo Caruso: I due cuori di un emigrante*, an equally handsome and substantial production, again matched by the translated version, *Carmelo Caruso: The two hearts of an immigrant*, by Jan Dickinson. All four volumes, brought out by the same publisher in uniform format, are vivid archival repositories, reproducing a wealth of documents and photographic illustrations of people, events and places, as well as being vigorous narrative texts, rich in incident, with strong memorial and affective recall in relatively straightforward chronological sequence.

The earlier autobiographical work in particular engagingly dramatises key incidents in the author's family and personal history, beginning with his childhood in Licodia Eubea, near Catania in Sicily, where he started work in a stone quarry at the age of twelve [Caruso 1999: 69]. With remarkable candour, Caruso recounts his difficulties with his overbearing father, whom he kept in the dark when, not yet twenty-one, he emigrated to Australia in 1950, slipping off in secret, "like a thief" [Caruso 1999: 109]. Likewise, he does not cover up his estrangement from his first sweetheart, whom he left behind at Licodia upon emigrating, nor that from his first wife. He is able to recollect his feelings of guilt: "My behaviour seemed despicable to me …" [Caruso 1999: 141].

Starting arduously as a tailor in the small North Queensland town of Ayr, Caruso right away commits himself to support networks, charity events and services for incoming Italian migrants and for disaster relief in Italy, as well as newspaper and radio reporting. Moving his tailoring business to the Queensland capital, Brisbane, he extends his activities to include agency work for travel between Italy and Queensland and Italian magazine and music programs for radio. He eventually establishes himself as a prominent travel entrepreneur and property developer, winning both Italian and Australian honours. His was the first radio program in a language other than English to be heard in Queensland [Caruso 1999: 224].

His books, like the success stories of other first-generation Italian Australians, are an assertion and a re-enactment of the integration in his own life of the two societies, succinctly expressed in his 2008 subtitle, *The Two Hearts of an Immigrant*, and of devoted voluntary service to both societies.

Meet Me at the Top! is the uninhibited title of the autobiography of the glamorous Sarina Russo, whose charismatic portrait beams from the book's front cover. Her "Introduction" infectiously opens with an account of her hosting ex-President Bill Clinton at a Brisbane City gala dinner:

> … in my wildest dreams I could never have imagined this happening …
>
> I was the kid from the working-class side of the tracks, the kid who came to Spring Hill, Brisbane, as a five-year-old from Sicily, the kid whose migrant Dad was a bridge worker and carpenter, the kid who couldn't speak English, the kid who was scorned at primary school because she ate Parmesan cheese and salami sandwiches, the young woman who was fired from several jobs after leaving school (and failing junior and senior English exams). [Russo 13-14]

And she disarmingly asks: "But is this description of my evening with a US president really worth the opening chapter of a book? Is it an exercise in Vanity?"

Writing very pointedly in the aftermath of the attack on the Twin Towers in 2001, Russo largely disclaims the intention of producing a self-serving and self-congratulatory autobiography. She certainly celebrates her own success quite uninhibitedly, but does so in service to others and to the world at large. She avows that she "felt obliged to go along with the publisher's wishes" in writing the book in the first person (rather than leaving it to her co-author, Russ Gleeson, to write about her using the third person) [Russo vi]. Ex-President Clinton comes into the book not merely to boost Russo's celebrity status by his dealings with her, but precisely as an answer to the shock of September 11, 2001, by reason of his peace message and his perspective on world-wide interdependence, to which Russo devotes a substantial portion of her book [Russo 86-91].

Throughout the book she makes it clear that her purpose is also to share what she has gained and learned, to help and encourage others to emulate her, to overcome perceived disadvantages and early setbacks and failures and, by sheer bold resolve, achieve their goals.[39] Each chapter ends by spelling out "lessons" for living and self-fulfilment. Part Two of the book, eighty pages out of a total of 224, is titled "How to succeed in business" and is what it says it is, a business success manual which draws on the experiences recounted in the autobiographical first part – both the setbacks and the bold moves, and particularly Russo's focus on the interests of her clients. A large part of Russo's business success involves inspired property deals, but her core business is in fact educational – secretarial training – out of which developed also a secretarial employment agency. An educational mission is therefore integral to her entire business enterprise, her life's work, in fact, and therefore to her life story as written in this book, an autobiography that goes beyond autobiography.

The Italian dimension figures significantly in this life project and in this life writing project. The postmodern transformation of Sarina Russo from family-bound Sicilian girl to globally mobile entrepreneur could have taken place in Sicily as well as in Australia, since the last quarter of the last century was a period of social and socio-economic transformation in both places, but the Sicilian or Italian flavour is very marked in this Australian story. The domineering,

---

39 See Terry Robson, *Failure is an Option: How setbacks breed success*, Pymble (NSW): ABC Books, 2010, which argues that initial or interim failures should be regarded as learning experiences on the way to eventual successful achievement.

patriarchal *padre padrone* figure of Sarina's father is pivotal in this process, as it is in the stories of several other Italian Australians of southern Italian origin – such as Damian Tripodi, Carmelo Caruso and Domenico Cacciola – but also some from the north of Italy such as Rino Baggio and Franca Arena. As in all instances, it is a conflicted story of devotion.

From her primary school years, Sarina helps her father run his rental properties and labours in his vineyard at weekends, while also doing domestic chores, and is subject to a strict regime of surveillance which denies her any autonomy in her social life outside the family circle. She describes her near-despair which her Australian friends could not understand, as, at the age of twenty-six, she agonised over the almost unthinkable decision to escape from her family prison, her "culture trap" [Russo 18-19]. But, once the step has been taken, family affection reasserts itself and the father-daughter relationship is restored [Russo 22], though Sarina continues to live independently away from home and, perhaps even more significantly, avoids permanent ties with a male partner: "… I didn't want to be anyone else's possession. I had not escaped from the restrictions and disciplines of my father's household only to lose my freedom to another man" [Russo 23]. Sarina Russo makes it to the top as a single, independent woman, but nevertheless is grief-stricken by her father's death, which confirms her in her career: "It was really hard to carry on after he died. The two years following I would burst into tears whenever I thought of him, which was often. Even today memories of him can bring tears to my eyes. I escaped my grief by throwing myself into my business with even greater urgency and passion" [Russo 52].

"My life has been a party … It's way too early to declare this party over" [Venuti and Hogan 296-7]. Thus, at age 70, Maria Venuti – not the operatic Italian American, but the Italian Australian singer and showbiz artiste, an Australian approximation to Madonna – suspends her life story, *A Whole Load of Front*, whose title puns on her larger-than-life personality and her physical attributes, which figure prominently on the book's jacket and in her narrative. This is conducted by Venuti and her co-author, Christine Hogan, with great flair, in a style that is hip, savvy and slick. Born in Australia in

1941, but to a Sicilian father like Carmelo Caruso and Sarina Russo, and to an Italian mother who had grown up in Egypt, Venuti, like Caruso and Russo, but far less agonisingly, had to resist and flout Sicilian patriarchal control and respectability in order to pursue her passionately chosen calling in the entertainment industry, in which she achieved national success and high public honours. A liberated woman without being a militant feminist, her life story undemonstratively celebrates her fully emancipated lifestyle (including an abortion [Venuti and Hogan 154]) without sacrificing close family bonds with her parents and her daughter (though her erstwhile husband drops out of the picture along with numerous lovers). The unabashed openness with which she presents all this is its own vindication, but further vindication emerges when she discovers, long after her father's death, that he had had a previous, unofficial, family before his marriage to her mother. This does not precipitate any sort of crisis, as it does in some other autobiographies that deal with "the secret lives of fathers" [cf. Porter 2011]. In keeping with her general attitude, Maria not only seeks out and embraces her newly discovered half-sister, now living in northern Italy, but revels in sharing her discovery with her readership [Venuti and Hogan 199-211].

Maria wears her Italianness lightly. There is relatively brief mention of the risk to her father of wartime internment and his actual service, briefly, in the Civilian Alien Corps [Venuti and Hogan 25-8], and even briefer mention of her changing school to avoid racial vilification [Venuti and Hogan 34]. For the rest, being Italian in post-war Sydney appears to involve no more than a keen appreciation of Italian cuisine among other appetising cuisines and occasionally singing in Italian to an appropriate audience. The musical and showbiz circles in which she moved seem commendably immune to ethnic prejudice. Venuti's own lack of prejudice extends so far that she even invites the anti-immigration politician Pauline Hanson, along with very unlike-minded ladies, to play a prominent role in one of the many charitable fundraising events in which Venuti played a part, with an entirely benign outcome [Venuti and Hogan 233].

Her Italian genealogy only belatedly, after both her parents' deaths, arouses Maria's curiosity, and it is at a relatively advanced age, when her own daughter, Bianca, has reached adulthood, and they have both been globetrotting, that the two of them first go and visit Maria's father's family in Messina and the nearby mountain village of Rapano, and then her mother's family in Cairo. The autobiographer admits: "Once again, I deeply regretted the fact that I had never asked my father about his childhood, about what had taken him away from Sicily, about how he felt about that loss" [Venuti and Hogan 267], and is less convincing, except perhaps as expressing a retrospective emotion, in commenting on the family reunion in Sicily: "This was the pinnacle of my trip to Europe. This is what I had longed for over the years" [Venuti and Hogan 268]. Retrospective genealogical curiosity is further teasingly equated with identity after the visit to Egypt: "... I don't want to feel as though the mystery is completely solved – I want to go back and I want to remain involved in the continuing process of discovering my identity" [Venuti and Hogan 278]. *A Whole Load of Front* fairly casually presents ethnicity as a relatively incidental, though positive, component of identity, and of living, and the life narrative ends with Maria achieving Italian citizenship to complement her Australian citizenship.

At least two Italian names figure brilliantly in the annals of that most spectacular of sports, Australian Rules Football. One is Ron Barassi, whose great-great-grandfather, born in 1826, came from Lombardy via the Swiss Canton Ticino to the Victorian goldfields in 1855. Ron's paternal forebears in Australia all married non-Italian women, and Ron grew up fully Australianised, his Italian origins no more than a hazy folk memory [Barassi and McFarline 1995: 16-17]. The most traumatic day in his life came at the age of five, in 1941, when a telegram informed Ron's mother that her husband, who had volunteered for the Australian army, had been killed at the siege of Tobruk, on Libya's Mediterranean coast [Barassi and McFarline 1995: 15, 19]. Ron's co-authored auto/biography remarks that he had gone "to fight an old enemy in an unknown country" [Barassi and McFarline 1995: 16], not mentioning that a new enemy was also involved, the land of the Barassis' origins, Italy. Italianness is not an issue or a theme in what is a straightforwardly informative and celebratory life history of a sporting great. As for Peter Lalor's

400-page *Barassi: The biography* [2010], it is sporting hagiography.

Another Melbourne-based Australian Rules star of Italian lineage whose life story has been written is Stephen Silvagni, whose father, Sergio, had also been an outstanding player of the game. Stephen's auto/biography, co-authored with Tony De Bolfo [2002], is a quilted text, his own snatches of narrative being stitched in among testimonial snippets from a multitude of other people, beginning with his grandparents and their generation reminiscing about their origins in northern Italy around the time of the First World War, and moving through the decades right up to the end of the century. The generational shift from Italianness to Australianness manifests the inevitability of gradualness, but also the snagging with English of the first generation to go through school in Australia, followed by a more accommodating multiculturalism which developed from the 1970s onwards [Silvagni and DeBolfo 2002: 15]. The quilting of many voices, somewhat like Pallotta Chiarolli's *Tapestry: Interweaving lives*, neutralises the individualistic presumptions of auto/biography and projects the individual life as part of a social continuum. (This is hinted at in Stephen's prefatory "Reflections" [Silvagni and De Bolfo 2002: xxvii].)

The success stories of Italian Australians, except in Alfredo Strano's cautionary life of Ezio Luisini, are offered by their authors as models, some implicit, others explicit, of self-fulfilment realised through philanthropy towards the place of origin and the place of adoption, or, in the case of Sarina Russo, through service to society, local and global, recognition and self-recognition intertwining. *Pietas* is the justification of individualism.

Chapter 5

Autoethnography

Ivano Ercole gave to his account of the Catholic Italian Federation of Australia the title *Un'infinità d'esperienze: un'unica storia*. Literally this translates as "an infinity of experiences: one single (hi)story", making a point which fades somewhat in the title actually given to the English version of his book: *A Living History*. Italian Catholics may be a slightly less heterogeneous group than Italians generally, but in either case the presumption of a collective Italian identity is problematical, as evidenced by the proliferation of Italian community organisations in Australia based on the particular point of origin, ranging from the tiny constituencies of the Isole Eolie and the town of Sortino in Sicily, to large regional organisations like the Veneto Club and the Abruzzo association.

Gianfranco Cresciani's study of emigration to Australia from Trieste, *Trieste goes to Australia* [2011], shows how problematical it is to achieve a unified group identity even for a single city and its immediate hinterland. He uses interviews with a large number of individuals to illustrate the range of experiences and reactions involved: first in the painful, albeit hopeful, departure, and then upon first arrival and the endeavour to settle in Australia, as well as in the more or less successful struggles to gain a livelihood or establish a career. And he elicits retrospective judgements about the wisdom or otherwise of that initial decision and varying attitudes to Australia and to Trieste or Italy.

Life writing is here projected through the reverse end of the telescope, subsumed in minimalist quotations from numerous informants or in succinct summaries of the life trajectories of distinguished individuals, many having little bearing on Triestine or Italian identity. Even in such a tightly constructed group identity, individual outcomes prevail.

Nevertheless, "Italy" does exist both as a political entity, a national State, and as a conglomerate of local identities, and virtually, if not quite, all of the written lives studied in this present book express a broad sense of Italian identity and belonging. Moreover, Piero Genovesi explicitly presents the migration history of the Pitruzzellos as part of a national epic of Italian migration, and the title of his translation of Diana Ruzzene Grollo's account of her family's migration history, *Noi gente d'emigrazione* (We emigrants), sounds the same note. From an Australian point of view, immigration from the Italian area is but a part of an even more variegated phenomenon of migration from over a hundred different nations, ranging from England to the Sudan, including Chinese and Irish, Sri Lankans and Colombians. And, in turn, immigration into Australia is part of population movement world-wide.

Perspectives, then, are infinitely variegated, but the present study, pragmatically, takes Italians in Australia as a sufficiently meaningful social grouping, however heterogeneous, and presents their life writing as being, collectively, an illuminating exemplar of the experience of immigrants from another country making their home in Australia and learning to belong. Each life writing text therefore contributes insights into the social history of migration as experienced by the individuals concerned – not only circumstances and events, but also attitudes, interactions and reactions.

Collectively, the texts studied here are a restricted, self-selecting and privileged sample, as not everyone writes her or his autobiography or has his or her life story written by someone else, and not every life that has been written finds its way into print. The writing requires considerable literate skills and sufficient leisure, resources and motivation, and publishing what has been written requires even more of the same. In this respect, Ilaria Serra's survey of Italian American autobiographies is broader than my survey of Italian Australian life writing, in that the former covers mainly unpublished texts preserved in family or public archives, while mine is restricted to published works. On the other hand, this study includes a spectrum ranging from autobiographies to biographies, many of them quite lavishly produced, some of them republished, usually in revised or translated versions. It also extends to the second and later generations. With reservations about their representativeness, however, we can view these texts as works of auto-ethnography or ethnography of the Italian presence in Australia. This is *not* to accept that the writing of Italian Australian lives is to be relegated to the status of oral history and ethnographic documentation, though this may be an important dimension of such texts.

One text which positively invites viewing in this light is Valerio Borghese's *Appunti di un emigrato* [1996], a title which could be translated as "Observations of an emigrant". It is part reflective migrant autobiography and part commentary on Australia as seen through Italian eyes. It thus offers a systematic account of the migration experience both from the personal point of view of the experiential subject and from the point of view of the relatively detached observer.

The author's personality is well fitted to this dual role. A Triestine, Borghese was not part of the well-defined Triestine exodus of the 1950s which we have seen described in Cresciani's *Trieste Goes to Australia*, but a lone clerical worker of limited schooling and largely self-taught, attached to his native town, but impelled to leave it at the age of thirty-five in 1960 by the perceived dearth of prospects in Trieste and glowing reports of life in Australia. He harbours ambitions to be a writer and contributes journalistic pieces, sketches and stories to the Italian press in Australia. Curiously enough, the bulk of these *appunti* were written during Borghese's first ten years in Melbourne, up to 1970, but were not to be published until quarter of a century later, with an updated supplement, and were presented by the publisher, Tom Padula, as an educational handbook making for understanding and friendship between ethnicities, immigrant and Australian-born.

Borghese's is a chatty, buttonholing style, gently humorous and witty, and its autobiographical element is minutely detailed, making the material and human circumstances – housing, neighbours, a great variety of work-places and fellow-workers, the texture of

Australian life in the 1960s – vividly real, while on the other hand the ethnographical element is systematically pursued in brief thematic chapters on Melbourne's urban landscape (non-residential city centre and sleepy characterless suburbs), transport and people. No other Italian Australian life story that I have read gives such an intimate, close-grained portrait of an increasingly multiethnic Australian society, recording interactions between the author and others of varied provenance, Australian-born and immigrants from various parts of Italy and from various European countries (Australia was then still pursuing a "White Australia" policy). Only Marie Alafaci's *Savage Cows and Cabbage Leaves* has some of the same fine-grained rendering of the concrete minutiae of the immigrant's experience of Australian life. Borghese's despondent acceptance of Australia gives a sobering insight into the deep-seated alienation which the immigration experience meant to so many immigrants. Despite a vocation for sociability, Borghese did not join the local Triestine association or any other Italian club, possibly because of problems of time, transport and expense, but he does appear for some time to have joined a "Migrants' Welcome Group" which was set up in response to a letter which he wrote to the Melbourne *Herald*, pleading for friendlier relations between the Australian-born and immigrants [Borghese 1996: 86-91].

All the texts studied in this present volume can in fact be viewed to a greater or lesser extent in an ethnographic light, without being reduced to this flat dimension. Collectively, they map out a paradigm that starts, spatially and chronologically, with the place of origin and leads, through various stages, to settlement in Australia and the observing and writing present.

Liliana Belardinelli's autobiographical *Destination Australia* ends with the author's arrival in Australia, and says nothing about the experience of living as an immigrant in Australia. But, as we have seen, it does offer a highly individual explanation of the circumstances and motives that led an upper middle-class Italian to leave Italy and choose Australia as her destination. All the texts centred on first-generation migrants, and many of those centred on the migrants' children, whether born in Italy or in Australia, record their place of origin and their reasons for emigrating. Some, like Genovesi's account of the Pitruzzellos and Armstrong's account of the de Pieri brothers, Triaca's account of her grandmother Amelia and Baggio's account of his family and Alcorso's autobiography, dwell, either lovingly or with mixed feelings, on the place of origin or, like Adele Bentley, discover it or rediscover it emotionally upon returning home. The brothers B. A. and Joseph N. Santamaria (both born in Melbourne, between the two World wars, of Sicilian parents) in their respective autobiographies are most reticent as regards their place of origin. B.A. (Bob) Santamaria devotes his monumental account entirely to his political and intellectual mission. Dr Joe's lighter work is devoted in part to his mission as a doctor combating the scourge of alcoholism, but mostly to wryly wise and humorous reminiscences. Both write as comfortably established Australians, and only secondarily as carriers of an Italian heritage.

Emigration is always an adventure, as well as in some sense an escape, and some texts dwell more on the one aspect, some on the other. Adventure predominates in the stories of those who migrated before forming families of their own; hard necessity is more to the fore for those already with children, but all working-class immigrants faced hard times, especially prior to the expansion of the Australian economy which took off during the 1950s.

While all the texts here studied are rich sources for social history, several present themselves mainly in that light, dwelling less on subjectivity and individualism. Lucchesi's history of Joe Maffina, discussed in chapter 1, is one such text, and something rather analogous may be said of Robert Pascoe's earlier work on Luigi Grollo, which combines the author's geo-historical scene-setting, from Grollo's Trevisan peasant origins in the Veneto to his roving life of labour in Victoria's construction industry, with translations of the transcripts of the recordings of Grollo's own matter-of-fact and self-effacing account of his experiences and activities from the 1920s on. This traces a paradigm of at first slow, then increasingly rapid upward socio-economic mobility as Grollo evolves from being a labourer to an entrepreneur in his own right on an ever-larger scale. Photographic illustration, of course, complements the documentary account, as in virtually all Italian Australian life narratives.

Domenico Stella's bilingual volume, *Pages of my Life / Pagine della mia vita*, supplements the recollections of Luigi Grollo, going all the way back to the First World War when the author, of peasant family, was growing up right on the Asiago battlefront facing the "unredeemed" territory of Trento. The foot-soldier, as he is soon to become, shows an acute interest in military strategy before taking the reader along with him to Australia and decades of peregrinations across Victorian towns and country areas in pursuit of employment as a labourer and the establishment of a family. Franco Zaccariotto's reminiscences take us jauntily through his experiences as a prisoner of war of the British during the Second World War and his emigration to Australia, to his rise as a building entrepreneur, while Rolando (Ron) D'Aprano's *Le mie due patrie* (My two homelands) (1990) takes him from Ventosa, near Latina in the Agro Pontino, to Melbourne in 1948, aged twenty-one, leading to naturalisation as an Australian and a busy working life including involvement in local politics. Carlo Coen, introducing the volume, characterises D'Aprano's ramshackle opinionated account as "cronaca", a "source" to be read critically, or, we might say, as raw auto-ethnography. D'Aprano himself in his "Prefazione" disclaims any literary or intellectual pretensions: "È uno scritto semplice, di un uomo semplice: uno scritto per gente semplice" ("It's simply written, by a simple man, for simple folk.") D'Aprano's account does, however, encompass a remarkably compendious paradigm of the migrant experience in its manifold episodes and aspects, and displays wisdom in the perspective in which he combines his two homelands [see Kupfersin 1998].

Just as Robert Pascoe records the recollections of Luigi Grollo, in *Nicolina's Story: A woman of the land* (2002), D. A. Davies records those of La Contadina Nicolina (Nicolina the Peasant Woman), an industrious outdoor countrywoman born in Calabria in 1930 into a model hard-working farming family, who sets up another such in a succession of farms around Swan Hill in Victoria, to which she migrated in 1948, until her family's educational aspirations led them to move to Melbourne in 1970, where they ran a milk bar. Difficulties with English seem to present no serious impediment, either during the early stages of settlement or in the course of the children's schooling. A tantalisingly casual remark hints at the ancestral Italian peasant tradition: "It was the winter of 1967. Our vegetable land in Swan Hill was resting until the next season and the position of the moon was right to plant the new crops" [La Contadina Nicolina 103]. Vitality and cheerfulness are the keynote of Nicolina and her family, as with Emma Ciccotosto, and are not dimmed even by the fact that a daughter, Grace, was born with a hole in her heart. Not expected to survive infancy, Grace had a life of love and joy until the age of eighteen.

Martino's Story is in some sort the converse of *Nicolina's Story* – the life of a man of the land, Martino Bruno, from Nocera Inferiore, near Naples, written by an Anglo-Australian woman, Lyn Chatham. She is no self-effacing scribe, but interacts with her lively octogenarian subject and relays the give-and-take of her interviews with him, creating a rapport with him easily shared by the Australian reader. Writing and reading the life thus becomes an ongoing lived experience in itself, comparable, at a distance, with Helen Garner's interacting as an Anglo-Australian with Joe Cinque's bereaved parents. Martino's life story is not much more eventful or remarkable than Nicolina's, though he has been in the war in Libya and a prisoner-of-war in Egypt, India and finally Australia, where he is taken into farm service in western Victoria by a family with whom a strong friendship develops and which leads to his return to Australia from Italy after the war's end. Lyn Chatham's engaging style of interviewing and reportage draws out of Martino a wealth of reminiscences many of which may seem trivial but which capture the texture, the tone, and the humour-tinged drama of the life of this family man who devoted himself wholeheartedly to becoming Australian and who earned the warm appreciation of his rural community of Winchelsea and environs, and a far-flung reputation as a market gardener.

Giovanni Sgrò's *Australia per forza e per amore* (1995), published in his native Calabria, also has the virtue of simplicity and, like D'Aprano's life story, a political bent, but combines these with considerable impact, beginning with the title which translates as "Australia willy-nilly, and with love," referring to the fact that at age twenty-one in 1952 the boisterous Giovanni was shipped off to Australia against his will by his father, but then grew to love the place and married a characterful girl of Scottish Protestant background, who translated his autobiography with the less provocative title *Mediterranean Son: Memoirs of a Calabrian migrant* (2000). His account includes the turmoil in the Bonegilla immigrant holding centre (previously an Army camp) in 1952, then Sgrò's adapting to life in the country around Cobram in Victoria without any knowledge of English, then his employment in the house-painting and bricklaying trade in Melbourne and his involvement in the grass-roots Italian immigrant welfare organisation FILEF (Federazione Italiana Lavoratori Emigrati e Famiglie) and in the Australian Labor Party. This saw him rise to a prominent position in the Victorian Parliament, where he made history by delivering his maiden speech partly in Italian, to drive home to the Parliament the hardship suffered by immigrants when faced by a strange language. He claims that this was the first time a language other than English had been used in the parliament of any English-speaking country anywhere in the world [Sgrò 2000: 79].

The globetrotting Franco Lugarini's *Mio padre mi chiamava zingaro* (My father used to call me a gypsy) more matter-of-factly, but with quiet satisfaction, mentions his political involvement in Melbourne, as well as his success as a fashionable ladies' hair stylist, after having described his youthful experiences in wartime Lazio.

There are also collections of shorter accounts of the migration experience of Italians in Australia which are straightforwardly and interestingly auto-ethnographical in character. One such is Morag Loh's 1980 collection *With Courage in their Cases: The experiences of thirty-five Italian immigrant workers and their families in Australia*, an early contribution to the field. Such auto-ethnographic writing is taken up again much later in the Yarra Valley Italian Cultural Group's 2009 *Dreams from a Suitcase (Sogni dalla valigia): Recollections of Italian settlers in the Yarra Valley*, in which the telling of life stories is presented as "good therapy for good health" for a now aging Italian immigrant population [Yarra Valley vii].

Such collections of brief lives do indeed offer a dialectic of heterogeneity within community, and assume a variety of configurations.

The Melbourne Community of the Asiago Highlands (*Comunità Montana*), for instance, has collected the brief life stories, none of them more than three pages in length, of a good two hundred individuals who came to Victoria from that small area of the Veneto. The book's title describes them as oral histories, and the stories exhibit quite a lot of individual, and even idiosyncratic, anecdotage and detail, in quite characterful writing, although many of the accounts are couched in the third person [Comunità Montana 7 Comuni di Melbourne, 2010)].

The volume compiled by Francesco and Morwenna Arcidiacono [2009] does things the other way round: it includes immigrants from all over Italy who settled in a small highland area of south Queensland, the so-called Granite Belt, centred around Stanthorpe. These are "family histories", but have very similar characteristics to the Asiago autobiographies. Both these handsomely produced and illustrated volumes open with panoramic histories – of the place of origin in the case of Asiago, and of the place of settlement in that of Stanthorpe.

Pino Bosi's bilingual volume, *L'emigrante ignoto / The Unknown Migrant* [2001], admirably projects the double belonging of some seventy Italians who made their homes in Victoria. The English and Italian accounts of each are free versions of one another, rather than translations, and Bosi's English is as lively and idiomatic as his Italian. Some of the seventy are indeed relatively "unknown" migrants, and, though few of the life stories are more than five or six pages in length, quite a circumstantial and varied overall picture of Victoria's Italian community emerges, with plenty of attention to the hardships endured. Half a dozen entries tell the stories of Italians who went back to Italy, most of them discovering that they had become quite Australian. Some life histories are told mainly by the subjects themselves, while in the cases of people whom Bosi knew well, a fascinating rapport is woven into his discourse, capturing the exhilarating timbre of Italian sociability in Australia. Bosi, as well as being a writer and journalist, is also an historian in his own right, a researcher and a populariser, specialising in the history of settlement in Australia and well versed both in Italian and in British history. He thus gives his miniature life histories a rich web of geo-historical and cultural reference, so that the volume as a whole builds up to a composite portrait of Australia and of Italy and of the Italians in relation to Australia.

The book that comes closest to the "unknown migrant" is Tony De Bolfo's remarkable *In Search of Kings* [2002]. De Bolfo has researched the lives of all of the one hundred and ten passengers from many different parts of Italy that disembarked in Melbourne from the liner *Re d'Italia* on Thursday, 24 November 1927. Uniquely, a complete cohort of immigrants thus comes under scrutiny, not as a coldly dispassionate study, but with a warm sense of the courage involved in facing such radical dislocation. The vast majority of this cohort consisted of adult males – one hundred and two – and of these an overwhelming majority again were described as farm labourers. It has not been my business in this present volume to discuss abbreviated life histories drawn predominantly from oral or comparable testimony provided by the descendants, but life writing of this sort must be kept in mind to counterbalance the selective and individualistically privileged full-length biographies and autobiographies that are discussed here. As might be expected, the hardships and setbacks encountered by these labourers, especially arriving as they did on the very brink of the Great Depression, receive greater prominence in these short accounts, though generally with an emphasis on endurance and achievement. In these shorter accounts the family emerges overwhelmingly as the most important life-determining factor, even more so than in the full-length life histories, and not merely because De Bolfo's investigations necessarily took him to descendants and relatives of those 1927 arrivals.

Vincent Moleta's self-effacing *Family Business: An Italian-New Zealand story* [2012] is a study of the place of origin – Sicily's Aeolian Islands – and of several generations of the Barnao family, some of whose members left there around the turn of the nineteenth century for the very different ambience of New Zealand. It draws on historical material and documents as well as family records and stories, especially those of the author's maternal grandfather, and is a classic tale of enterprise, adaptability and perseverance.

Some autobiographically and auto-ethnographically oriented works may, like the Yarra Valley collection, be presumed to have had a more immediate therapeutic and sustaining effect on others as well as on their authors in the earlier years of the impact of the migration event. The title of Valeria Gorlei Aliani's *Le mie avventure in Australia* [1989], though gently jocular, strikes a significant note which tends to be missed by some in the host country who stereotype many immigrants as pathetic and desperate refugees from hopeless economic conditions in the country of origin. Aliani had certainly suffered devastating blows: a business collapse brought about the loss of the family's factory and house in Viareggio on the Tuscan coast and the death through heart failure of Valeria's husband, giving her no alternative but to leave her mother and aunt in a retirement home and seek a livelihood in Melbourne with her two young daughters, having reached the age of forty without any previous employment experience. Remarkable as is the sheer fact of a single mother of two migrating to the other side of the world with little knowledge of English, it is hardly more remarkable than the equanimity and humour with which the trials and challenges and setbacks, large and small, as well as the acts of kindness and the achievements, are recounted, as the little family gradually establishes itself in suburban Melbourne and adapts to Australian ways without losing its Italian character, to the extent that Aliani publishes the entertaining and uplifting tale of her own experiences in Italian, with illustrations and technical inputs by her growing daughters. This is auto-ethnography looking in on itself.

Similarly engaging are Alessandro Faini's sketches of middle-class life in the Melbourne suburbs and the surrounding countryside, *Quadretti di un italiano in Australia* (1984), in which the narrator humorously tracks the gradual adaptation of the immigrant to the quirks of Australian living, to the point at which he feels estranged from life in Italy.

The mutually supportive auto-ethnographic impulse continues into the second generation of the mass migration from Italy of the

1950s and 1960s. The title of the 1993 collective volume *Growing up Italian in Australia: Eleven young Australian women talk about their childhood* declares it to be a work of auto-ethnography – the self-description of a reasonably well-defined social group: second generation Italian Australian women. That it is a selective sample of that group is clear from the fact that all write faultless English. Several pieces are straightforwardly and perceptively auto-ethnographical. Collectively, they address a considerable range of experiences and situations in Australian suburbia towards the end of the twentieth century. The first piece, "The memories file" by Joanne Travaglia [*Growing up Italian* 1-18], offers reflections about the immigrant experience and group identity: "The more you argue against stereotyping, the more you run across common experiences and concerns. … We meet people all the time who have had similar experiences …" [*Growing up Italian* 16]. And Travaglia comments on generational drift away from Italian origins: "Somehow the rewards never make up for the losses" [*Growing up Italian* 17]. These losses are implicitly addressed in the Italo-Australian Youth Association's 2002 volume *Doppia identità. I giovani: conoscerli per capirli: Stories by young Italo-Australians*. The Italian part of this title may be translated as "Dual identity: Getting to know today's youth so as to understand them." The stories themselves are in English, but focus on the sense and varying degrees of Italian belonging on the part of the authors.

Zoë Boccabella's *Mezza Italiana* (Half Italian) [2011] brings us close to a provisional conclusion. A third-generation Italian Australian born of an Anglo-Australian mother, Zoë throughout her childhood and well into adulthood has done her best to disavow and suppress the Italian peasant component of her identity and has married an Anglo-Australian husband, showing no interest in her grandfather's ancestral line rooted in Fossa dei Marsi in the Abruzzo and her grandmother's from Calabria. Her book, however, opens and closes with a Prologue and an Epilogue foregrounding the earthquake that devastated the Abruzzo region on 6 April 2009, including the Boccabella ancestral home. The first chapter, "Antique linens", focuses on her Calabrian *nonna*, whom the young Zoë insists on addressing by the Anglo-Australian title Nanna Francesca, and who regularly presents her with traditional Italian bed-linen items for her bridal trousseau or glory-box – items which the young Zoë receives with impatient disinterest.

The discourse of *Mezza Italiana* unfolds as an interweaving of narrative, reminiscence and reflection on Zoë's initially grudging rediscovery of her Italian, especially Abruzzese, heritage, beginning with a reluctant but obligatory first visit to Fossa with her much more enthusiastically Italophile (but non-Italian) husband, Roger. The couple are overwhelmed by the warmth of family feeling, the spectacular landscape of the Abruzzo, its historic aura, its rich material culture – domestic architecture, household objects, and above all, food.

The Italian culinary heritage is well established, even in academic discourse, as a strategic identity marker and value category for people of Italian ancestry, and *Mezza Italiana*, like Emma Ciccotosto's *A Recipe for Life* and Judith Armstrong's biography of the de Pieri brothers, sports some regional Italian recipes. There is a remarkable similarity between *Mezza Italiana* and another book that appeared in the same year, Angela Di Sciascio's *Finding Valentino: Four seasons in my father's Italy*. The author is also, like Boccabella, the descendant of a peasant farmer from the Abruzzo (in this case, her father) and an Anglo-Australian mother. She, too, had in her youth tried to expunge the Italian component of her identity, but sought to reclaim it at a maturer age, spending a year in Italy, mostly in her father's native village, but also touring other parts of Italy. The book is predicated on recovering her father's lost past as he is gradually succumbing to Alzheimer's disease. Di Sciascio does this by experiencing the material conditions of Abruzzese peasant subsistence agriculture, revolving overwhelmingly around the production, preparation and consumption of food, with local recipes profusely interspersed in the narrative. The "recipe for life" paradigm has established itself as a niche micro-genre within Italian Australian life writing, no doubt powered in considerable measure by tele-chef programs, supplemented by genealogically inspired travelogues.

In Boccabella's *Mezza Italiana*, too, there is an expanding travelogue, exploring the Abruzzo region and Calabria and Italy generally, varying from the homely to the touristy, with interludes in Zoë and Roger's home town of Brisbane. Personalities abound, the dominant one being that of Zoë's charismatic, larger-than-life grandfather Anni (Annibale). Zoë ends up by confessing: "I did not plan to write of something so personal I had hidden for so long, but my hand seemed guided, perhaps by my ancestors" [Boccabella 345]. The at first involuntary exploring of her family heritage has changed her sense of self but, interestingly, her non-Italian husband Roger embraces an Italian identity even more decisively than she does.

This third-generation Italian Australian, and her husband, both of them university graduates and high school teachers, are well equipped for this expansion of self, and Zoë as author aligns herself in effect with those who have theorised a "third space" of in-betweenness or hybrid identity:

> I did not realise until I travelled that the migrants had become a different race to the natives of the birth countries they left behind. This was not a race belonging to any particular country or continent: it was the race of what I would term "migrancy". [363]

And:

> Whether I am standing in Fossa or Beutelsbach, Lincoln or Brisbane, I sense all those that have been before me, who are immortal because their blood continues to flow through my veins, through my heart. I hope future descendants will have the freedom to be proud of their heritage from an early age and do not spend decades surrendering part of themselves as I did. Forsaking migrant heritage because of racism or other pressures means denying the existence of people who worked hard and made sacrifices. There is an honour in remembering. [364]

The celebratory ethnographic apotheosis of Italian Australian living comes with Giulia Giuffrè's *Primavera or, The Time of Your Life* [2011], whose 700 engagingly light-hearted pages chime in with the Australian vogue for things Italian around the turn of the millennium. The Italian inflexion is very much taken for granted and under-emphasised, and the book is an acute and whimsical wisdom miscellany of family reminiscences, reflections, *divertissements* spanning three generations over more than half a century, penned by a high-flying literary academic in an unpretentious buttonholing style, the writer effacing herself in a third-person Giulia. Ethnic grievances are nowhere to be seen as the canonical progression from the Italian peasant self-sufficiency of the maternal grandparents to marriage to a non-Italian husband and Australian upper middle-class affluence almost imperceptibly evolves in a discursive structure that embeds micro-narratives in a tidal flow that dissembles its own macro-narrative forward movement through time, embodying the gradualness of ethnological change with a maximum of domestic intimacy conveyed through conversational exchanges within the family, so that the reader shares or re-lives the experience, and Italian Australia enters the mainstream at the level of everyday ordinariness and effervescence.

Rebecca Huntley's *The Italian Girl* [2012] is a parting glance at a century of Italian life in North Queensland, focusing on the author's Ballini family of origin, in the Innisfail area, in the wake of her grandmother's passing. The book chronicles the author's quest through the first decade of the twenty-first century to reconstruct the life-experience of previous generations of Italian Australians in the sugarcane area by dint of eliciting the memories of her older surviving relatives and scouring localities and archives, to find that the Italian identity component has been bred out, as is symbolically attested by the author's own change of surname and by the few dubious snippets of Italian language that enter her text.

Chapter 6

Fosco Antonio's *My Reality*

Beyond autobiography?

Fosco Antonio's *My Reality* is an extraordinary, perhaps a scandalous, text, and is much more than an autobiography. If it is, in one important dimension, immigrant autobiography, it is also, in an even more commanding dimension, an enactment of a whole society's entrapment in the transition from one civilisational configuration to another.

My Reality jumps out of several of the conventions of writing and publishing, as it jumps out of any familiar or straightforward mode of autobiography. It is textually unstable, having appeared in two editions, with considerable textual differences, the first self-published by the author in a plain white cover in 2003 and the second by Total Cardboard in 2007, with a dazzlingly illustrated cover showing a dark and stormy watery landscape. The author's name is given as Fosco Antonio, but the book is copyrighted under the name of Fosco Ruzzene. It is therefore not so much a pseudonymous as a pseudo-pseudonymous autobiography. The narrator identifies himself simply by the first person singular pronoun throughout, except for certain narrative sequences that are conducted impersonally. On a couple of occasions he makes problematical play with his first name which translates roughly as "murky" or "dim" [28, 170; 29, 143].[40]

---

40 In referring to *My Reality*, where appropriate I show the page number in the 2003 edition first, followed by that in the 2007 edition. Quotations, unless otherwise indicated, are from the 2003 edition, and may differ or disappear in the 2007 edition. However, individual copies of the 2003 edition vary in typeface, composition, font size and pagination, therefore page references given here to my copy might not apply exactly to other copies.

The first edition is replete with typographical and orthographical irregularities, including, for instance, repeated mentions of someone called "Hilter" and of the "Scared Heart" as an object of Catholic devotion, and is couched in splintered syntax rather than orchestrated sentences. The typographical irregularities are mostly eliminated from the second edition, and sentence structures are made more connected and fluent, but errors and oddities of language are by no means absent. Are we dealing with a semi-literate writer? Or with a writer who doesn't care about correctness? Or with a rebel against the rules of language? Or all three at once?

Both editions of *My Reality*, the first more markedly than the second, yoke together and intertwine a variety of different discourses: episodes of the migration of a peasant family from the rural Veneto to suburban Melbourne in the mid 1950s and of the narrator's subsequent life-experiences through the education system and in Melbourne society; sporting sagas about cricket and Australian football, in which the narrator plays no part except as a spectator and amateur commentator; the narrator's imaginary encounters with Australians from the historical past; his stocktaking of the history of Christianity and of Europe, culminating in the "twentieth century European Death Orgies" and "the Great Walk-Out" in the 1960s from Christian belief, in Europe and other parts of the Western world, signally including Australia; his critique of Australian modernity and of many of its personalities, and his interrogation of sanctity and sexuality within the Western tradition in his quest for a loving humanity; sequences about the Redneck and about the Prime Minister, Mundy, who ends up being liquidated by the Media Patriarch. The earlier version has an impersonally narrated "Triumph March of Historical Grandeur" through Melbourne's central Collins Street, featuring Adolf, Big Julius, Bonaparte, Cleo, Marilyn, Elvis, a large brown horse ("the Greatest Australian", i.e., the unbeatable racehorse, Phar Lap), Albert, and, finally, Paul (the apostle) [2003: 38-52].

A mixture of autobiography, social commentary, spiritual enquiry, fantasy and fiction, *My Reality*, in either version, defies straightforward definition, as the paratexts of the two editions emphasise. The second edition carries the dedication "For Jesus, John Lennon and Germaine Greer". The first edition is subtitled "Autopsy of a soul in crisis" and is prefaced by an eighteen-line free-verse poem about "the sojourners of the night", casting a metaphysical light on the text that is to follow, while the back cover sports a "what they say" blurb consisting of fourteen one-liners by authorities who had pre-deceased the book's publication, including Nietzche [*sic*] ("this book gives me hope"), Jesus ("he misunderstands me"), Phar Lap ("an absolute horse laugh"). The front cover of the first edition carries the legend "This is not a political Manifesto. This is not Literature. This is table top dancing." Both the negatives and the affirmative are quizzical, as the book certainly carries a political charge and also defies the literary, while the table top dancer is developed as a symbolic motif identified with the anguished exhibitionism of the autobiographical "I" [92, 93, 132; 69, 70, 109].

Clearly, the author is a joker, even more so in the 2003 edition than in the 2007 one, so that we are bound to ask how seriously we are to take him, as well as what to make of *My Reality* as an autobiography – a life writing text – and how to deal with the disparities between the two editions. Also, since *My Reality* is so much more than a conventional autobiography because, as its title implies, self and world, subjectivity and objectivity, are intimately fused, another question we are bound to ask, if we accord this dual text full seriousness, is what light it throws on the scope of life writing and, in particular, of course, of autobiography.

Alone, among the fifty or sixty Italian Australian life narratives that I have read, *My Reality* recalls the personal experience of discovering the appalling historical injustice perpetrated against Aboriginal Australians [2003: 121-3; 2007: 97-100] (though the Italian Australian poet, Lino Concas, gives it full recognition in his poetic *oeuvre*). Striking as this is in itself, what is even more striking is the way this discovery is re-enacted in terms of the personal experience and shock, first, of the young Fosco's elder sister, then a school-girl, and subsequently of their entire family, as an encounter with a hitherto suppressed Australian reality which they experience not merely as immigrants, but as Australians, as evolving members of Australian society, and which, indeed, is presented as their effective introduction to engagement with civic awareness, participation and responsibility more generally. "She [Fosco's sister] had a choice. Reject her newly given knowledge to preserve a moral worldview. Or accept that the world is not moral" [2003: 121; 2007: 98]. The processes of confronting this issue in personal, family, group and societal terms, including the media interface, are canvassed by Antonio in three richly articulated pages.

The Aboriginal theme is picked up on two further occasions, first when Fosco acknowledges learning from a Koori woman of the age-old significance of the local rubbish tip: "She told me that in finding my way to the tip, I had found my connection to the authentic Australian Story. The woman had profound knowledge of the wounds in the Australian psyche" [85; 61]. And then in the final chapter, when Fosco updates the deceased Manning Clark on the latest political developments regarding the status of Aborigines [250-1; 206].

To a much greater degree, then, than any other Italian Australian written life narrative, Fosco Antonio's *My Reality* is an engagement with Australia, a dramatic portrait or a radiography of a society, a projection which is dynamic and mobile and problematical, rather than monumental and static. It is much more, indeed quite other, than a chronicle of a single person's experiences and a construction of an individual's longitudinal identity. The engagement with Australia clearly explains the sporting divagations and Fosco's arresting imaginary encounter with Australia's first saint, Mary McKillop, in the Old Melbourne Gaol [159-66; 134-8], and his other, equally arresting, imaginary encounter with Henry (Lawson), the foundational storyteller of the Australian bush, and the inspirational historian, Manning (Clark), in the former gold-mining settlement of Walhalla which gives its name to the book's brief concluding chapter. It also explains the fictitious Mundy narrative which is spliced in among the book's other narrative and non-narrative components for almost its entire length, and in which Fosco does not figure among the *dramatis personae*.

Opening and origin

The main text opens dramatically and strategically with the words "We had arrived!", which mark it clearly as an immigration narrative. The pregnancy of the moment is captured in its suspensefulness:

> We were clinging to the side railing of the ship, anchored at Station Pier. We were waiting to disembark. We were pondering the people standing on the pier. Their psyche was stationary. Ours was in movement. We were still on a journey. It was autumn, back in the 50's.
>
> I was the second youngest, aged five. I was impatient. I sensed something had already started. Maybe the football? Whatever it was we were late.
>
> Our journey was about to end. Something new was about to begin. We did not know what. We were ignorant. We were wogs. We were desperate. And we were here. [5; 5]

As well as a moment, a self-characterising idiom or idiolect is also established, an idiosyncratic English – an Australian English, but with a difference: there is the staccato syntax; there is the distinctive terminology ("pondering the people", "Their psyche was stationary"); there are the jumps outside the temporal frame ("Maybe the football?", "We were wogs"). Such idiosyncrasies are more marked in the 2003 than in the 2007 edition, but in both versions the existential drama of the moment is established by this peculiar use of language.

And, a couple of lines on, narrative chronology is disrupted, zooming instantaneously into a remote past, forwards again to the moment of writing, and then back again to the narrator's peasant childhood in northern Italy:

> My soul is anchored in the millenniums of peasant existence. Yet within me there is brokenness. There is disconnection. A contradiction. My psyche is over seventy generations deep in peasantry. Yet my intellect was told a different story-telling, recited in an alien language.
>
> My communal working life began in the traditional way of the peasant, in the stable, holding the tail of the family cow, while my brother milked. [5; 5]

This freedom with time and space and mode of discourse characterises the entire book. Autobiographical episodes from early childhood to the narrator's present are strung out throughout the book, but do not make a connected chronological sequence: the linear chronology of individual life is not a privileged signifier in *My Reality*; the self is not developed as a coherent entity, but as a cluster or mish-mash of problems. If this is autobiography modelled on the *Bildungsroman*, it is a highly original *Bildungsroman* indeed. The seven chapters that constitute the book have a (barely definable) forward movement in trans-historical terms and in terms of the discourse of the psyche, and all except the last are variously subdivided by time of day (Dawn, Morning, Noon, Afternoon, Evening, Midnight), without any obvious rationale. The 2007 edition labels each chapter with the days of the week, beginning with Monday. This seems to emphasise existential enclosure in recurrent time, in the repetitive routines of daily and weekly living which underlie the vagaries or convulsions of history.

The first chapter is titled "Holding the Cow's Tail", highlighting the difference between Australia and the peasant Italy from which Fosco's family has come. Its first section, "Morning", elaborates on the significance of the cow and of holding the cow's tail in the peasant ideology and the peasant economy, and also dwells on the peasants' subjection to the feudal power of the *Conte*, the Count or country squire, and to the religious control of the *prati* (more correctly, *prete*), the priest. The rebel against this subjection is the *matto*, the half-naked madman of Fosco's childhood memory, whom he saw running down the village street waving an axe with which he meant to kill the Count. The reminiscing Fosco sees a "primal" gender politics in the village women's disarming and restraining of the madman and their clothing of his nakedness: the women prevent the liberating act, and perpetuate their own subjection. Fosco avows: "I experience deep, primal 'urges' to run semi-naked to Sydney North Shore with an axe. I feel a deep sense of wholeness with il 'matto' [*sic*], with his mission. To complete that which he began" [7; 7-8]. This is a rogue autobiography that readily flaunts a rogue autobiographical

"I". Sydney North Shore stands, in *My Reality*, as the home of the media barons.

But this is immediately followed by the final sub-section of the "Morning" section of this first chapter, and the beginning of the next section, "Afternoon". These jointly address societal mayhem of vastly greater proportions than a lone axe-wielding lunatic: "Spiritually, the journey to Australia began in the winter of 1943, at the Russian Front …" [8; 8]. Fosco's father, drafted into the Italian army, "passed personal judgement on European history. A judgement passed in his soul. He concluded that the European Story was invalid." This determines his departure and that of his family for Australia [9; 10].

Selective quotation cannot adequately represent the twists and turns of Fosco's writing. Occasional samples will have to serve. Here is one such, following fairly close on Fosco's report of his father's decision:

> My enemies say all this is illusion! And that I show symptoms of victim self-absorption and self-hate.
>
> I do have enemies. I hear them. I hear their voices. they speak to me. when I am alone in my room. my room is courageous. my room is art. my room expresses my inner reality … wallpaper is peeling … the air is foul … flaws glare at me … my mirror is covered. my self-image terrifies me. my window is locked. covered. no light is allowed to enter.
>
> I sleep fully clothed … my psyche is on full alert. yet there is no threat. but there is the more threatening threat of a threat. I search for meaning in my mind. but find only runaway thoughts. [punctuation as in 2003 edition] [9; 10]

These internalised enemies and their voices recur in various guises and contexts throughout the book, which is by turns preposterous and unnerving. The discourse shifts from points of family history, situated in a historical time before the narrator's birth, to the narrator's present self at the time of writing which, if the reader is to judge by the date of publication, would give him an age of around fifty. In one swoop, we have been taken from the war-torn steppes of Russia to a squalid room presumably somewhere in Melbourne, and in less than a page further on we are into the insomniac night of the fictive career politician called Mundy and then of the media Patriarch, in Sydney. Connections are thus incessantly and busily set up between things, some of which have a close and clear relationship with one another while others would seem to have none, until it appears that the psyche of the individual, Fosco, and of other individuals, some of whom he encounters in person, some in imagination, and some not at all, is part – a recalcitrant part – of the collective psyche of a whole society, Australia, both the individual psyche and the collective being unstable, contradictory. The connections between all these psychic states and the variegated textual strands and slabs that carry them thus act like the synapses of the brain and, within a few opening pages, they take us into the thick of the psychic morass which is Fosco's, or the world's, "reality".

Perspectives

After the short opening chapter, the second is titled "History", and opens with the "brokenness" sensed as the narrator's family depart from Italy to emigrate to Australia, and felt particularly by his mother [16; 16]. This is followed by a programmatic introduction or manifesto, full of ironic (or disingenuous) disclaimers and avowals:

> But this is no bleeding heart "wog" story. This is no wog-Lit! This is no wank essay for the wank literati. This is no search for cultural identity. This is not the Great Australian Novel. Nor am I going Confessional.
>
> …
>
> I will perform live. I will give my troubles the full authority of the "I" voice. There will be no schizophrenic separation. I warn readers they will be left vulnerable. Sometimes I may well lose control of my narration. For those who cannot go the journey I offer counsel. Try Harry Potter.
>
> …

I am also to be in a cultural "place and time". To be immersed in the Story of a people. So here I am in the Great Australian Story. I am to enter the womb of the psyche of Nation. Already I see great troubles.

…

Am I a crack-pot? Who gives me authority to speak? … Well, I will answer this right here! I "speak" because I've "been there". I've walked the water's edge. I have heard the silent howl of humanity. [16-17; 16-17]

Clearly, "I" is a conscious performer, and has warned the reader that this is no simple-minded, supposedly transparent, transcript of a life. Disconcertingly, the immediately following segment of his text, after mentioning his absorption in a shop-lifted copy of Manning Clark's *Short History of Australia*, crosses over to a narrative account of a short journey he makes in a Melbourne tram, during which he becomes aware of two large incongruous figures, one male and one female, who suddenly reveal themselves to be ticket-inspectors [17-20; 18-20].

The melodrama and bathos of this episode is overwhelming in its pettiness. This is first of all due to the narrative finesse with which the narrator reads the interconnected behavioural codes of body language, eye movements, and what he consistently calls "street theatre": a *bravura* which he displays in all comparable sequences throughout the book. But it also suggests the media-induced pettiness of life as lived by the *popolo bue*, the oxen-like dumb herd which the narrator is shortly to discuss, and of life as experienced by the narrator himself, who is immersed in that society. It is a banal, but telling instance of the weakest in society being victimised, as the "Underclass" passenger is caught without a ticket. The episode is a first, rock-bottom version of "the Great Australian Story", which will gradually evolve in a slowly ascending spiral in a series of other encounters, some of them imaginary, in the course of the book. Interestingly, the autobiographical subject, the Fosco who uses the "I" voice, and who is distracted by the incongruous couple on the tram from his pondering over the uncertainty principle, is only an observer, not an actor, in this scene, but nevertheless his account of it concretises his persona for the reader. Portraying the other can be a way of portraying the self.

But Fosco, immediately following this sequence, takes matters to preposterous extremes in his diatribe first against "the Aussie Bloke", and then against the Greek male. The former, Fosco writes, "claims the King Penis throne in the great Australian story", and he elaborates at some length on his historic crimes, with ludicrous genetic profiling. For the Greek male he professes utter contempt and detestation, either having internalised the Aussie Bloke's contempt for wogs, or slyly parodying it and presenting a self-caricature [20-3; 21-3].

Impersonal history predominates in the rest of the chapter, with intermittent first-person autobiographical flashes. The Catholic Church is singled out for demolition, first with a one-page scene of a funeral mass in the cathedral, attended by all the diocesan clergy, for one of their number who has turned out to be a paedophile, and, in effect, for the death of the church institution itself [26; 26-7]. This is followed by a sardonic primer on Church governance and ecclesiastical career management [27-8; 27-8] and leads to Fosco's assertion about "the Great Walk Out" from Christian belief during the 1960s [29; 30] and, in the following chapter ("Oh God"), an account of his schoolday experience of sadistically imposed Catholicism [57-61; 39-47]. From this point on, various narrative threads pursue Fosco's key learning or questing experiences, mostly outside the education system. On the way there, Fosco engages his dispute with feminism, which looms large as a personal problem for him throughout the rest of the book [33-8; 33-6], and presents his trans-historical fantasy, or "night vision of history", the "Triumph March of Historical Grandeur" (omitted from the 2007 edition) [2003: 38-52]. The book now takes on the character of a quest for meaning and value, which have been voided by the European Death Orgies and the Great Walk Out from institutional Christianity.

Ethnic identity?

So intricately interwoven are the multifarious strands that make up the text of *My Reality* that separating them out is a desperately artificial and probably arbitrary exercise. Contradictions and denials within the text complicate the task still further, but might be subsumed and transcended in Fosco's gradual progression towards sharing the brokenness of others and placing his own brokenness within the more general one, until he arrives at the "being together" which closes the book.

From this perspective, the ethnic brokenness of the migrant child who leaves one (peasant) subaltern culture (to use the Gramscian term) for another ethnically subaltern culture whose language and attitudes are alien and incomprehensible is but a part of an all-embracing subjection to a system of mind-control which itself has moved on, in Antonio's analysis, from that of the Church, exercised through the pulpit, through State propaganda as perfected by Goebbels, especially through radio, to the present omnipotence of the electronic media "Patriarchs", with a television in every bedroom. Thus the traumatic transition from a peasant culture mediated through a dialect of Italian is compounded by the anthropological transformation into what Guy Debord and the Situationists of the 1960s theorised as "the society of the spectacle", where reality is manipulated into media image. Fosco Antonio not only articulates this argument pervasively in the course of his book, but also projects it in psycho-narrative form in the account of the career politician and Prime Minister, Mundy, and his political annihilation by the Patriarch – a story which otherwise would appear to have little to do with the life-experience of Fosco himself.

The link between this focus on mind-control and Fosco's Italian peasant ethnic background is his childhood memory of the village *matto* who wants to take an axe to the local wielder of mind-control, *il Conte*, and Fosco's own declared impulse to do the same on Sydney's North Shore, home of the Media Patriarch [7; 7-8]. The link here between "Italianness" and "Australianness" seems to be one of continuity rather than discontinuity. This would bear out Fosco's disclaimer: "This is no bleeding heart 'wog' story … This is no search for cultural identity" [16/16]. Yet the first edition goes on to assert the contrary: "Here I am in the Great Australian Story. I am to enter the womb of the psyche of Nation" [17; omitted in the 2007 edition]. The oscillation and the rupture within the psyche caused by being interpellated by two different systems of meaning and value – apparently ethnic, but essentially systemic – are one of the structuring elements of *My Reality*.

The narrative strand that relates the arrival in Melbourne of Fosco's family in fact dwells consistently on the ethnic – or perhaps, more precisely, the anthropological – divide, the newcomers' ignorance of what awaits them [5; 5], their "brokenness" [16-17; 16-17], the key moment before stepping on Australian soil: "We were still Italians. We had not yet become migrants," and then encountering a new kind of human being in the person of the customs official [25-6; 25-6]. The landing completed, Fosco's Melbourne-based Italian uncle strikes him by his very Australian disregard for officialdom, and Fosco's "old" (i.e., Anglo-)Australian aunt also impresses him by her difference, her devil-may-care irreverence for authority, particularly expressed in her boisterous laughter [53; 37], a motif which is subsequently expanded upon [66; 48] and further developed in contrast with Fosco's mother [75; 54-5] in explicitly ethnic terms.

Fosco reflects on the growing children's language shift:

> A small breaking was happening. We were leaving our parents. Our departure was not generational change. Gradually English became the spoken language among ourselves. Only when speaking to our parents would we return to the dialect of our beginnings.
>
> Our parents had chosen migration. A human event with breaking at its core. They could not offer us continuity of tradition. Migration is a one generation experience [75-6; 55].

English remains subtly alien, affecting Fosco's writing style:

> I cannot spell. My grammar is hopeless. More importantly, I do not possess the rhythm of the English language. I can never have this possession. Language has its rhythm written in the psyche of its culture. Which can only be learnt from one's parents. Together with their culture's pain. Formal institutions do not enter this scared space.
>
> The Sisters had taught me to speak English. But not

communicate. Speaking expresses the mind. Communication expresses the psyche.

["scared" appears thus in both editions] [111; 90]

On the other hand, standard Italian, as opposed to the peasant
Venetian dialect spoken in the family, is even more alien, and is
embodied in the reviled "Royal Personage" visiting from Italy, who
looks down on the benighted emigrant [69; 50].

This class antagonism against the privileged Italian elite even
manifests itself with regard to a charismatic and utterly admirable
visitor from Italy, Luciano [170-4; 142-7], though he is presented
speaking in English, with a beguiling Italian accent. The narrator
dwells on the fact that Luciano's name, signifying "light", stands in
contrast to Fosco's, signifying "gloom". The narrating Fosco does full
justice to his opposite: "Luciano's Italian positivity blossomed in the
Australian desert" [171; 144]. "The two women … liked Luciano.
Unstated, but malignantly present was a question. Why was I not
like Luciano? Why the maligned malcontent, immersed in a fear(ful)
migrant psyche?" [172; 144]. Luciano's entrance at Brunetti's fashionable café is "Marcello Mastroianni in style, charm, energy and
appearance" [172; 144], leading Fosco to muse: "Who would I have
been if my parents had not migrated?" [172; 145]. Yet Fosco sees
in Luciano's lordly way of talking and in his way of dealing with
the waiter a person immersed in Italian Catholic spirituality, and
remarks: "The old *padrone* appeared in Luciano, the old brute Fascist
of the Italian male psyche" [173; 145].

The ethnic identity of Fosco's Italian peasant origins thus acts as a
complicating marker of a sense of exclusion and inferiority which is
essentially class based. This is most vividly represented in his attachment to the tip:

> During childhood I did find a place of refuge. Refuge
> from the psychological slaughtering of primary school,
> family poverty, migration with its cultural backwardness,
> forced assimilation policies of the Menzies government
> and the Cold War. I found the tip.
>
> I would walk for hours around the tip, lost amongst its
> ruins. My salvation. There, I would be left alone. I was

just a dirty, dago kid down the tip [85; 61].

This explains the low, self-abasing fellowship Fosco comes to feel, after an initial dismissiveness, for a Buddhist monk expounding his religious practice. The monk describes himself, in perfect English, as having emigrated from Italy: "The Buddhist monk was an ethnic. An Italian ethnic like me" [138; 115]. Apparently, however, "Whatever Italianness had existed in his being had long dissolved" [143; 121]. But Fosco asks him a spoiling question, challenging the relevance of his Buddhism to a struggling working-class family. "His language changed. It had been authoritative and precise. A migrant English emerged. Bring[ing] a touch of accent and non-ownership of language. He is still a wog, I thought. A fellow wog" [144; 122].

Fosco acts the part in these cases, and relives it in the telling, of one who has internalised the stigma of supposed ethnic inferiority. This is part of his "existential psyche crisis", a crisis to which he is attached and which he feels is part of his authenticity ("I prefer to be in the panic of crisis") [135; 113]. Here, midway through the book, he presents himself as a gambler, addicted to losing:

> Lately I have been feeling a deepening of my own existential psyche crisis. I have lost the courage to gamble. I have gambled and lost already. I can no longer risk-take. My confidence shattered. Gambled and lost on migration. Gambled and lost on Catholicism. Gambled and lost on education. Career came to nothing. Failed migrant. Failed human being. My spirituality in crisis. My masculinity in crisis. My sexuality in crisis. [134; 111]

What does this mean? In what sense has Fosco gambled (and lost) – on migration, on Catholicism, on education? They are investments he was born into rather than chosen by him. There is an invisible centre here, an unexplained core, perhaps related to his "urge" to imitate the village madman and take an axe to those who exert mind-control. This black hole is further deepened by that laconic reference to "Career came to nothing". For *My Reality* tells us nothing about Fosco's attempt at a career, if there has been any. Male identity in autobiography is typically centred around a career, worldly or unworldly. Nothing as coherent as a career is discernible in *My Reality*. Rather, it is replete with contempt for the "rational humanist narrative" of the "Economic Myth". A quest for meaning and value is Fosco's nearest approach to a constructive project, coupled with his vocation for seeking out fellow human beings in crisis. *My Reality* reads like a rejection of success or worldly achievement as a value, or at least like a deeply ambivalent attitude to it, a complex of desire and revulsion. At its most negative, Fosco's vocation could be seen as a vocation for failure.

In the book's concluding chapter, "Walhalla", the ethnic and migrant theme reappears briefly but eloquently, transformed into a positive. Manning approvingly recognises Fosco as not British and as contributing to the process of making Australia "more Australian" [249; 204]. "'Migration' he summarised authoritatively, 'is not the story of grand heroics but the simple heroism of ordinary people and ordinary lives.'"

Imaginary encounters

Many passages in *My Reality* are concerned with what Fosco perceives as the crisis in gender relations, with feminism playing a crucial role in bifurcating the psyche between the goals of careerism and sexual gratification – goals which he himself does not achieve and which he rejects. Loneliness and emptiness are seen as the result for the individual in the many encounters which Fosco describes. The quest for an alternative comes to a head in two of the last three sections of the penultimate chapter. In the "Evening" section, Fosco describes a death-of-God theology lecture in which the lecturer discards all the major tenets of Christianity. A young man in the audience asks: "what's left?" [213; 178]. Several pages later, the narrator, Fosco, faced with a derelict street-dweller suffering from terminal cancer, gives the answer: "… well, we are" [224; 186], which ends the "Evening" section.

The following section, "An autumn breeze", briefly, but pointedly, recalls the deaths of Fosco's parents. This is followed by "Night", the last section in the sixth chapter, after which comes the brief final chapter, "Walhalla". The concluding pages of the "Night" section

[244-6] conduct a discussion which leads up to the Pauline theme of love: "St Paul says our being is anchored in love. Does 'God' then exist? … well, perhaps when we bring love into situations 'He' exists; when we don't we take our chances!" [244; 200]. The narrator then moves on to describe a feedback session for trainee volunteers (including the narrator) working in a crisis call-centre. One trainee ends her remarks with a question "… 'what do the people who phone here really want?'" Her question reverberates through the text for the next fifteen lines, until the team leader, Gary, slumping, replies "'… to be loved …'" [246; 202], bringing the long sixth chapter to an end and linking up with the final chapter.

In the final section of the fifth chapter, one of Fosco's peregrinations across Melbourne takes him to visit the Old Melbourne Jail: "God can be there too. If He wants to! Possibly He won't. Whether God was ever there nobody knows. Possibly not!" [160; 134]. Fosco muses on the executions by hanging, their underwriting of compliant respectability, the abiding impression they leave in the prison. Attracted to the strangely lit condemned cell, Fosco sees there a young man asleep and, watching over him, a woman dressed in black whom he recognises "from historical photographs" as Mary McKillop [162; 136], who died in 1909, had been beatified in 1995, and was canonised as Australia's first saint in 2010.

Fosco and Mary have a low-key conversation in which Fosco updates Mary on the current crisis of Catholicism, the rise of feminism and the quandary of idealism, and then tells her of a young woman he had known, caught between devotion to others and spiritual striving: "She was struggling with her own individual pain. Struggling with a death in her soul" [166; 137]. "'… yes …'", replies Mary, "'we were at the two ends, good works and spiritual devotion. Something was neglected …'" and tears roll down her face [166; 138]. Fosco leaves, and this fifth chapter ends: "It was still very cloudy. I wondered whether God could see through the clouds" [166; 138]. The next chapter is titled "The house becomes empty".

This imaginary encounter thus rehearses or recapitulates (more fully in the four and a half pages of the 2003 edition than in the bare two shorter pages of the 2007 edition) the most troubling concerns that have exercised Fosco Antonio's text thus far: the collapse of religious faith and of allegiance to the church institution, gender relations in the power structures of society and in sexuality, the moral and existential viability of the self. As in Fosco's other encounters with others, which are presented as presumptively factual rather than imaginary, the imaginary encounter with Mary McKillop projects Fosco's existential concerns outwards, as concerning others rather than himself – reflective people generally, women (and especially feminists), a particular young woman of his acquaintance, and Mary McKillop herself. Notably, this is done by engaging, with full respect, an iconic Australian figure, but one which is signally and uniquely also Catholic.

Just as the fifth chapter of *My Reality* closes with the imaginary encounter between the autobiographical subject and Mary McKillop in the Old Melbourne Jail, the book as a whole closes with another imaginary encounter (again foreshortened in the 2007 version) in the brief seventh chapter, "Walhalla", which is the only one not divided into sub-sections. The encounter takes place in the former gold-mining hill town of Walhalla in eastern Victoria, and specifically in its hilltop cemetery. This encounter is doubly counterfactual, as compared to the one with Mary McKillop, in that Fosco here meets two historical figures whose life spans hardly overlapped – the historian of Australia, Manning Clark (1915-91), and the writer of the Australian bush narrative, Henry Lawson (1867-1922) – and yet Manning appears in the text as apparently the older of the two, performing a protective role with regard to Henry. Fosco describes the "strange sight" of the two men walking towards him: "There was no physical contact between the two men yet there was a sense of togetherness" [248; 203-4]. The same note is struck in the concluding words of the sequence and of the book as a whole: "There was a gentleness in their being together …"

Again, as in the scene with Mary McKillop, both narrative and dialogue are low-key, understated. The scene starts with Fosco musing on the symbolism of the cross on the tombstones. This musing is interrupted by the appearance of the two men. Manning notes with approval the increased non-British immigration since the war, which he says has made Australian society "more Australian" [249; 204], but remarks, "'We are all still very European'" (including his own English connection) [250; 205]. The two men touch on the injustice done to Aborigines or, rather, Kooris, and then ponder on a tombstone commemorating the death of an Irish-born five-year-old child. But the dominant focus of the scene, when Henry moves away for a while, becomes Manning's account of his painful relationship with the insatiable emotional demands made upon him by Henry, a desperately broken man. Fosco introduces the word "love" into the conversation, and Manning muses that "'God is love'", adding "'through people'". This picks up the drift, and the close, of the preceding sixth chapter of *My Reality*. The theme is worked through as Henry returns and togetherness is quietly re-established, and as the two part company with Fosco, Henry unexpectedly embraces him, as also does Manning. The narrator comments: "The small ritual was not an expression of leaving but a thanking. For a small time we had been brought together. Perhaps by love. I do not know. Certainly, at least, by a person's pain." The 2007 edition omits the last three sentences, leaving the point implicit [254; 209]. One of the apocryphal "what they say" quotations on the back cover of the 2003 edition has Manning Clark exclaim: "A beautiful book about love".

Such imaginary encounters are virtually unprecedented in autobiographical writing. The towering exception is Dante's *Commedia*, if we take it as an autobiographical text, for it is wholly imaginary, and composed entirely of encounters with figures of the past but, by that token, cannot be taken as factual autobiography. What is distinctive about Fosco Antonio's text is that most of the narrative is factually plausible and convincing (and tallies at every relevant point with the wholly factual autobiography, *Growing Through the Brick Floor*, written by his sister, Diana Ruzzene Grollo), except for the narrative sequences that are clearly counterfactual, involving, as they do, personalities that have already passed away, and the Mundy narrative, that is clearly fictive and in any case does not involve the autobiographical subject.

My Reality thus stretches the autobiographical genre by including imaginary encounters in order to articulate in dramatic form decisive moves in the argument mounted by the autobiographical author. The very fact that *My Reality* is visibly constructed as an argument places it in a forward position, at the outer limits, in the topography of the genre, in the company (at least in this respect) of few other autobiographical works, of which the most prominent is Augustine's *Confessions*. Fosco's imaginary encounters enable the autobiographer to engage with Australian history, going back a century, as well as with carefully selected interlocutors with whom he can plausibly establish a sympathetic understanding and a meaningful dialogue. The figures of Mary McKillop, Manning Clark and Henry Lawson, as they appear in *My Reality*, are made to stand for the disinterested and non-sexual love and service to others and togetherness and care for common humanity which Fosco's quest throughout *My Reality* has been seeking to realise. The counterfactual companionship between Clark and Lawson presented in *My Reality* is psychologically convincing in the light of Clark's well-attested admiration and affection for Lawson, and particularly of his affectionate and intensely subjective biography *In Search of Henry Lawson*.[41] The title of Fosco Antonio's book takes on ironic meaning in light of the extremely virtual nature of these components of his "reality".

Rogue autobiography or total autobiography?

My Reality is clearly a rogue autobiography in terms of the literary genre, with its mixture of modes – experiential narrative combined with imaginary, fictional and fantasy narrative, disquisition, invective, satire, confession – and its unstable "I" with its contradictory postures, often preposterous, at other times deeply serious, sometimes silly, often brilliant. Its glaring faults make it easy to dismiss, yet the penetration of its critique commands attention.

It is also clearly a rogue autobiography in terms of the theme

---

41 Manning Clark, *In Search of Henry Lawson*, South Melbourne: Macmillan, 1978. Brian Matthews makes a great deal out of Clark's interest, approaching hero-worship, in Lawson and the value of "mateship" in the latter's literary work. Matthews also quotes Clark's article of faith, "Hell is for those who can neither love nor be loved." See B. Matthews, *Manning Clark: A life*, Crow's Nest, NSW: Allen & Unwin, 2008.

of migrant ethnicity and marginalisation: almost uniquely among Italian Australian immigrant autobiographies, it does not uphold the dignity of the culture of origin, which is seen as having subscribed to the European Death Orgies. It includes the Catholic Church in this complicity, pillorying it as *puttana* (strumpet), and compounds this by associating the Catholic Church in Australia with the concealment of paedophilia among its clergy. What is perhaps even more shocking to the writers of integrated Italian Australian lives is that Antonio, despite his university education and his intellectualism, appears to have achieved nothing, but ekes out a sullen existence as a down-and-out.[42]

My Reality cannot even be said to qualify as a *testimonio* text, speaking for a submerged group with what is in effect a collective voice.[43] Fosco may in a sense represent the silent group of Italian Australians who have not felt at home in Australia, but he shows no solidarity with them. Most of the people he interacts with in *My Reality*, apart from family members, are not identified as Italian. In fact, though no career or life-project emerges in the course of the

---

42 Drawing particularly on Bataille and Mauss on the one side and on Geertz, Rawls and Shklar on the other, William Boelhower argues, of immigration from developing countries into the United States, that the parental act of immigration is a sacrificial wager which does not relinquish personal sovereignty but is to be redeemed or fulfilled by the achievement of personal sovereignty by the parents' children in the new country not merely in the economistic, but in the moral, sphere of the gift exchange economy deriving from the country of origin and its authentic traditions [Boelhower 2007]. Fosco Antonio's *My Reality*, and his sister Diana Ruzzene Grollo's autobiography, *Growing Through the Brick Floor*, are, of Italian Australian immigrant autobiographies, the most circumstantially informative about the conceptualisation, by both parents and children, of the migration act, but neither of them support the notion of either a sacrificial wager by the parents or gift exchange by the children.

43 Sidonie Smith [1993: 20-1] cites Cora Kaplan's notion of "out-law" genres, interestingly, in the context of resisting autobiography and transnational subjects [cf. Kaplan 1992]. Kaplan's argument is predicated on group identity, which only partly applies to Fosco Antonio's *My Reality*. See also John Beverley [1992] for *testimonio*.

book, neither does a deep commitment to personal relationships, which is the usual alternative model for an autobiographical text. Fosco is an isolated individual. To be sure, *My Reality* is full of tense and engaging encounters with other people, but no continuing relationship is developed with any of them. Fosco's mother is the person who recurs most frequently, but without any close or sustained rapport. In fact, it is striking that the persons with whom Fosco communes most deeply are dead – Mary McKillop and Manning Clark.

Autobiography is typically an agnostic genre, unless explicitly religious. But in *My Reality* God is a problem character, neither present nor absent. Fosco is on the lookout for him – on the way to and from the Old Melbourne Jail, among the graveyard crosses at Walhalla. It is no accident that these are the two occasions when Fosco converses with the dead. *My Reality* is a death-of-God autobiography, total autobiography, that cannot be entrammelled by genre rules, distinctions between fact and fantasy, a coherent self, ethnic identity. This is in keeping with Fosco's Pauline vocation, his sacerdotal role, communing with numerous individuals without tying himself to any, his pursuit of secular sainthood.

Autobiography and biography constitutionally canonise the self, the category of individuality and individualism, by which the twin genres are structured and framed. Fosco Antonio's *My Reality* deconstructs the self, but does not subsume it into a social group or class or collectivity or ethnicity. Rather, the deconstructed, chaotic self is interfused, or con-fused, with a chaotic humanity perceived as a society in fragmentation.

Chapter 7

Overview

Imagining the Italian Australian

The inaugural text of Italian Australian autobiography is Nino Culotta's *They're a Weird Mob*, which appeared in 1957. (The next was Osvaldo Bonutto's lone work of 1963, followed by a trickle in the 1980s before a growing stream from the 1990s.) *They're a Weird Mob* became Australia's record-breaking best-selling book, with around a million copies sold well before the end of the century [David Carter 2004: 62; McQueen 2007]. The catch is that no such person as Nino Culotta (a joke surname) ever existed under that or any other name, as the book's author was an Australian of Irish antecedents by the name of John O'Grady. His first book, *They're a Weird Mob* was a hoax of a kind or, better, a tongue-in-cheek game with the reading public and the formerly non-reading public, pursuing a dual agenda: that of viewing rough-and-ready but honest working-class Australians from the outside (or a supposed outside) in all their apparent strangeness as a "weird mob" and in their real virtues; and that of accepting the supposed outsider as a potential member of that same weird Australian mob.

The second of these agendas is based on an improbable fiction and on an all too real racism. The fiction is that the supposed Italian first-person narrator, Culotta, a journalist, speaks classy educated English of the British variety but volunteers to live the life of an Australian building labourer so as to be able to write a reportage for his newspaper in Italy on Australian working-class life which many Italian migrants were then experiencing. The racism is that of an Italian northerner against the southerners of his nation, whom he refers to in Italian as "Meridionali" – a racism of which we have encountered traces from time to time in this study, notably in Peter Dalseno's *Sugar, Tears and Eyeties* – mirroring the racism of "white" Australia against those deemed less white:

> … There are many kinds of people in the world.
>
> But at that time I thought the worst kind were what we call Meridionali. These are Italians from the south of Italy. They are small dark people with black hair and what we considered to be bad habits. We are big fair people with blue eyes and good habits. Perhaps it is a matter of opinion, and an Australian would lump us all together and call us 'bloody dagoes', but we didn't like Meridionali, and they didn't like us [John O'Grady 1957: 10].

Tongue-in-cheek and even parodistic as this may sound, as well as curiously nuanced ("at that time"), discourse about Dagoes recurs through the book, even involving the then Pope [John O'Grady 1957: 184], yet we have here a truly weird instance of what we may call collaborative autobiography (of a fictive kind) in which a supposed Italian is seen through Australian eyes and Australians are seen through supposed Italian eyes. The nature of such collaboration in Italian Australian life writing will change radically as the corpus develops from some thirty-odd years later, but it is as well to keep in mind the presence of this widely read spurious intertext or subtext (which is explicitly mentioned only in Rino Baggio's *The Shoe in My Cheese* [Baggio 1989: Preface]) as we consider the more factual Italian Australian life histories that come later.

Nearly forty years after the appearance of *They're a Weird Mob*, just as the caravan of Italian Australian life writing is getting properly under way, a very different perspective is mooted. The feminist theorist of the "nomadic subject", Rosi Braidotti, founds that theory and propounds her own subjectivity autobiographically on her experience as an Italian Australian, having been born in the Veneto and having grown up in Australia before the advent of multiculturalism, in fact during the period of the spectacular popularity of O'Grady's book. Braidotti's book, *Nomadic Subjects: Embodiment and sexual difference in contemporary feminist theory*, opens with the declaration: "This book traces more than an intellectual itinerary; it also reflects the existential situation as a multicultural individual, a migrant who turned nomad" [Braidotti 1994: 1] and, in less than a page, recalls the "inner turmoil within the Australian psyche and way of life" due to the erasure from mainstream consciousness of the Aboriginals, as well as her own ambiguous status as a "white" Australian in relation to those less white, but as "off-white", a "wog" or "dago", as compared to Anglo-Celtic Australians [Braidotti 1994: 9]. It was in Australia, she writes, that she discovered herself as a European, with all the "historical contradictions" that that designation fails to hide.

Braidotti's vocation is to be a nomad and a polyglot, rather than an exile or a migrant. She defines herself not in terms of a lost origin or an adopted place of belonging, but in terms of the freedom to cross borders and languages, and, in fact, as an academic, she works in several countries and across – or through – several languages. But the nomadism she professes is not merely spatial or geographic, but intellectual. She systematically criss-crosses borders between academic disciplines – philosophical, epistemological and theoretical borders – essaying to be pluralistic without being merely eclectic or relativistic. Her academic project is existentially predicated, and in this sense can be seen in terms of conative autobiography, a striving to construct an identity.

Braidotti's notion of the nomadic subject has been eagerly but often indiscriminately embraced by students of the literature of migration. This present survey of the published life histories of Italian Australians has turned up very slight instances of nomadism. Most of these histories at most dwell on two-way links between the Italian place or places of origin and the Australian places of arrival. Contact with Aboriginal Australians is almost totally absent from these narratives and, where it is mentioned, is at best vestigial, except in Fosco Antonio's *My Reality*. This near-total silence regarding Australia's first peoples in Italian Australian life writing is thrown into relief by Chris Sarra's *Good Morning, Mr Sarra*, whose author is one of the children born of an Aboriginal mother to an Italian father who emigrated from the Abruzzo in the 1950s to the Cherbourg district of rural south-west Queensland. The author has been prominent in raising the expectations of Aboriginal schoolchildren, but has also visited his Italian relatives in the Abruzzo and established bonds with them. Interactions between Italian Australians and other non-Anglo-Celtic immigrants likewise appear minimal in Italian Australian life writing, and even hostile (as in the possibly provocative case of Fosco Antonio's *My Reality*), and even the presentation of interactions between different Italian groups is sometimes marked by hostility.

The Italian Australian generation

The desire to be Australian as well as Italian is always implied in the Italian Australian life writing texts under study. Cappiello's *Paese fortunato* is the glaring exception, and it is significant that it was first published in Italy in 1981, where it first achieved celebrity before doing so also in Australia and being translated into English as *Oh Lucky Country* in 1984 [Maher 2011: 21-49]. Cappiello's book thus made a stir before Italian Australian life writing had got under way, in the latter 1980s. Only Bonutto's autobiography, in its essayistic earlier version, had been published before then, and it had apparently not been widely noticed, while B. A. Santamaria's political memoir, *Against the Tide*, which appeared in 1981, hardly (or invisibly) qualifies as Italian Australian life writing. There is therefore a possibility that Cappiello's book, with its rubbishing of Australian multiculturalism and of the integration of Italianness with Australianness, may have triggered an impulse to valorise the Italian Australian experience through the writing of immigration narratives. It is remarkable that there was virtually no straightforwardly biographical or autobiographical writing about Italian Australians until the late 1980s, since when there has been a notable spate of such publications. This may have been affected by the slightly earlier spate in Australian life writing generally.

In many if not most of the texts studied in this present volume, bicultural belonging to Australia and to Italy is explicitly, even strenuously, asserted. But this is not always the case. In several texts the adventure or the trials of living are sufficient to exhaust the life writing project, and the dual affiliation to Italy and Australia is taken for granted, but not asserted. The brothers Joe and B. A. Santamaria in their respective autobiographies nod their acknowledgement of their Italian origins but accord their primary loyalty to Australia and get on with the business of writing about how they live their versions of the Australian life. Born in Melbourne of Sicilian parents shortly after the First World War, enjoying upward social mobility and tertiary education, and escaping the internment net during the Second World War, they were already sufficiently integrated. Joe Maffina and Osvaldo Bonutto, who came to Australia as young men, one before and one after the First World War, were, as we have seen, not so lucky, and even Amelia Tilbury, who had arrived at the turn of the nineteenth century, was to voice, through her narrating granddaughter, her recriminations against anti-Italian feeling, as was Rino Baggio, who was born in rural Victoria in the 1930s.

Likewise, for Italians arriving in Australia in the decades following the Second World War, differences in life writing arise depending upon the age of the immigrant on arrival or whether she or he was born in Australia, and in precisely which decade, as the hostility to mass migration from Italy in the 1950s and 1960s gradually subsided with the rise of multiculturalism. These differences can be tracked in the individual life histories, which nearly all appear in the last decade of the twentieth and the first decade of the twenty-first century, with no clear-cut category distinctions.

All the texts examined, however, have in common that they recount the life experience of first or second generation Italian Australians, in other words, those involved in the process of becoming Australian, while more recently life histories have been appearing from a later generation of Italian Australians more interested in rediscovering their Italian origins. The only exceptions are Desmond O'Grady's biography of the nineteenth-century adventurer and gold-digger, Carboni, who was in Australia for only a year, through the Eureka Stockade experience, and Liliana Belardinelli, whose account comes to an end as she sets foot in Australia, while Rosa Cappiello's semi-fictional *Paese fortunato* (*Oh Lucky Country*) enacts a rejection of Australia after a year's experience of the Sydney sweat-shops and multi-ethnic underclass. The few first-generation Italian Australians sufficiently literate and sufficiently leisured and motivated to tell their own story (Bonutto, Alcorso, Caruso, Domenico Stella) are followed by a second generation who recount their own and their parents' struggle to integrate and establish themselves (Baggio, Russo, Cacciola, Bentley, Pallotta-Chiarolli, Ruzzene Grollo), and by a third generation or by other biographers who retrieve that life story (Triaca's life of her grandmother, Amelia Tilbury; Geoff Easdown's biography of Gualtiero Vaccari). Zoë Boccabella is the first Italian Australian life writer of the third generation who narrates the recuperation of her Italian identity component after having been well on the way to monocultural assimilation. Those of the first generation, especially the socio-economically and educationally and linguistically underprivileged, have to endure the initial hardship, sometimes amounting to trauma, of migration and the struggle to establish themselves, or at least gain a foothold, in the new society. It is essentially the second generation, the children born of Italian parents but who have grown up and been schooled in Australia, that are caught between the two cultures and the two languages, and have to negotiate, more or less painfully, the relationship between the two. Relatively few of these texts can be said to bear out Whitlock's remark that "Biographic writing confirms eminence in the dominant culture" [Whitlock 2000: 241], but there is clearly a striving towards acceptance in life histories written or translated into English. This is quintessentially the Italian Australian generation.

Ilaria Serra's absorbing study of Italian-American immigrant autobiography presents many differences from this present study. Her title, *The Value of Worthless Lives*, presents a first set of differences. She mainly discusses unpublished manuscripts which carry no presumptions of importance beyond the autobiographical authors themselves and their families and possibly an intimate circle of friends, and are often couched in non-standard Italian. Serra's title encapsulates her argument that these unpretentious texts are an assertion of the authors' "quiet individualism", of dignity, perseverance and survival of the trauma of being detached from their organic and collective social culture and individualised by the experience of migration [Serra 1-48].

This "quiet individualism" is to varying degrees visible in the texts we have been looking at. Our corpus, however, differs from Serra's not only geographically and historically (her texts mostly belong to an earlier period than ours), but also in that she restricts herself methodically to first-person autobiographies by first-generation migrants – those who have had the actual experience of migration. My approach, on the other hand, attenuates the distinction between autobiography and biography, emphasising the frequency and importance of collaborative life writing. It also emphasises the transgenerational continuity of the migration experience, with its associated traumas, into the second generation. And it focuses on published life writing texts, which corroborate and extend Serra's argument against what she sees as Bourdieu's socio-cultural "determinism", according to which social groups and classes are trapped within the conventional limits of their social culture and must "jump a double hurdle of class and ethnicity" [cf. Serra 27-8]. (The spread of literacy and of various forms of publishing – especially electronic self-publishing – has in some respects outdated Bourdieu's postulates.) But Serra's book and this present one share a common interest in charting the autobiographical or biographical subject's degree and kind of self-determining agency, the subject's sense of or search for identity, whether in individual, social, ethnic or cultural terms.[44]

As Leigh Gilmore, echoing Betty Bergland, argues, "the assimilationist policies that entrap the immigrant and ethnic autobiographer are replicated in criticism that would make a select group of autobiographers into 'representative voices'" [Gilmore 1994: 10; Bergland 1994: 130-66]. The trap consists in canonising (or "naturalising") such voices, rather than seeing them as more or less statistically significant outcomes across a spectrum of possibilities. Bergland, considering the hypothesis of "double-voiced discourse" in immigrant autobiography (and we might here also include immigrant biography), urges her readers to "question any easy relationship between discourse and the speaking subject, particularly the assumption that *experience* produces a *voice*", arguing that "the metaphor

---

44 Most of the foregoing distinctions also apply to the differences between this present study and that by Camilla Cattarulla, *Di proprio pugno: Autobiografie di emigranti italiani in Argentina e Brasile*, Reggio Emilia: Diabasis, 2003.

of double-voiced discourse … risks naturalising these categories" [Bergland 1994: 134]. We have seen in the contrasting accounts of wartime internment by Dalseno and Alcorso how an apparently identical experience can result in quite different voices dictated by a prior narrative.

Drawing on David Palumbo-Liu, Eva Karpinski discusses the "minority model discourse" of Asian immigrant writing in North America which, in one reading, strives for acceptance through conformity and compliance. This is a reading which may apply quite widely to the writing of Italian lives in Australia:

> As the product of a particular mode of reading and subject construction, model minority discourse addresses potentially explosive issues of racism, sexism, and class differences in ways acceptable to a liberal audience. Such texts usually participate in the rhetoric of depoliticised self-healing that suppresses material differences and sees change as the function of individual adjustments required of ethnic subjects. To the dominant group, model minority discourse offers a sign of possible recovery from racism; to other immigrants, it represents patterns of assimilation that other groups ought to imitate. According to Palumbo-Liu, Asian American literature has been exploited as model minority discourse in order to affirm dominant ideologies of the self and of success, popularizing the liberal notion that racial minorities can only blame themselves for their alienation in America [Palumbo-Liu 400]. The dominant function of model minority discourse is to reproduce specific minority subject positions within the hegemonic order, reinforcing the dominant culture's normative expectations of conformity and a larger ideology of individualism. [Karpinski 113]

Whitlock sounds a somewhat similar note. Of Australian life writing generally, with its characteristic attention to childhood narrative, she asks: "What are the politics of innocence? What are the complicities between the genre of self-portrait autobiographies and processes of assimilation? … critics, writers and readers can no longer claim innocence. The uses of these genres and inventions of the self are ethically, morally, socially, politically held to account, and at the heart of ways Australians respond to their unsettled past" [Whitlock 2000: 254-5].

Collaborative life writing

This study of Italian Australian life writing has not been able to make any clear-cut distinction between autobiography and biography. There is a whole spectrum of writing positions. Gillian Whitlock canvasses this issue in her essay "From biography to autobiography", which surveys Australian life writing generally, Cappiello being the only Italian mentioned. "Because the forms of literary biography and autobiography are interdependent and interactive, this writing can be imagined as a spectrum, a linkage of separate yet related forms." And she covers the field as a "traverse" from the biographical "grand portrait" to the writing of "fluid autobiography" [Whitlock 2000: 233].

At one extreme, the subject of the Italian Australian life story writes her or his own narrative in the first person with little or no visible participation by any other hand. This is the case with the autobiographies written in English by Claudio Alcorso, Sir James Gobbo and Franca Arena, among others, with no mention of any role played by publisher or copy-editor. The same is true of the autobiographies written in Italian by Giuliano Montagna, Olga D'Albero-Giuliani, Fernando Basili and Luigi Strano. At the opposite extreme are the biographies written about individuals already deceased, as in Desmond O'Grady's life of Raffaello Carboni, Catherine Dewhirst's account of Giovanni Pullè, Alfredo Strano's life of Ezio Luisini, and Helen Garner's investigation into Joe Cinque. However, even in these third-person accounts, the first person of the biographical subject can also speak out directly in quotation, as is spectacularly the case with Carboni, who is quoted frequently in his own words. Most third-person biographies of people known to the author during their lifetime draw largely on interviews or remembered or tape-recorded conversations, and the speaking voice of the biographical subject, or an approximation to it, is often heard, as in Piero Genovesi's presentation of Sebastiano Pitruzzello and his family and Judith Armstrong's double biography of the de Pieri brothers. This latter is also liberally garnished with recipes and poems written by the brothers themselves.

The biography of a living person is, in all the cases studied here, a collaborative endeavour between the author and the subject of the biography. As in autobiography, therefore, the main thrust of these third-person accounts is to delineate an identity and a life-project by telling a life history: the main difference between autobiography and biography is that an external perspective on the individual, and particularly on the environments s/he encounters and the context of the life experience is more marked in biography than in autobiography (although virtually all the autobiographies we have studied attempt objective self-portraiture and depict their geographical and historical setting in more or less detail). This occurs more readily when the biographer has a high degree of autonomy. Thus a remarkable instance of collaborative biography is Flavio Lucchesi's biography of Joe Maffina, conducted along dual lines, with Lucchesi's broad socio-historical narrative alternating with that of Maffina's daughter, translated from the English. The non-Australian biographer projects a stark picture of the hardships endured by the Italian immigrant and a sharp critique of Australian xenophobia, sometimes evident at a demotic level and sometimes at an institutional level.

Genovesi's biography of the Pitruzzellos, as we have seen, projects their migration in an epic light, which might not have reflected the consciousness of the protagonists, or which they might have not themselves presumed to voice. The non-Italian biographers, Judith Armstrong and Helen Garner, noticeably deploy an Australian perspective, at once panoramic, societal and intimate, which is peculiarly sensitive to the mode and degree of the integration and interaction of their Italian subjects with the Australian milieu.

What brings biography and autobiography even closer together in the corpus of Italian Australian life writing texts is the fact that several of the autobiographies are also markedly collaborative texts. The collaboration may take different forms. Maria Triaca tells the story of her grandmother, Amelia Tilbury, a compulsive storyteller, in the first person, and in impeccable English, which may or may not reproduce Amelia's idiom. Do we call this biography or autobiography? The distinction dissolves. And this is not an isolated case. Michal Bosworth also tells the story of Emma Ciccotosto in the first person, or Emma tells her own story which is put into English as "a translated life" by Michal. And Carlo Zaccariotto's life story is in effect a conversation between himself and Pino Bosi. An imperfect command by autobiographers of either or both of standard English and standard Italian or of compositional skills necessitates a helping hand, which in some cases may amount to wholesale delegation of the scribal role. Thus Des Tobin appears as author of the biography of Michael Tricarico and Irene Sampognaro as that of Carmel Caruso, while Sarina Russo, Maria Venuti and Domenico Cacciola acknowledge co-authors of their autobiographies.

In several cases, indeed, undecidability affects the very motivation to write a life. Amelia Tilbury, Emma Ciccotosto and La Contadina Nicolina all appear to have been compulsive (and compelling) storytellers, remarkably vital oral autobiographers who inspired their entranced and literate Anglophone helpers to transcribe their life stories in English. It must be these scribes who shape the accumulated anecdotes into a connected history, and this must mean that autobiographies of this kind are characterised by dual authorship, one author being the oral *raconteur* of anecdotes and incidents and episodes, and the other being the one who says "I" on her behalf, and delivers the autobiographical enterprise as a coherent project. A special case is the Anglo-Australian Vivien Stewart's story of her marriage to Eliseo Achia, which is both biography and autobiography and which has gone through radical structural and other changes, largely suggested by third parties.

Translation adds a further dimension to the collaborative endeavour. We have seen above how Walter Musolino's translation of Piero Genovesi's account of the Pitruzzellos moves the discourse closer to Australia and gently downplays Sicilian differences and autonomy. Several of the life stories we have covered appear both in an English and in an Italian version: besides the book on Pitruzzello, this applies to Ruzzene Grollo's *Growing Through the Brick Floor*, to Lucchesi's book on Joe Maffina, to the two life narratives on Carmelo Caruso, to Damian Tripodi's bilingual volume *Words of my Father*, to the autobiography of Giovanni Sgrò and to Cristina's *Secrets of a Broken Heart*, this last having gone through three, four or five pairs of hands in each of the two languages. Fernando Basili writes his memoir of protest with equal vigour in both languages, first in Italian, then in English. The bilingual address clearly seeks an Australian audience and an Italian one, whether in Australia or in Italy. One curious case is that of Luigi Strano's autobiography, which appears in Italian and in French, but not in English, both versions brought out by the same publisher in Italy.

Life narratives published in only one language – the great majority – clearly imply a statement about which language world or social culture they most intimately belong to or most ardently wish to belong to. Thus English is obviously the obligatory language of those life narratives seeking rehabilitation from the stigma of internment as "enemy aliens" – Alcorso, Bonutto, Dalseno, while Maffina's story has to wait for vindication in Italian before returning to English. Of these, it is notable that Dalseno's book distances the protagonist from his Italian origins, which are marked by abandonment by a perfidious father, a problematical mother, confinement to an English-language boarding school, and some sordid aspects of the community in which the boy is brought up. Dalseno's overriding concern is to be accepted as an Australian. This is the case with all second and later generation Italian Australian (auto)biographers, though these also vigorously assert their Italian identity component.

Do the texts studied here approximate to the models of collaborative life writing that have been found elsewhere? There are undoubted elements of the "mirror talk" identified by Susanna Eagan [1999] in virtually all the autobiographers, whose selves are partly defined by what they see in others close to them (overbearing parents, especially), and in all the biographers, who impart something of their own personality to the subject whose life they are writing and draw something back in return. The extreme case here is Giuliano Montagna's deliberate modelling of his own life in imitation of, and in dialogue with, that of his father Giovanni Guareschi, whose paternity his autobiography passionately claims, beginning with its very title. Some collaborative texts appear to fit along the spectrum mapped out by G. Thomas Couser [2001], some of them approximating, but not at all closely, to the ethnographic model in which the recorder controls the text, others approximating more closely to the celebrity model, where the protagonist of the biography or autobiography is mostly in control. But for the most part, in these Italian Australian life writing texts, there is a sympathetic balance between the two roles, justifying the definition of these texts by the label used by Eagan, "auto/biographies". Couser's remark on the "nearly oxymoronic status" and "inherently ventriloquistic" character of such collaborative life writing works neatly fits many, though not all, Italian Australian texts, which work towards acceptance and accommodation within an implied Australian sociocultural mainstream:

> Although the process by which the text is produced is dialogical, the product is monological; the two voices are allowed to engage in dialogue only in supplementary texts – forewords and afterwords – and even there the dialogue is managed and presented by the nominal author. [Couser 2001: 222]

However, a mediating dialectic, if not a dialogism, between the biographer's discourse and that of the biographical subject can often be sensed.

What does *not* happen is the identification of the auto/biographical subject with the group in a spirit of solidarity and resistance to redress a social grievance or injustice, as envisaged in the contributions to the collective volume edited by Julia Watson and Sidonie Smith, *De/Colonizing the Subject* [1992]. In spite of the bitter wartime internment experience to which Australia's Italian community was subjected, and in spite of widespread hostility and discrimination over long periods of time, and in spite of the bitterness engendered in the Bonegilla immigrant reception camp in the 1950s, these autobiographies address social grievance, if at all, overwhelmingly within an individual dimension, signalling their inscription in the ideology of individualism. Even a text like Fosco Antonio's *My Reality*, which figures "brokenness" in multiple dimensions of collective experience – peasant life, "the twentieth-century death orgies", working class migration, socio-economic subordination, religious disillusionment – remains trapped within the dimension of impotent individualism. Only Zelda D'Aprano (married to an Italian, but not herself Italian) turns her life story into what Carol Boyce Davies [1992] calls a "crossover genre", speaking for the empowerment of women formerly silenced, or what Caren Kaplan [1992] calls an "out-law genre" in a similar sense (though Fosco Antonio's text might be counted here). None of these texts qualifies as "testimonio" [see Beverley 1992], again in a similar sense, nor, to turn to another model, an "ideographic memoir" [Quinby 1992], where selfhood is configured not in terms of coherent autonomy and stable plenitude but of refractions of multifarious influences and experiences coming from outside the self. Nor is there much sense of families participating collectively, and across the generations, in the broader history of their nation of origin [cf. Davis 2011].

These Italian Australian life histories are predicated on individual survival or achievement, putatively the "comic plot" central to autobiography and celebratory biography (though not always fully realised). They leave in the dark the lives of many who, if they had their time again, would choose not to come to Australia. These lives are not published and have not been much researched [see Thompson 1980; Vasta 1985], but occasionally one comes across significant anecdotal evidence such as that provided by Mariastella Pulvirenti [1996] and discussed in chapter 3 regarding the members of a club in the Melbourne suburb of Brunswick, who unanimously declared their experience of migrating to Australia to have been hell.

An oblique bearing in this regard is offered by a curious and extraordinary text – an autobiography in the form of a *roman fleuve* – an endless novel. This is the first generation Italian Australian Tony Troiani's *Journey Around Myself*, published in three volumes amounting to nearly a thousand pages in length. The title seems to promise boundlessly self-engrossed individualism, and indeed the narrator pontificates on a myriad issues with an air of oracular authority and with a fine disregard for syntax. He calls the book a novel and at the same time opens the "Author's Introduction" as follows:

> I would like to stress the point that the events in this story are true. However the events are not necessarily my own experiences, but experiences of other people put together that led to the development of the fictitious character Tony Troia. [Troiani 2003: xii]

It is one of the jokes of the work that Troia means "slut" or "whore", compounding the equivocation between documentary autobiography and fiction. The narrative style is racy and the pace is brisk but the forward movement through time is leisurely, constituting a grand tour through innumerable manifestations of Italian Australian social life through family and schooling, work and leisure, a variety of occupations, institutions of all sorts, visits to Italy, encounters with a hundred characters of varied ethnicity, provenance and calling, all done with spectacular irreverence towards authority of every kind except the freedom of thought, enquiry and expression.

But the individualism is a *trompe l'oeil* – a trick of perception or an optical illusion. Through his composite alter ego – Tony Troia – and the many people he encounters, the narrator anarchically presents an unnerving caricature of multicultural Australia, including its Italian component, across the second half of the twentieth century and the start of the twenty-first, and the individual protagonist-narrator himself seems a caricature. This must be one of the most compendious and most circumstantial portraits of Australian, and certainly of Italian Australian, society ever attempted, and it is couched in the demotic, but not wholly uneducated, mode. In Troiani's texts, as in hardly any others, the individual is indistinguishable from the sociological.

Framing Italian Australian life writing

A frame defines primarily by exclusion. My frame catches published full-length biographies and autobiographies of Italian Australians that aim to present a recognisable person in terms of origins, experience and achievement – that is, some sort of plenitude at the individual level, within a composite and heterogeneous Italian space and a composite and heterogeneous Australian space, with their corresponding subjectivities, but it excludes other spaces and their corresponding composite subjectivities – for instance, out of an open-ended array, Aborigines, English, Irish, Germans, Vietnamese, Sri Lankans, Somalis or Chileans.

That is one self-evident arbitrariness of my chosen frame. Another, equally arbitrary, consequence of my frame is the emphasis on the individual. The moment you step into biography or autobiography, you get embroiled in the ideology of individualism. This privileges the individual subject or agent, makes the individual stand out from the social group or groups she or he belongs to, tends to regard the individual as self-determining and self-validating. Should the auto/ biographical subject, the person, be conceptualised in Cartesian terms, as a rational, free agent? Or in anti-Cartesian terms, as a prod-uct of prevailing ideologies? As a discursive construct? Or in terms of Slavoj Žižek's Ticklish Subject, problematical, but potentially realisable? These are questions to which I don't have preconceived answers, and therefore my frame needs to be pitched interrogatively, rather than categorically.

Within the Italian Australian catchment, my frame – categori-cally considered – excludes the overwhelming majority, that is, those Italian Australians whose lives do not become the central focus of a published text. Some of these lives – mainly those of family members of the biographical or autobiographical subject – may enter more or less prominently into the life writing discourse. Others may not appear at all: they are framed out of the life writing texts, but are extra-textually present in their absence, part of the ambience in which the written lives are lived. They may, of course, figure in other kinds of text, more partial texts – interviews, oral history, documentaries, ethnographic surveys and the like. Several collections of these brief life-narratives have been mentioned in chapter 5. The unwritten lives of Italians who have returned to Italy from Australia, and those who have remained in Australia but wish they had never come, as instanced earlier in this book in the anecdote reported by Mariastella Pulvirenti, must also problematise the chosen frame.

The same is true of those outside the Italian Australian catch-ment, some of whom may appear more or less fleetingly in the life writing texts which I examine, while the overwhelming majority usually remain significantly absent and invisible. The frame therefore has to be conceived as including what it excludes if it is not to falsify its object, given that the insertion or non-insertion of "Italians" into "Australia" will not neatly (if at all) correspond to the insertion or non-insertion into Australia of non-Italians. Conversely, Italian Australian framing centres attention on the relation between Italian and Australian ethnicity or identity, whereas in some texts that relationship is not central, and other concerns are to the fore.

My frame is in two respects unusually inclusive. Firstly, it includes biography as well as autobiography, and, secondly, it encompasses the immigration experience not only of those who actually underwent the move from old homeland to new – first generation immigrants – but also of the next generation, and even the third or successive generations. Biographies are included for two main reasons. First, because there is often no clear demarcation between autobiography and biography. Putative autobiographies are often collaborative works in which a family member of the autobiographical subject – usually a daughter or granddaughter – plays an important part, even the major part, in writing the life story. Almost equally often, someone not related at all performs that role; while a biographer of a living person is usually dependent on inputs by the biographical subject. It has repeatedly been demonstrated that the discursive ego of autobiography projected in a first-person account is no less socially conditioned than the subject of a biography, though it may be more selective.[45] A second reason for including biographies as well as autobiographies is that different vantage points interestingly illuminate the acculturation of the immigrant into the receiving society.

On the other hand, I have excluded both autobiographically based fictions and also other forms of life writing such as memoirs, diaries and journals, epistolary correspondence, interviews and oral

---

45 Mark Freeman, for instance, remarks: "'My story' can never be wholly mine, alone, because I define and articulate my existence with and among others, through the various narrative models – including literary genres, plot structures, metaphoric themes, and so on – my culture provides" [Freeman 2001: 287].

histories and other texts which do not present a holistic portrait of the subject.

The inclusion of second and later generations in immigrant life writing springs from the perception that the immigrant experience, understood as the acculturation into the receiving society, is in fact a transgenerational experience, and that the negotiation of a balance between different societal identities may continue or recur across several generations, the case of Catherine Dewhirst's link with her great-great-grandfather Giovanni Pullè and his legacy, being the furthest remove – perhaps an extreme one – that I have encountered. Certainly, many Italian Australian autobiographies are written by second generation subjects who devote considerable attention to the challenges involved in trying to reconcile or to balance the social cultures, value systems and languages of their Italian parents and the Australian milieu. A recent work in which an Italian Australian retrospectively explores her father's Italian identity carries a poignant blurb:

> Angela Di Sciascio's father can no longer describe his past, lost in a world ravaged by Alzheimer's disease. Deciding not to let his story fade, Angela embarks on a voyage that takes her through four seasons in her father's Italy, reconnecting to her ancestry and absorbing all of its chaos, beauty and style.
>
> Meal by meal at her father's family table and step by step through the Italian countryside, she slowly comes to understand the young Valentino who left for the new world. [Di Sciascio 2011]

This particular item poses a peculiar problem for my chosen frame, since it explores the father's Italian identity *before* his transfer to Australia, yet it suggests an oblique renegotiation of the dual Italian Australian identity both by the daughter and on behalf of the father. Should I frame it out as being too exclusively Italian, or should I frame it in as being predicated on the effort required of an Australian identity to accommodate the Italian difference? By mentioning it here, I have it both ways.

In including biography as well as autobiography, and also in spanning the generations, then, my study differs from Ilaria Serra's study of Italian American immigrant autobiographies, which confines itself to first-person accounts of individuals who actually crossed the Atlantic to make a new home in the United States.

Sau-Ling Cynthia Wong takes William Boelhower to task for his "conceptually problematic telescoping of first and second generations into a single 'immigrant experience'" [284], but the "conceptual problem" disappears if the frame changes from the individual's geo-cultural relocation to the family's transgenerational adaptation from one society to another. Studying the individual's experience of immigration is one thing, studying the experience of dual or multiple identity as a result of migration, is something else again: book titles are revealing. As I subtitle my book "Italian Australian life writing", so Shen Yuanfang's *Dragon Seed in the Antipodes* is subtitled *Chinese-Australian autobiographies* and Richard Freadman's *This Crazy Thing A Life* is subtitled *Australian Jewish autobiography* [2007]. Both Shen Yuanfang and Freadman, like Serra and Boelhower, limit their studies to autobiographies, but do not limit them to the immigrant generation. Rocío G. Davis has recently extended the transgenerational family frame still further in her *Relative Histories: Mediating history in Asian American family memoirs* [2011]. Family history in relation to national and international history occasionally surfaces in Italian Australian life stories and is most prominent in Diana Ruzzene Grollo's *Growing Through the Brick Floor* and Fosco Antonio's *My Reality*.

Most Italian Australian life histories, especially first-person accounts, touch on the difficulties of living between two different linguistic and cultural codes, but none thematise this aspect as systematically as Eva Hoffman's *Lost in Translation: A life in a new language*.

Generally, these narratives fit into a neat and regular longitudinal paradigm: they start by describing the place and family of origin, and then proceed with the decision to emigrate, the emigrants' struggle to establish themselves in Australia, support from fellow-Italians in Australia or from non-Italian helpers, achievements, links with Italy. Most texts aim at a well-shaped straightforward narrative structure and limpid expression, whether in English or Italian, obeying the perceived norms of the genre, often with great narrative verve and grace.

A few flout these norms to a limited degree, disturbing symmetry with excursions into history or linguistics or ethnic politics. Angela Napolitano's *Liborio, My Great Love* is adroitly structured as a courtroom drama to do with her husband Liborio's asbestos-related disease and death, each chapter coupling one stage in the lawsuit with a stage in Liborio's life history. Helen Garner's *Joe Cinque's Consolation: A true story of death, grief and the law* is an investigative reportage of a Canberra murder case, in which the author tries to retrieve the life of the victim. Both these texts are centred on Italian Australians, but they do not focus primarily on issues of dual ethnic identity, and much less does the non-narrative *Secrets of a Broken Heart*, by an author named simply as Cristina, which is an anguished cry or prayer for redemption from the trauma of childhood incest. Giuliano Montagna's [2004] *Mio padre Giovannino Guareschi: Dal Po all'Australia inseguendo un sogno* (My father Giovanni Guareschi: From the Po to Australia in pursuit of a dream) focuses on the author's lifelong determination to prove himself worthy of being his father's son, though unrecognised as such. Acquiring an Australian identity, in addition to his Italian identity, is an almost incidental part of the story.

These texts challenge the formal and ideological mould of longitudinal life writing, presenting original alternative paradigms, but they do not transform the conventional paradigm from within. Maria Pallotta-Chiarolli's work, *Tapestry: Interweaving lives*, goes much further, including the author's life experiences in among those of five generations of her own and her husband's family members in a quilting pattern that criss-crosses from epoch to epoch, from location to location, from person to person, transcending the individualistic paradigm with a familial and societal network. Individuality, however, is by no means down-played: personalities and voices stand out from one another. And something similar can be said of the quilted polyphony of the life story of the Australian Rules footballer Stephen Silvagni, even though the book's title – *Silvagni* – appears to flag the opposite.

Conative auto/biography

The striving to establish a sense of self, assert an identity, assess the degree of agency in one's attempt to master or endure circumstances, to make sense of one's own existence and to find a meaning in life is always present in life writing, be it in the first person or in the third person. Often, the self is not problematised, but more or less taken for granted, and life viewed as an adventure or a series of adventures buoyantly embraced or crises stalwartly faced, or a quest steadfastly pursued. Many biographies are of this kind – those of the Pitruzzellos, of the de Pieri brothers, of Gualtiero Vaccari, even perhaps Alfredo Strano's life of Ezio Luisini, *Luck Without Joy* – but so also are several autobiographies which might be expected to be more introspective and interrogative: we might include here those by Sir James Gobbo or Luigi Strano (though the latter admits to having contemplated suicide during his early years in Australia [L. Strano 44-5]). And those of Angela Napolitano and Domenico Cacciola are sagas of strenuous self-affirmation against mighty odds. Yet some apparently very four-square personalities do describe undergoing fairly radical changes: witness the existential shift to feminism, from markedly differing starting-points, of Olga D'Albero-Giuliani on the one hand and Zelda D'Aprano on the other.

But these are not quests to find or to forge the self, which is taken as given, though subject to change (and Italianness is often, but not always, seen as part of that given). We have seen instances of such questing in the autobiographies of Claudio Alcorso and Liliana Belardinelli. For Alcorso (years after the profound trauma of his wartime internment) this questing may manifest itself in an epiphany which transports him from a quiet back-street somewhere in China to his infancy in Rome, or else in a sense of metaphysical estrangement and lostness. This leads him to end by speculating on degrees of determinism or self-determination and to conclude inconclusively with his title, *The Wind You Say.* For Belardinelli also her conclusion is suspended in her title, *Destination Australia*, and the questing may be an indeterminate urge to re-establish her sense of identity after the double void opened up (but not dwelt on in her text) by the disappearance first of her father and then of the great love of her life.

Alcorso's and Belardinelli's are somewhat muted instances of what may be called conative autobiography – texts in which the writing itself enacts the endeavour to establish a self. The most strenuous and forceful instance of this conative urge within the corpus of texts studied here is Cristina's *Secrets of a Broken Heart*, whose textual extremity of incantatory self-persuasion, prayer and insistent quotation of biblical texts is ultimately addressed to a God whose presence is ardently and desperately desired and for whom we the readers stand in as public witness.

More quietly, but with a very different, almost acrobatic, textual versatility, Fosco Antonio's *My Reality*, in its two variant redactions, enacts a not too dissimilar brokenness in the conative endeavour to reach a viable God, which is also to say, a viable self. Fosco, like Cristina, though in less agonisingly individual terms, sees himself and the society he lives in as victims of brokenness, of disenchantment or desacralisation, of a loss of connection with nature, with age-old traditions, with spirituality, with some sort of authentic selfhood, in fact. Trapped in the critical scepticism of "rationalist humanism" and the accompanying loss of faith in God and Marx, he nevertheless seeks for signs in existing or imagined society of a more satisfactory mode of being, which does not separate self from society. I therefore see *My Reality*, along with *Secrets of a Broken Heart*, as a strong instance of conative autobiography, as compared to the weak instances of *The Wind You Say* and *Destination Australia*, while most other autobiographies can be called conative only in a much looser sense.

Fosco Antonio's *My Reality* is the one text that problematises all aspects of the Italian Australian life writing paradigm. *My Reality* is predicated on brokenness – brokenness both in the societal shift from north Italian peasantry to Australian industrial society, and brokenness in Australian society itself, as indeed in western civilisation in its entirety, and brokenness in the individual. The migration narrative is fragmented in a multiplicity of epiphanic moments, interspersed riotously and kaleidoscopically with a variety of other types of discourse: epiphanic encounters with numerous members of Australian society, some of them resurrected from the past; invective;

polemics on feminism, sexuality and love; diatribes against the Catholic hierarchy and Catholic school education and against media power; fictional narrative.

My Reality is a veritable farrago in which brilliantly perceptive and savagely satirical passages alternate with preposterous ranting. Serious engagement with Aboriginal Australia contrasts with caricatural contempt for Australia's Greeks. The stance and status of the rogue narrator-protagonist are radically unstable, as he oscillates between being a suicidally inclined loser and a self-assured and arrogant critic of his world, seeking a new humanist spirituality. *My Reality* destabilises the precarious certainties on which our world rests, and goes a long way beyond issues of Italian or Australian identity, though it also addresses these issues caustically.

To know Australia, to know its contemporary society and its recent history, and for Australia to know itself, it is necessary to know its component ethnic groups not as static, ghetto-like communities, but as interacting dynamically with each other and with the hitherto dominant, and itself composite, Anglo-Celtic group. The mainstream is no longer Anglo-Celtic, nor even predominantly European, but comprises the whole medley, including Indians, Chinese, Vietnamese, Sudanese, Lebanese and all the others – among them, Italian Australians. Published life histories are a relatively narrow but revealing frame through which to view these component groups – one frame among many, but one that is directly accessible and invaluable for the chroniclers and analysts of this country, or for any interested reader.

Thus, finally, we can consider the historical frame of this study. It covers a period – centrally, the decades of the 1990s and the 2000s – when the ethnic integration of Italians into Australian society has run its course from difficult beginnings in the first half of the twentieth century, most particularly in Queensland and Western Australia, through the period of mass influx of the 1950s and 1960s, and on to the multicultural turn of the 1970s and 1980s. Since then, the reduced numbers of Italians arriving in Australia have been able to fit into established structures within a transformed economy and a more receptive and variegated society. Fresh inflows of immigrants to

Australia from new countries, especially from Asia and Africa, find themselves in a situation not very similar to that encountered by the main waves of Italian immigration. It is unlikely that the Italian immigrant experience multifariously conveyed in the life stories discussed in this book will be repeated in closely resembling terms either by future immigration flows into Australia from Italy or from other parts of the world.

Italian Australian Life Writing Texts Cited

Achia, Vivien [2013] *Marrying Italian: When love is not enough*. Melbourne: Hybrid Publishers.

Alafaci, Marie [1999] *Savage Cows and Cabbage Leaves: An Italian life*. Alexandria, NSW: Hale & Iremonger.

Alcorso, Claudio [1993, 1994] *The Wind You Say* [*An Italian in Australia: The true story of an inspirational life*]. Pymble, Sydney: Angus & Robertson.

Aliani, Valeria Gorlei [1989] *Le mie avventure in Australia*. Melbourne: Valeria Gorlei Aliani.

Antonio, Fosco [2003, 2007] *My Reality*. Clifton Hill (Victoria): Fosco Ruzzene; revised ed. Melbourne / London: Total Cardboard.

Arcidiacono, Francesco and Morwenna Arcidiacono (eds.) [2009] *Echoes of Italian Voices: Family histories from Queensland's Granite Belt*. Stanthorpe, Qld: published by the editors.

Arena, Franca [2002] *Franca: My story*. Roseville, NSW: Simon and Schuster.

Armstrong, Judith [2001] *The Cook and the Maestro: Two brothers, two countries, two passions*. [*The story of Sergio & Stefano de Pieri*], South Melbourne: Lothian Books.

Baggio, Rino A. [1989] *The Shoe in My Cheese: An immigrant family experience*. Footscray (Victoria): Footscray Institute of Technology (Humanities Dept.).

Barassi, Ron, and Peter McFarline [1995] *Barassi: The life behind the legend*. East Roseville (NSW): Simon and Schuster.

Basili, Fernando [2004] *Vita vissuta: Esperienze di un emigrato ("Perché?" "Perché")*. [No publication details.] English version: *A Migrant's Experience ("Why?" "Because")* [2006]

Belardinelli, Lilian L. [2002] *Liliana Lucia: Destination Australia*. Lilian L. Nelson.

Bentley, Adele [1996] *Between Two Cultures – Italian-Australian: An autobiography*. Roleystone, WA: Grosnells Print.

Boccabella, Zoë [2011] *Mezza Italiana*. Sydney: Harper Collins.

Bonaccorso, Ian [2008] *"Addio Italia" – "Hello Australia": Stanthorpe Italian pioneers*. Brisbane: CopyRight Publishing.

Bonutto, Osvaldo [1963, 1994] *A Migrant's Story: The struggle and success of an Italian-Australian, 1920s-1960s*. H. Pole and Co. Pty., Ltd., 1963; 2nd ed., St Lucia: University of Queensland Press, 1994, with "Foreword" by Don Dignan and postface, "The wartime treatment of Italians in South Queensland," by Neil J. Byrne.

Borghese, Valerio [1996] *Appunti di un emigrante*. Brunswick West (Victoria): Insegna Publishers.

Bosi, Pino [2001] *L'emigrante ignoto / The Unknown Migrant*. Brunswick (Victoria): Santo Aiello.

Bosi, Pino [2012] *Ajò in Australia – Let's go to Australia: History of the Sardinian migration to Victoria, with 53 interviews collected by Dott. Saverio Minutolo*. La Trobe University, Melbourne: Italian Australian Institute.

Cacciola, Domenico (with Carmelo Cacciola and Ben Robertson) [2009] *The Second Father: An insider's story of cops, crime and corruption*. St Lucia: University of Queensland Press.

Cappiello, Rosa. [1981, 1984] *Paese fortunato*. Milan: Feltrinelli, 1981; as *Oh Lucky Country*, trans. Gaetano Rando, St. Lucia: Queensland University Press, 1984.

Caruso, Carmelo [1999] *Under Another Sky: The life and sentiments of an Italian emigrant* and in Italian [1998] *Sotto un altro cielo: vita e sentimento di un emigrante*. Galatina (Lecce): Mario Congedo Editore.

Chatham, Lyn [2005] *Martino's Story*. Highton (Victoria): Peter Bruno.

Ciccotosto, Emma, and Michal Bosworth [1990, 1995] *Emma: A translated life*. Fremantle: Fremantle Arts Centre Press, 1990; 2nd extended edition, *Emma: A recipe for life*. Fremantle: Fremantle Arts Centre Press, 1995.

Comunità Montana 7 Comuni di Melbourne Inc. [2010] *L'Altopiano di Asiago terra delle nostre radici: A collection of oral histories from the* Altopianesi *of Victoria*. Rosanna East (Victoria): Comunità Montana 7 Comuni di Melbourne Inc.

Cresciani, Gianfranco [2012] "'Socialismo per la generazione presente'. Rifugiati politici italiani e movimento socialista australiano", in *Italian Historical Society Journal*, Carlton (Victoria), vol. 20, pp. 25-49.

Cristina [2003] *Secrets of a Broken Heart* and *Segreti di un Cuore Spezzato*. Thornleigh, NSW: Bridge to Peace Publications.

D'Albero-Giuliani, Olga [1994] *Piccola quercia: La vita di Olga*. Two vols in one. West Brunswick (Victoria): Insegna Publishers.

Dalseno, Peter [1994] *Sugar, Tears and Eyeties*. Bowen Hills (Brisbane): Boolarong Publication.

D'Aprano, Rolando (Ron) [1990] *Le mie due patrie*. Melbourne.

D'Aprano, Zelda [1977, 1978, 1995] *Zelda: The Becoming of a woman*. Melbourne (Australia) and Norwalk (CTT): Visa. Revd. ed. [1995], *Zelda*. North Melbourne: Spinifex Press.

De Bolfo, Tony [2002] *In Search of Kings*. Sydney / Auckland / Toronto / New York: HarperCollins Publishers. (Edition used, 2004).

De Matteis, Cloris [2008] *An Italian Down Under: A migrant woman's tale*. ISBN: 978-0-646-49724-2.

Di Sciascio, Angela [2011] *Finding Valentino: Four seasons in my father's Italy*. Carlton, Victoria: Victory Books.

Easdown, Geoff [2006] *Gualtiero Vaccari: A man of quality*. Melbourne: Wilkinson Publishing.

Faini, Alessandro [1984] *Quadretti di un italiano in Australia*. Melbourne: Co.As.It.

Garner, Helen [2004] *Joe Cinque's Consolation: A true story of death, grief and the law*. Sydney: Picador Pan Macmillan Australia.

Gatto, Mick, with Tom Noble [2009] *I, Mick Gatto*. Carlton (Victoria): Victory Books.

Genovesi, Piero [2003] *Sebastiano Pitruzzello: l'uomo – la famiglia – l'industria*. Thomastown (Victoria): Pantalica Pty Ltd, 2003; 2nd ed. 2004. English translation by Walter Musolino, *Sebastiano Pitruzzello: The man – his family – his company*. Thomastown (Victoria): Pantalica Pty Ltd, 2003.

Giuffrè, Giulia [2011] *Primavera or, The Time of Your Life*. Sydney: GAG Enterprises.

Gobbo, Sir James [2010] *Something to Declare: A memoir*. Carlton (Victoria): The Miegunyah Press.

Growing up Italian in Australia: *Eleven young Australian women talk about their childhood* [1993] (with intro. by Franca Arena). Sydney: State Library of New South Wales Press.

Huntley, Rebecca [2012] *The Italian Girl*. St Lucia (Queensland): University of Queensland Press.

Italo-Australian Youth Association [2002] *Doppia identità. I giovani: conoscerli per capirli. Stories by young Italo-Australians*. Beverly Hills, NSW.

La Contadina Nicolina (with D. A. Davies) [2002] *Nicolina's Story: A woman of the land*. BEA*MAR Productions.

Lalor, Peter [2010] *Barassi: The biography.* Crows Nest (NSW): Allen & Unwin.

Loh, Morag (ed.) [1980] *With Courage in their Cases: The experiences of thirty-five Italian immigrant workers and their families in Australia.* Carlton, Victoria: FILEF.

Lucchesi, Flavio [2002, 2007] *Cammina per me, Elsie: l'epopea di un italiano emigrato in Australia.* Milano: Guerini e Associati, 2002, 2008. English translation by M. Downing, *Walk for Me, Elsie.* Macleod (Victoria): Italian Australian Institute, 2007.

Lugarini, Franco [undated, between 1998 and 2003] *Mio padre mi chiamava zingaro.* Eliotecnica.

Moleta, Vincent [2012] *Family Business: An Italian-New Zealand story.* Christchurch NZ: Canterbury University Press.

Montagna, Giuliano [2004] *Mio padre Giovannino Guareschi: Dal Po all'Australia inseguendo un sogno.* Reggio Emilia: Edizioni Diabasis.

Napolitano, Angela [2006] *Liborio: My great love.* Tuart Hill, Western Australia: Angela Napolitano.

O'Grady, John [1957, numerous reprints] *They're a Weird Mob: A novel by Nino Culotta.* Sydney: Ure Smith; Wellington: Reed's.

O'Grady, Desmond [1985, 2004] *Stages of the Revolution: A biography of the Eureka Stockade's Raffaello Carboni.* Prahran (Victoria): Hardie Grant Books: 2004. (Revised version of *Raffaello, Raffaello!*, Hale and Iremonger, 1985.)

Pallotta-Chiarolli, Maria [1999] *Tapestry: Interweaving lives.* Milsons Point, NSW: Random House Australia.

Pascoe, Robert [1988] *The Recollections of Luigi Grollo.* Northland (Victoria): Grollo Australia Pty. Ltd.

Pascoe, Robert [2012] *Nat Bonacci: No ordinary Australian.* Ballan (Victoria): Connor Court Publishing Pty Ltd.

Russo, Sarina (with Russ Gleeson) [2002] *Meet Me at the Top!* North Melbourne: Crown Content.

Ruzzene, Fosco – see Antonio, Fosco.

Ruzzene Grollo, Diana [1997, 1999] *Growing Through the Brick Floor.* Thornbury (Victoria): Gro-Set, 1997; translated by Piero Genovesi as *Noi gente d'emigrazione: ricostruire un cammino.* Thornbury (Victoria): Gro-Set, 1999.

Ruzzene Grollo, Diana [2004] *Cooper's Creek, Gippsland: The Trevisani.* Also in Italian: *Cooper's Creek, Gippsland: I Trevisani.* Thornbury (Victoria): Mure.

Sampognaro, Irene [2008] *Carmelo Caruso: I due cuori di un emigrante* and trans. by. J. Dickinson as *Carmelo Caruso: The two hearts of an immigrant.* Galatina (Lecce): Mario Congedo Editore.

Santamaria, B. A. [1981, 1997] *Santamaria: A memoir.* Melbourne: Oxford University Press. 1997 (updated ed. of *Against the Tide*, 1981).

Santamaria, Joseph N. [2006] *The Education of Dr Joe.* Ballan (Vic): Connor Court Publishing.

Sarra, Chris [2012] *Good morning, Mr Sarra.* St. Lucia (Queensland): University of Queensland Press.

Sgrò, Giovanni [1995] *Australia per forza e per amore.* Vibo Valentia (Italy): Qualecultura. Trans. by Anne Sgrò as *Mediterranean Son: Memoirs of a Calabrian migrant.* Coburg (Victoria) [2000].

Silvagni, Stephen, and Tony De Bolfo [2002] *Silvagni.* Pymble (NSW): HarperSports.

Stella, Domenico [2010] *Pages of my life (Pagine della mia vita).* Edited by Piero Genovesi, English translation by Margaret Downing. Macleod (Victoria): Italian Australian Institute.

Strano, Alfredo [1973] *Prigioniero in Germania.* Cittadella di Padova: Rebellato.

Strano, Alfredo [1986] *Luck Without Joy: A portrayal of a migrant.* Trans. Elizabeth P. Burrows. Fremantle: Fremantle Arts Centre Press.

Strano, Alfredo [2001] *Lo sguardo e la memoria: diario di un emigrato in Australia.* Cittadella di Padova: Rebellato.

Strano, Luigi [1999] *Rocciosa è la via: memorie.* Also in French trans. by Geneviève Immé as *Rocailleux est le Chemin: Mémoires.* Milan: Edizioni Pergamena.

Tobin, Des [2009] *Michael Tricarico: The journey not the destination.* Malvern (Victoria): Killaghy Publishing.

Triaca, Maria [1985] *Amelia: A long journey.* Richmond (Vic): Greenhouse Publications.

Tripodi, Damian [2003] *Parole di mio padre: Il sogno d'un emigrante / Words of My Father: A migrant's dream.* Published by Damian Tripodi.

Troiani, Tony [2001, 2003, 2008] *Journey Around Myself.* Melbourne. Published by the Author in three volumes.

Vellar, Ivo [2008a] *Adventures in Two Worlds: My battles with the D word.* North Balwyn (Victoria): Ivo D. Vellar.

Vellar, Ivo [2008b] *From Camporovere to Carlton: The story of five families.* Richmond (Victoria): Publishing Solutions.

Vellar, Ivo [2012] *Thomas Fiaschi, Italo-Australian Patriot, Surgeon, Soldier and Pioneer Vigneron.* North Balwyn (Victoria): Publishing Solutions.

Venturini, Venturino Giorgio [2007] *Never Give In: Three Italian anti-Fascist exiles in Australia.* Surry Hills (NSW): SEARCH Foundation.

Venuti, Maria with Christine Hogan [2011] *A Whole Load of Front.* Sydney / Auckland / London / Cape Town: New Holland Publishers (Australia) Ltd.

Volpe, Daniela [2005] *From Tuscany to Victoria: The life and work of Pietro Baracchi, Carlo Catani, Ettore Checchi*. Macleod (Victoria): Italian Australian Institute.

Yarra Valley Italian Cultural Group [2009] *Dreams from a Suitcase (Sogni dalla valigia): Recollections of Italian settlers in the Yarra Valley*. Burwood East (Victoria): Memoirs Foundation.

Zaccariotto, Carlo [1987] *"Me Ricorde …"* narrato da Pino Bosi. Sydney: Kurunda.

Zammit, Paul [2006] *The Life and Times of John (Jack) Iori*. Sydney: Zammit Publishing.

Other Texts Consulted

Aaron, Daniel [1964, 1985] "The hyphenate American writer", *Smith Alumnae Quarterly* (July 1964), pp. 214-17; revised as "The hyphenate writer and American letters", in *Rivista di Studi Anglo-Americani*. 3.4-5 (1984-85), pp. 11-28.

Alcorso, Caroline, and Claudio Alcorso [1992] "Italians in Australia during World War II", in S. Castles, Caroline Alcorso, G. Rando and E. Vasta (eds.), *Australia's Italians: Culture and Community in a Changing Society*, North Sydney: Allen & Unwin, pp. 18-34. Italian version by Davide Panzieri: "Gli italiani in Australia durante la seconda guerra mondiale", in *Italo-australiani: la popolazione di origine italiana in Australia,* a cura di S. Castles, Caroline Alcorso, G. Rando ed. E. Vasta, Turin: Edizioni della Fondazione Giovanni Agnelli [1992], pp. 51-68.

Anderson, Benedict [1983, 1991] *Imagined Communities*. London: Verso, 1991.

Arrighi, Michael (ed.) [1991] *Italians in Australia: The literary experience* (with intro. by Gaetano Rando). Wollongong (New South Wales): The University (Department of Modern Languages).

Ashley, Kathleen, Leigh Gilmore, Gerald Peters (eds.) [1994] *Autobiography and Postmodernism*. Amherst: The University of Massachusetts Press.

Baldassar, Loretta [1994] "Migration as transnational interaction – Italy re-visited", in Antonina Bivona (ed.), *Proceedings of "Italian Towards 2000: The Role of Italian Studies in Australian Universities – Prospects for the Future", International Conference, 20-22 September* 1994, Melbourne: Victoria University of Technology, pp. 42-53

Baldassar, Loretta [2001] *Visits Home: Migration experiences between Italy and Australia,* Carlton South: Melbourne University Press.

Baldassar, Loretta, Cora Vellekoop Baldock and Raelene Wilding [2007] *Families Caring across Borders: Migration, ageing and transnational caregiving*. Basingstoke: Palgrave Macmillan.

Baldassar, Loretta, and Ros Pesman [2005] *From Paesani to Global Italians: Veneto migrants in Australia*. Crawley, WA: UWA Press.

Baldassar, Loretta and Donna R. Gabaccia [2011] *Intimacy and Italian Migration: Gender and domestic lives in a mobile world*. New York: Fordham University Press.

Bannister, Roland [2007] *Music and Love: Music in the lives of Italian Australians in Griffith, New South Wales*. Melbourne: Italian Australian Institute (La Trobe University).

Baracchi, Paolo [2012] "Interview with Sir James Gobbo", in *Italian Historical Society Journal,* Carlton (Victoria), vol. 20, pp. 5-11.

Barbaro, Francesco [1993] "Italian Workers: Contributions, prospects and progress", in Desmond O'Connor and Antonio Comin (eds.), *The First Conference on The Impact of Italians in South Australia, 16-17 July 1993: Proceedings*. Adelaide: Italian Congress Inc. & Italian Discipline, The Flinders University of South Australia, 1993, pp. 187-95.

Battistini, Andrea [1990] *Lo specchio di Dedalo: autobiografia e biografia*. Bologna: Il Mulino.

Battiston, Simone [2012] *Immigrants Turned Activists: Italians in 1970s Melbourne*. Kibsworth Beauchamp (Leics.): Troubador.

Benjamin, Walter [1923]. "Die Aufgabe des Übersetzers", translated by Harry Zohn as "The task of the translator", repr. in L. Venuti (ed.), in *The Translation Studies Reader*, London and New York: Routledge, 2003, pp. 15-23 (with Steven Rendall, "A note on Harry Zohn's translation", pp. 23-25).

Bergland, Betty [1994] "Postmodernism and the autobiographical subject: Reconstructing the 'Other'", in Ashley, Gilmore and Peters (eds.), 130-66.

Besemeres, Mary and Anna Wierzbicka (eds.) [2007] *Translating lives: Living with two languages and cultures*. St. Lucia (Queensland): University of Queensland Press.

Bevege, M. [1993] *Behind Barbed Wire: Internment in Australia during World War Two*. St. Lucia (Queensland): University of Queensland Press.

Beverley, John [1992] "The margin at the center: On *Testimonio* (testimonial narrative)" in Watson and Smith (eds.), 1992, pp. 91-114.

Boelhower, William [1982] *Immigrant Autobiography in the United States: Four versions of the Italian American self*. Verona: Essedue Edizioni.

Boelhower, William [2007] "Shifting forms of sovereignty: immigrant parents and ethnic autobiographers", in Rosalia Baena (ed.) *Transculturing Auto/Biography: Forms of life writing*. London and New York: Routledge, pp. 1-17.

Bosworth, M. [1992] "Fremantle interned: the Italian experience", in Bosworth, R. and Ugolini (eds.), pp. 75-88.

Bosworth, R. [1992] "Oral histories of internment", in Bosworth, R. and Ugolini (eds.), pp. 105-116.

Bosworth, R. and R. Ugolini (eds.) [1992] *War, Internment and Mass Migration: The Italo-Australian experience 1940-1990*. Rome: Gruppo Editoriale Internazionale.

Boyce Davies, Carol [1992] "Collaboration and the ordering imperative in life story production", in Smith and Watson [1992], pp. 3-19.

Braidotti, R. [1991] *Itinéraires dans la dissonance. Patterns of Dissonance: A study of women in contemporary philosophy*, translated by Elizabeth Guild. New York: Routledge.

Braidotti, R. [1994] *Nomadic Subjects: Embodiment and sexual difference in contemporary feminist theory*. New York: Columbia University Press.

Braidotti, R. [2002] *Metamorphoses: Towards a materialist theory of becoming*. Cambridge, UK; Malden, MA: Polity Press in association with Blackwell Publishers.

Braidotti, R. [2006] *Transpositions: On nomadic ethics*. Cambridge, UK; Malden, MA: Polity Press.

Brockmeier, Jens and Donal Carbaugh (eds.) [2001] *Narrative and Identity: Studies in autobiography, self and culture*. Amsterdam and Philadelphia: John Benjamins Publishing Co.

Broughton, Trev Lynn (ed.) [2007] *Autobiography*. 4 vols. London / New York: Routledge.

Burns, Jennifer. [2003] "Frontiere nel testo: autori, collaborazioni e mediazioni nella scrittura italofona della migrazione" / "Borders within the text: authorship, collaboration and mediation in writing in Italian by immigrants", in J. Burns and L. Polezzi (eds.) *Borderlines: Migrazioni e identità nel Novecento*. Isernia: Cosmo Iannone Editore, 2003, pp. 203-12; 387-94.

Byrne, N. J. [1994] "The wartime treatment of Italians in South Queensland", in Bonutto [1994], pp. 91-9.

Carter, David [2004] "O'Grady, John, see 'Culotta, Nino': popular authorship, duplicity and celebrity. (*They're a Weird Mob*)." *Australian Literary Studies*, 21.4: 56-74.

Carter, Paul [1992] "Lines of communication: Meaning in the migrant environment", in Gunew, Sneja and Kateryna O. Longley (eds.) *Striking Chords: Multicultural literary interpretations*. N. Sydney: Allen & Unwin, pp. 9-18.

Caruth, Cathy (ed.) [1995] *Trauma: Explorations in memory*. Baltimore and London: The Johns Hopkins University Press.

Cattarulla, Camilla [2003] *Di proprio pugno: Autobiografie di emigranti italiani in Argentina e Brasile*, Reggio Emilia: Diabasis.

Clark, Manning [1978] *In Search of Henry Lawson*. South Melbourne: Macmillan.

Colmer, John [1989] *Australian Autobiography: The personal quest*. South Melbourne: Oxford University Press Australia.

Couser, G. Thomas [2001] "Collaborative Life Writing", in *Encyclopedia of Life Writing: Autobiographical and biographical forms*, ed. Margaretta Jolly. London: Fitzroy Dearborn, Vol. 1, pp. 222-3.

Cresciani, Gianfranco [1988] *Migrants or Mates: Italian life in Australia*. Royal Exchange, Sydney: Knockmore Enterprises.

Cresciani, Gianfranco [1992] "The bogey of the Italian fifth column: internment and the making of Italo-Australia", in Bosworth and Ugolini (eds.), pp. 11-32.

Cresciani, Gianfranco [2011] *Trieste goes to Australia*. Published by the author in Lindfield, NSW.

Dalziell, Rosamund [1999] *Shameful Autobiographies: Shame in contemporary Australian autobiographies and culture*. Carlton, Victoria: Melbourne University Press.

Damasio, Antonio [2003] *Looking for Spinoza: Joy, sorrow, and the feeling brain*. Orlando: Harcourt, Inc.

D'Aprano, Charles [1995] *From Goldrush to Federation: Italian pioneers in Victoria, 1850-1900: the story of the first wave of Italian migration to Australia.* Pascoe Vale South, Victoria: INT Press.

Davidson, Alastair [1997] *From Subject to Citizen: Australian citizenship in the twentieth century.* Cambridge: Cambridge University Press.

Davine, Annamaria [2006] *"Vegnimo da Conco ma simo Veneti" – A study of the immigration and settlement of the Veneti in Central and West Gippsland 1925-1970.* Melbourne: Italian Australian Institute (La Trobe University).

Davine, Annamaria [2008] *"Building Community": Fifty years of the Pastorelle Sisters in Australia.* Melbourne: Italian Australian Institute (La Trobe University).

Davine, Annamaria [2009] *"Neither Here Nor There": Italians and Swiss Italians on the Walhalla Goldfield, 1863-1915.* Melbourne: Italian Australian Institute (La Trobe University).

Davis, Rocío G. [2011] *Relative Histories: Mediating history in Asian American family memoirs.* University of Hawaii Press.

Davis, R. D., J. Aurell and A. B. Delgado [2007] "Ethnic life writing and historical mediation: Approaches and interventions", in Davis, Aurell and Delgado (eds.) [2007], pp. 9-21.

Davis, R. D., J. Aurell and A. B. Delgado (eds.) [2007] *Ethnic Life Writing and Histories: Genres, performance and culture.* New Brunswick and London: Transaction Publishers.

De Lacey, P. R. and Millicent E. Poole (eds.) [1979] *Mosaic or Melting Pot: Cultural evolution in Australia.* Sydney: Harcourt Brace Jovanovich.

Dewhirst, Catherine [2002] "Giovanni Pullè: Pioneer and founding father of Italian ethnicity", in David Moss (ed.), *Italian Figures in Australian Landscapes*, Supplement to *Spunti e Ricerche*, Vol. 17, 2002, pp. 26-49.

Dignan, Don. [1992] "The internment of Italians in Queensland", in Bosworth and Ugolini (eds.), pp. 61-74.

Dignan, Don [1994] "Foreword" to O. Bonutto, 1994, pp.vii-x.

D'Intino, Franco [1998] *L'autobiografia moderna: storia, forme, problemi*. Rome: Bulzoni.

Douglass, W. A. [1992] "Images and adages: Anglo-Australian perceptions of Italians in Queensland", in Bosworth and Ugolini (eds.), pp. 33-60.

Eagan, Susanna [1999] *Mirror Talk: Genres of crisis in contemporary autobiography.* Chapel Hill: University of North Carolina Press.

Elkner, C. [2005] "The internment of Italian-Australians: A perspective from Melbourne, Victoria", in Elkner, Martinuzzi O'Brien, Rando, Cappello, pp. 1-13.

Elkner, C., I. Martinuzzi O'Brien, G. Rando and A. Cappello [2005] *Enemy Aliens: The internment of Italian migrants in Australia during the Second World War.* Bacchus Marsh (Victoria): Connor Court.

Ercole, Ivano [1985] *Un'infinità di esperienze: un'unica storia;* translated into English by Vicki Gare and Oriella Romanin as *A Living History: The first 25 years of the Italian Catholic Federation in Australia.* Bulleen, Victoria: Federazione cattolica italiana.

Field, Robin E., and Parmita Kapadia (eds.) [2011] *Transforming Diaspora: Communities beyond national boundaries.* Madison / Teaneck: Fairleigh Dickinson University Press.

Fitzgerald, Ross [2003] (with the assistance of Adam Carr and William J. Dearly) *The Pope's Battalions: Santamaria, Catholicisim and the Labor split.* St. Lucia (Qld): University of Queensland Press.

Folkenflik, Robert (ed.) [1993] *The Culture of Autobiography: Constructions of self-representation.* Stanford, Calif: Stanford University Press.

Freadman, Richard [2001] *Threads of Life: Autobiography and the will*, Chicago and London: University of Chicago Press.

Freadman, Richard [2007] *This Crazy Thing a Life: Australian Jewish autobiography*. Crawley (WA): University of Western Australia Press.

Freeman, Mark [2001] "From substance to story: Narrative, identity, and the reconstruction of the self", in Brockmeier and Carbaugh (eds.), pp. 283-98.

Gadamer, Hans-Georg [1960] *Wahrheit und Methode*. 4th ed., Tübingen: Mohr Siebeck, 1975. As *Truth and Method*. New York: The Crossroad Publishing Co., 1988.

Gardaphé, Fred L. [1996] *Italian Signs, American Streets: The evolution of Italian American narrative*. Durham and London: Duke University Press.

Gardaphé, Fred L. [2004] *Leaving Little Italy: Essaying Italian American culture*. Albany: State University of New York Press.

Gilmore, Leigh [1994] "The mark of autobiography: Postmodernism, autobiography, and genre", in Ashley, Gilmore and Peters (eds.), pp. 3-18.

Gilmore, Leigh [2001] *The Limits of Autobiography: Trauma and testimony*. Ithaca and London: Cornell University Press.

Glenn, Diana [2004] "Experiential narratives of a group of first-generation Italian-Australians in South Australia: Preliminary findings", in Desmond O'Connor (ed.) [2004] *Memories and Identities: Proceedings of the second conference on the impact of Italians in South Australia*. Adelaide: Australian Humanities Press, pp. 119-29.

Gregory. M and S. Carroll [1978] *Language and situation: Language varieties and their social context*. London: Routledge and Kegan Paul.

Gunew, Sneja [1985] "Rosa Cappiello's *Oh Lucky Country*: Multicultural reading strategies", in *Meanjin*: 44.1: 517-28.

Gunew, Sneja [1994] *Framing Marginality: Multicultural literary studies*. Carlton (Vic.): Melbourne University Press.

Halliday, M. A. K. [1978] *Language as Social Semiotic*. London: Edward Arnold.

Hammerton, A. James and Alistair Thomson [2005] *Ten Pound Poms: Australia's invisible migrants*. Manchester and New York: Manchester University Press.

Henke, Suzanne [2000] *Shattered Subjects*. New York: St. Martin's Press.

Hermans, Theo [2002] "Paradoxes and aporias in translation and translation studies", in Riccardi, pp. 10-23.

Hoffman, Eva [1989] *Lost in Translation: A life in a new language*. New York: E. P. Dutton.

Hooton, Joy [1994] "Australian autobiography and the question of national identity: Patrick White, Barry Humphries and Manning Clark", *a/b: Auto/Biography Studies* 9 (Spring 1994), pp. 43-63.

House, Juliane [2002] "Universality versus culture specificity in translation", in Riccardi, pp. 92-110.

Idini, Fabiana [2012] "The experience of Italian assisted migrants in Australia during the economic crisis of 1952", in *Italian Historical Society Journal*, Carlton (Victoria), vol. 20, pp. 16-24.

Jurgensen, Manfred [1985] review of Rosa R. Cappiello, *Oh Lucky Country*, in *Outrider*, June 1985: 243-6.

Kaplan, Caren [1992] "Resisting autobiography: Out-law genres and transnational feminist subjects", in Smith and Watson (eds.), 1992, pp. 115-38.

Karpinski, Eva C. [2012] *Borrowed Tongues: Life writing, migration, and translation*. Waterloo (Ontario): Wilfrid Laurier University Press.

Kirkby, Joan [1996] "Abject discourse and the imperial gaze in Rosa Cappiello's *Oh Lucky Country*", in Maes-Jelinek, Hena, Gordon Collier and Geoffrey V. Davis (eds.) *A Talent(ed) Digger: Creations, cameos and essays in honour of Anna Rutherford*. Amsterdam: Rodopi, pp. 221-6.

Koch-Emmery, Erwin [1953] "On understanding New Australians", *MLTAV Newsletter* (Modern Language Teachers' Association of Victoria), Nº 20 (October, 1953), pp. 16-20.

Kupfersin, Paola [1997-1998] *Due patrie: autobiografie di italiani emigrati in Australia*. Degree Thesis, Università degli Studi di Trieste, Facoltà di Lettere e Filosofia.

Kyrkilis, Joanne, Toula Nicolacopoulos and George Vassilocopoulos [2004] "From epistemological indeterminism to ontological integrity: Ethnicity and generational differences in collaborative life history writing", *a/b: Auto/Biography Studies*, 19: 1 & 2, Summer 2004, pp. 275-85.

Lamidey, N. [1974] *Aliens Control in Australia (1939-1945)*. Sydney.

Lefevere, André [1990] "Translation: Its genealogy in the West", in *Translation, History and Culture*, London: Pinter Publishers, pp. 15-27.

Lukács, Gyorgy [1980] "Reportage or portrayal?", in *Essays on Realism*, London: Laurence and Wishart.

Luzi, Alfredo [1991] "Espressionismo linguistico ed emarginazione sociale: la scrittura di Rosa Cappiello", in Marchand, Jean-Jacques (ed.), *La letteratura dell'emigrazione: Gli scrittori di lingua italiana nel mondo*. Turin: Edizioni della Fondazione Giovanni Agnelli, pp. 539-45.

McInnes, William [2010] *The Making of Modern Australia*. Sydney: Hachette Australia.

McQueen, Humphrey [2007] "Laying our cultural foundations", *The Age* (Melbourne), 17 November, A2: 19.

Maher, Brigid [2011] *Recreation and Style: Translating humorous literature in Italian and English*. Amsterdam / Philadelphia.

Manzin, Gregoria [2009] "Storie al femminile di un esilio dimenticato: la comunità istro-dalmata in Australia", in *Studi Emigrazione*, 176, ed. Matteo Pretelli, on *Gli italiani in Australia. Nuovi spunti di riflessione*.

Martinuzzi O'Brien, I. [1992] "The internment of Australian born and naturalized British subjects of Italian origin", in Bosworth and Ugolini (eds.) [1992], pp. 89-104.

Martinuzzi O'Brien, I. [2005] "Internment in Australia during World War Two: Life histories of citizenship and exclusion", in Elkner, Martinuzzi O'Brien, Rando, Cappello [2005], pp. 13-33.

Matthews, Brian [2008] *Manning Clark: A life*. Crow's Nest, NSW: Allen & Unwin.

Mayne, Alan [1997] *Reluctant Italians? One hundred years of the Dante Alighieri Society in Melbourne, 1896-1996*. Melbourne: Dante Alighieri Society.

Musolino, Walter [1989] Review of R. A. Baggio, *The Shoe in My Cheese: An immigrant experience* [*sic*]. *Spunti e Ricerche* 4-5 (1988-89), pp. 141-5

O'Connor, D. [1996] "War and internment", in *No Need to Be Afraid: Italian settlers in South Australia between 1939 and the Second World War*. Kent Town (S. Australia): Wakefield Press, pp. 173-95.

Ozolins, Uldis [1993] *The Politics of Language in Australia*. Cambridge / New York / Melbourne: Cambridge University Press.

Paganoni, Anthony [2003] *Valiant Struggles and Benign Neglect: Italians, church and religious societies in diaspora – The Australian experience from 1950 to 2000*. New York: Centre for Migration Studies.

Pallotta-Chiarolli, Maria [2004] "Weaving textual tapestries: Weaving the 'Italian woman writer' into the social fabric", in Scarparo and Wilson (eds.) [2004], pp. 152-69.

Palumbo-Liu, David [1999] *Asian/American: Historical crossings of a racial frontier*. Stanford, CA: Stanford University Press.

Papalia, Gerardo [2010] *"Hic sunt leones*: a dynamic Italian Australian villa", in *La Questione Meridionale / The Southern Question*, 1.1: 101-20.

Parati, Graziella [2005] *Migration Italy: The art of talking back in a migration culture*. Toronto / Buffalo / London: Toronto University Press.

Pascoe, Robert [1987] *Buongiorno Australia: Our Italian heritage*. Richmond (Victoria): Greenhouse Publications.

Ponzanesi, Sandra and Daniela Merolla (eds.) [2005] *Migrant Cartographies: New cultural and literary spaces in post-colonial Europe*. Lanham, MD: Lexington Books.

Porter, Roger J. [2011] *Bureau of Missing Persons: Writing the secret lives of fathers.* Ithaca and London: Cornell University Press.

Pretelli, Matteo [2010] *Il fascismo e gli italiani all'estero.* Bologna: CLUEB.

Pulvirenti, Mariastella [1996] *Casa mia: Home ownership, identity and post-war Italian Australian migration.* University of Melbourne Ph.D. thesis.

Quaquarelli, Lucia [2010] "Chi *siamo* io? Letteratura italiana dell'immigrazione e questione identitaria", in Quaquarelli, L. (ed.) [2010], pp. 43-58.

Quaquarelli, Lucia (ed.) [2010] *Certi confini: Sulla letteratura italiana dell'immigrazione*. Milan: Morellini.

Quinby, Lee [1992] "The subject of memoirs: *The Woman Warrior*'s technology of ideographic selfhood", in Watson and Smith (eds.), 1992, pp. 297-320.

Rak, Julie [2013] *Boom! Manufacturing Memoir for the Popular Market*. Waterloo (Ontario): Wilfrid Laurier University Press.

Rando, Gaetano [2004] *Emigrazione e letteratura: il caso italo-australiano*. Cosenza: Luigi Pellegrini Editore.

Rando, Gaetano [2005a] "Tales of internment: the story of Andrea La Macchia", in Elkner, Martinuzzi O'Brien, Rando, Cappello, pp. 35-53.

Rando, Gaetano [2005b] "Italo-Australians during the Second World War: some perceptions of internment". *Italian Studies in Southern Africa / Studi d'Italianistica nell'Africa Australe,* 18.1: 20-51.

Rando, Gaetano [2010] Review of Irene Sampognaro, *Carmelo Caruso: I due cuori di un emigrante,* in *La Questione Meridionale / The Southern Question,* 1.1: 153-5.

Ravenscroft, Alison [2004] "Recasting indigenous lives along the lines of Western desire", *a/b: Auto/Biography Studies,* 19: 1 &2, Summer 2004, pp. 189-202.

Ricatti, Francesco [2011] *Embodying Migrants: Italians in postwar Australia.* Bern: Peter Lang.

Riccardi, Alessandra (ed.)[2002] *Translation Studies: Perspectives on an emerging discipline.* Cambridge: Cambridge University Press.

Robson, Terry [2010]. *Failure is an Option: How setbacks breed success.* Pymble (NSW): ABC Books.

Rutherford, Jonathan [1990]. "Interview with Homi Bhabha: The Third Space", in Jonathan Rutherford (ed.) *Identity, Community, Culture, Difference,* London: Lawrence and Wishart, 207-21.

Scarparo, Susanna and Rita Wilson (eds.) [2004] *Across Genres, Generations and Borders: Italian women writing lives.* Newark: University of Delaware Press.

Scott, John A. [1991] "Il caso Strano: esperienze poetiche ed esperienze prosastiche", in Marchand, Jean-Jacques (ed.), *La letteratura dell'emigrazione: Gli scrittori di lingua italiana nel mondo.* Turin: Edizioni della Fondazione Giovanni Agnelli, pp. 555-64

Sengupta, Mahasweta [1995] "Translation as manipulation: The power of images and images of power", in Anuradha Dingwaney and Carol Maier (eds.), *Between Languages and Cultures: Translation and cross-cultural texts.* Pittsburgh and London: University of Pittsburgh Press, pp. 159-74.

Serra, Ilaria [2007] *The Value of Worthless Lives: Writing Italian American immigrant autobiographies*. New York: Fordham University Press.

Shen Yuanfang [2001] *Dragon Seed in the Antipodes: Chinese-Australian autobiographies*. Carlton South (Victoria): Melbourne University Press.

Sinopoli, Franca and Silvia Tatti (eds.) [2005] *I confini della scrittura: il dispatrio nei testi letterari*. Isernia: Cosmo Iannone.

Smith, Sidonie [1993] *Subjectivity, Identity, and the Body: Women's autobiographical practices in the twentieth century*. Bloomington: Indiana University Press.

Smith, Sidonie and Julia Watson (eds.) [1992] *De/Colonising the Subject: The politics of gender in women's autobiography*. Minneapolis: University of Minnesota Press.

Smith, Sidonie and Julia Watson [2001] *Reading Autobiography: A guide for interpreting life narratives*. Minneapolis: University of Minnesota Press.

Snel Trampus, Rita D. [2002] "Aspects of a theory of norms and some aspects of teaching translation", in Riccardi , pp. 38-55.

Sturrock, John [1990] "Writing between the lines: the language of translation", *New Literary History*, 21:993-1013.

Tamburri, Anthony Julian [1998] *A Semiotic of Ethnicity: In (re)cognition of the Italian / American writer*. Albany: State University of New York Press.

Tavan, Gwenda [2005] *The Long, Slow Death of White Australia*. Carlton North (Victoria): Scribe.

Thomas, Mark [1989] *Australia in Mind: Thirteen influential Australian thinkers*. Sydney: Hale & Iremonger.

Thompson, Stephanie Lindsay [1980] *Australia Through Italian Eyes*. Melbourne: Oxford University Press.

Toury, Gideon [1995] "The nature and role of norms in translation", in *Descriptive Translation Studies and Beyond*, Amsterdam and Philadelphia: John Benjamins Publishing Co.

Vasta, Ellie [1985] *"If you had your time again, would you migrate to Australia?" A study of long-settled Italo-Australians in Brisbane.* Canberra: Australian Government Publishing Service, Department of Immigration and Ethnic Affairs.

Venuti, Lawrence [1995] *The Translator's Invisibility: A history of translation.* London and New York: Routledge.

Venuti, Lawrence [1998] "The bestseller", in *The Scandals of Translation*, London and New York: Routledge, pp. 124-57.

Venuti, Lawrence [2002] "The translator's unconscious", in Riccardi, pp. 214-41.

Watson, Julia and Sidonie Smith [1992] "Introduction: De/ Colonization and the politics of discourse in women's autobio- graphical practices", in Smith and Watson (eds.), pp. xiii-xxxi.

Weinreich, Peter and Wendy Saunderson (eds.) [2003] *Analysing Identity: Cross-cultural, societal and clinical contexts.* London: Routledge.

Whitlock, Gillian [1996] "Introduction: Disobedient subjects", in Gillian Whitlock (ed.), *Autographs: Contemporary Australian autobiography.* St. Lucia (Queensland): University of Queensland Press.

Whitlock, Gillian [2000] "From biography to autobiography", in Elizabeth Webby (ed.), *The Cambridge Companion to Australian Literature*, Cambridge: Cambridge University Press, pp. 232-57.

Wilson, Rita [2008] "Excuse me is our heritage showing? Representations of diasporic experiences across the generations", *FULGOR* 3.3: 98-112.

Wong, Sau-Ling Cynthia [1991] "Immigrant autobiography: Some questions of definition and approach", in P. J. Eakin (ed.) *American Autobiography: Retrospect and prospect.* Madison: University of Wisconsin Press, pp. 142-70; repr. in Trev Lynn Broughton (ed.) *Autobiography.* London / New York: Routledge, 2007, vol. 2, pp. 279-304.

Yuval-Davis, Nira [2011] *The Politics of Belonging: Intersectional contestations.* London: SAGE Publications.

Index

www.ingramcontent.com/pod-product-compliance
Lightning Source LLC
Chambersburg PA
CBHW062212270326

41930CB00009B/1718